语言学论丛

现代汉语及物性研究

Studies in Modern Chinese Transitivity

龙日金 彭宣维 著
柴同文 译

图书在版编目(CIP)数据

现代汉语及物性研究/龙日金,彭宣维著. —北京:北京大学出版社,2012.9
(语言学论丛)
ISBN 978-7-301-18280-2

Ⅰ.①现… Ⅱ.①龙…②彭… Ⅲ.①现代汉语—研究 Ⅳ.①H109.4

中国版本图书馆 CIP 数据核字(2012)第 205575 号

书　　　　名:	现代汉语及物性研究
著作责任者:	龙日金　彭宣维　著
责 任 编 辑:	黄瑞明
标 准 书 号:	ISBN 978-7-301-18280-2/H·3127
出 版 发 行:	北京大学出版社
地　　　　址:	北京市海淀区成府路 205 号　100871
网　　　　址:	http://www.pup.cn
电　　　　话:	邮购部 62752015　发行部 62750672　编辑部 62754382
	出版部 62754962
电 子 信 箱:	zbing@pup.pku.edu.cn
印　刷　者:	三河市北燕印装有限公司
经　销　者:	新华书店
	650 毫米×980 毫米　16 开本　19.25 印张　304 千字
	2012 年 9 月第 1 版　2012 年 9 月第 1 次印刷
定　　　　价:	48.00 元

未经许可,不得以任何方式复制或抄袭本书之部分或全部内容。
版权所有,侵权必究
举报电话:(010)62752024　电子信箱:fd@pup.pku.edu.cn

写在前面的话

  1997年6月10日,龙日金教授赠与《汉语的及物性》(英文),半开玩笑地说,有时间将来译成汉语!他似乎只是随便说说;作为学生,我自然应允,只是并没有多想,毕竟当时聊着别的事,是附带说到翻译的,他似乎多少有些调侃的口吻。

  2007年8月,我因富布莱特访问项目即将赴美;临行前突然接到西南大学外国语学院院长李力教授电话,说龙日金老师病逝!我的心一瞬间给掏空了!因时间紧张,没能返渝看望老师最后一眼,遂嘱托文旭教授代为吊问。

  老师故去转眼间五年到了。过去五年,或是触景生情,或是夜深人静,每每念及往日师生情谊,总是心里作痛——就像一堆锯末木屑,内有火而外不见,隐隐中烧!

  回想1991年,我有幸考入西南师范大学,师从龙日金教授攻读硕士学位。入校后不久一个晚上,我和周军(现四川大学教授)第一次前去老师家,第一次听说到韩礼德其人,有些茫然。读本科时上过大学英语语法的课,课本是英国人的,何许人也,现在一点也记不起来了,印象最深的是与我们先前学的语法全然不同。也曾在校园马路边的旧书摊上买过一个破了封皮的《句法结构》(乔姆斯基著),深为其中那些优美的推导和演算着迷;还曾在本科毕业后的工作期间逗留学校图书馆浏览过夸克等人编写的语法书;可是,不曾听说过国际上曾经有人从汉语开始研究语言学,还独树一帜创立了学派。如果说这算是老师在我心中播下的一粒关于系统功能语法的种子,那也似乎只是一个名字。

  后来老师给我们开设系统功能语法课,教材是刚刚问世不久的《功能语法导论》(韩礼德著,1985年,第一版)。老师第一句话至今在耳:师傅领进门,修行在个人!因为之前已经把胡壮麟、朱永生、张德禄三位教授编著的《系统功能语法概论》(湖南教育出版社)拜读了n多遍了,所以学起来基本上没有费什么力气;而课余就反复啃两本来之不易的书:《英语的衔接》(韩礼德和韩如凯合著,1976年出版;现有张德禄教授等译本)和《作为社会符号的语言》(韩礼德著,1978年出版)。

再后来,老师调四川外语学院,我则转由陈治安教授指导毕业论文。但每逢周末回家路过烈士墓,我就要顺道去老师家请教问题。如果遇上吃饭时间,老师就做些好吃的留我一起享用,边吃边说,除了学习,什么都聊。

硕士学位获得后有四年时间,我把龙老师从澳大利亚留学带回的东西,分批次抱回家里系统阅读,如遇问题,下次还书借书时请教。其间承担的国家社科基金青年项目即运用系统功能语法理论进行英汉语对比研究,算是初步接触到了现代汉语(见《英汉语篇综合对比》,上海外语教育出版社,2000年出版)。后来跟随胡壮麟教授进一步学习,先前垫了底子,学习起来也不算费事。

博士学位获得后到了北京师范大学中国语言文学博士后流动站,师从王宁教授从事汉语研究。本该随王先生研究古汉语,但上承两位恩师研究现代汉语的夙愿一直未灭。得王先生应允,便运用系统功能语法理论,在两年时间内完成了博士后出站报告。其主体部分以《语言与语言学概论——汉语系统功能语法》为题,由北京大学出版社2011年4月刊行。余下10万字是关于汉语及物性研究的,这就是本书第二部分的基本内容。

本书两部分内容有承继关系:龙日金教授运用韩礼德的及物性早期模式首开现代汉语及物性研究之路;同门师姐周晓康博士在澳留学的博士学位论文"汉语官话的物质和关系及物性"则向纵深方向探索,同时融入了福赛特教授的思想,特别是计算描写。但周晓康博士的语料是直接从20世纪50年代以来各位主要汉语言学者那里借用的,目的是说明汉语的有关及物性现象;笔者的工作则是依据现代汉语的具体语料对周晓康博士相关模式进行修正,并进行了相关系统描写;还特地按照周晓康博士的思路补足了心理过程的研究。龙日金教授关于过程"范围"的描写,可在《语言与语言学概论——汉语系统功能语法》第七章看到定性解说。对比韩礼德教授及物性早期模式涉及的三个及物性过程(物质、关系、心理)与后来完善的六个过程(增补了言语、行为和存在三个次类),是很有启发意义的。

柴同文博士将龙日金教授的学位论文译成了汉语。这些年来,不断有师友同学来函索要龙老师的论文,但我总是自顾不暇,所以本书附上英文原文(也由柴同文博士整理校对),便于需要者引用之用。希望同行者在此基础上做进一步研究。

写在前面的话

  1998年离开重庆后，离老师远了，平时抽空打打电话，只有回渝探亲才有机会去看望他。早就知道他患上了哮喘，但谁也没有办法，只好安慰祈祷。最后一次见老师是2006年春节，他已经戴上了氧气罩！见我们一家人去了，他取了氧气罩，同我们聊了好半天，看得出来老师很高兴。但没曾想这竟是最后一面！

  在老师离世五周年之际，我和我攻读硕士学位时的同班同学（按年龄）夏日光、周军、楚军、张绍全、崔云红诸位，一并告慰老师：我们都继承了您的事业——教书育人；还有的也站到了您当年的位置上讲授系统功能语法。

  此外，感谢文旭院长就有关事宜多番联系龙老师后人。我也要借此机会祝愿母校诸位老师，特别是陈治安、刘家荣、李力、蒋家骏等教授，恭祝他们健康愉快！

  本书出版得到北京师范大学985项目支持；同时向北京大学出版社外语编辑部张冰主任和责任编辑黄瑞明女士由衷致意！

彭宣维
2012年3月26日
北京师范大学寓所

目 录

第一部分 汉语的及物性

前言 …………………………………………………………… (3)
符号使用说明 ………………………………………………… (4)
1. 语言的功能观 ……………………………………………… (5)
2. 及物性 ……………………………………………………… (6)
3. 过程 ………………………………………………………… (7)
4. 物质过程 …………………………………………………… (7)
5. 不同类型的物质过程 ……………………………………… (7)
6. 归属过程 …………………………………………………… (10)
7. 物质过程与归属过程 ……………………………………… (10)
8. 心理过程 …………………………………………………… (12)
9. 物质过程与心理过程之比较 ……………………………… (12)
10. 言语过程 ………………………………………………… (13)
11. 关系过程 ………………………………………………… (14)
12. "把"字句结构 …………………………………………… (16)
13. 被动句结构 ……………………………………………… (18)
14. 复合过程与双参与者 …………………………………… (19)
   14.1 无指向动作者过程＋无指向动作者过程 ………… (20)
   14.2 无指向动作者过程＋无指向受事过程 …………… (20)
   14.3 无指向动作者过程＋归属过程 …………………… (20)
   14.4 指向动作者过程＋无指向动作者过程 …………… (21)
   14.5 指向动作者过程＋无指向受事过程 ……………… (21)
   14.6 指向动作者过程＋归属过程 ……………………… (21)
   14.7 指向受事过程＋无指向动作者过程 ……………… (22)
   14.8 指向受事过程＋无指向受事过程 ………………… (22)
   14.9 指向受事过程＋归属过程 ………………………… (22)
15. 复合过程中的关系过程"成" …………………………… (23)

  15.1 无指向动作者过程＋"成" ················· (23)
  15.2 有指向动作者过程＋"成" ················· (24)
  15.3 受事过程＋"成" ························· (24)
  15.4 心理过程＋"成" ························· (24)
  15.5 归属过程＋"成" ························· (25)
  15.6 言语过程＋"成" ························· (25)
 16. 复合过程中的关系过程"在" ··················· (25)
  16.1 无指向动作者过程＋"在" ················· (25)
  16.2 受事过程＋"在" ························· (27)
 17. 复合过程里的指向动词 ························· (27)
 18. 复合过程、嵌入句和分枝句之比较 ··········· (28)
 19. 使役结构 ·· (29)
 20. 位相结构 ·· (32)
 21. 位相结构中的"有" ······························· (35)
 22. 受益者 ··· (36)
 23. 范围 ·· (37)
  23.1 同源范围 ···································· (38)
  23.2 度量范围 ···································· (38)
  23.3 结果范围 ···································· (40)
  23.4 处所范围 ···································· (40)
  23.5 工具范围 ···································· (41)
  23.6 过程范围 ···································· (41)
 24. 受事、施动者、动作者、目标和载体之比较 ··· (42)
 25. 受动受事和使成受事 ···························· (45)
 26. 句式过程及其参与者 ···························· (46)
 27. 句式过程中的受事/载体与属有格 ············ (48)
 28. 受事、目标和范围之比较 ······················ (50)
 29. 总结 ·· (51)
 附录 英文原文 ···································· (53)

第二部分 现代汉语及物性的进一步研究

第一章 小句的及物性(1)：物质过程和处所关系过程 ········· (157)
 1. 引言 ··· (157)

  2. 与及物性有关的基本问题 …………………………… (158)
  3. 物质过程 ……………………………………………… (166)
   3.1 物质过程的界定、分类及其相关理论描述 ……… (167)
   3.2 "施动者＋受动者"物质过程 ……………………… (173)
   3.3 唯施动者和唯中动者物质过程 …………………… (178)
   3.4 余论与小结 ………………………………………… (182)
  4. 处所关系过程 ………………………………………… (185)
   4.1 对周晓康系统模式的修正 ………………………… (187)
   4.2 处所类别 …………………………………………… (191)
   4.3 载体类别 …………………………………………… (194)
   4.4 小结 ………………………………………………… (200)

第二章 小句的及物性(2)：包孕关系过程
    和属有关系过程 ……………………………………… (202)
  1. 引言 …………………………………………………… (202)
  2. 包孕关系过程 ………………………………………… (202)
   2.1 单纯载体—包孕关系过程 ………………………… (203)
   2.2 复合载体—包孕关系过程 ………………………… (218)
  3. 属有关系过程 ………………………………………… (228)
   3.1 单纯载体—属有关系句 …………………………… (229)
   3.2 复合载体—属有关系句 …………………………… (235)

第三章 小句的及物性(3)：心理过程 ………………………… (248)
  1. 引言 …………………………………………………… (248)
  2. 心理过程 ……………………………………………… (248)
   2.1 基本感知者—现象过程 …………………………… (250)
   2.2 复合参与者心理过程 ……………………………… (264)
   2.3 以关系和物质过程的隐喻方式
     识解的心理过程 …………………………………… (268)

附录：主语是人际性的吗？——主语及主语结构
   的概念形式特征 ……………………………………… (273)
参考文献 …………………………………………………………… (292)

第一部分

汉语的及物性

前　言

　　本文试图运用韩礼德(M. A. K. Halliday)教授的系统功能语言学理论来分析汉语的及物性系统。

　　及物性的研究对象是小句中的"过程"，过程中的"参与者"以及与过程有关的"环境成分"。因篇幅所限，有关汉语"环境成分"的内容没有包括在内。

　　文中许多概念都是借自韩礼德教授，如：物质过程(Material Process)，心理过程(Mental Process)，言语过程(Verbal Process)，关系过程(Relational Process)，感知者(Cognizant)，现象(Phenomenon)，说话者(Sayer)，报告(Report)，识别者(Identifier)，被识别者(Identified)，载体(Carrier)，属性(Attribute)，受益者(Beneficiary)，范围(Range)等。有些术语是笔者为了分析汉语而创造出来的，如：动作者过程(Actor Process)，受动者过程(Patient Process)，归属过程(Ascription Process)，度量范围(Measurement Range)，处所范围(Location range)，结果范围(Result Range)，工具范围(Instrument Range)，复合过程(Complex Process)，双参与者(Double Participant)等。另外，还有一些术语虽然是借用，但却表达了不同的含义，如：动作者(Actor)，目标(Goal)，受动者(Patient)等。

　　借此机会，我要特别感谢导师韩礼德教授和马丁(J. R. Martin)博士。若没有他们前两年的耐心启发和引导，以及在整个论文写作过程中所给予的无私帮助和不倦教诲，本文是无法完成的。

符号使用说明

f. p.	前置语助词
i. a.	表始体
i. p.	疑问语助词
m.	度量词
m. s.	修饰后缀
n. p	名词化语助词
p. a.	完成体
pl.	复数后缀
p. p.	进化体语助词
p. s.	进化体后缀
*	不合语法的小句
…/…	……或者……

文中大写字母所标明的是小句的功能成分,如:动作者(Actor),目标(Goal),施动者(Agent),受动者(Patient)以及载体(Carrier)等。

文中每一个例句都用三行列出:首行为中文原文,次行为本文作者直译的中文小句,末行是对中文小句的英文翻译,详见括号内部分。

本文所用汉字都是根据其拼音系统(即在中国正式使用的、罗马化的一种体系)拼写的。

1. 语言的功能观

在功能语言学看来,语言系统的存在和发展是与它的功用紧密联系在一起的,而意义也只不过是处于一定语境下的功能而已。这一论断最初是由马林诺夫斯基(Malinowski,1935)提出来的。他在对太平洋特罗布里恩德群岛(Trobriand Islands)的实地考察中观察到了语言在土著人组织捕鱼作业等社会生活中所起的重要作用。他还发现,一种语言基本上根植于讲该语言的民族的文化、社会和风俗,而不同文化的术语或文本之间是不可能进行互相翻译的。但如果语言真像人们所说的那样具有自足性(self-contained)特征的话,这一点显然是解释不通的。在马林诺夫斯基看来,语言远不是一个自足的系统;它是在满足社会的特殊需要过程中形成和发展的,而它的本质和功用也恰恰反映了该社会的特征。正如马林诺夫斯基(Malinowski,1923:307)所言,"话语和情景不可分割地联系在了一起,而情景语境对理解词的意义特别重要"。换句话说,语言是"社会人"(social man)在其语言社区的特殊需要和活动中发展起来的。因此,人们只能在具体的"情景语境"(context of situation)和"文化语境"(context of culture)中推知某一话语的意义。据此,马林诺夫斯基区分了"情景语境"和"文化语境"两个概念。前者指的是与语言交际活动直接相关的客观环境,如时间,地点等;后者指的是语言交际活动参与者所处的整个文化系统。马林诺夫斯基(1923:309)指出:"一个词的意义不是从对该词的消极思考中获得的,而是源于对其功能的分析,其中就包括某些既定文化因素。"在此基础上,他区分了语言的三个主要功能:实用功能(pragmatic)、巫术功能(magical)和叙述功能(narrative)。

马林诺夫斯基关于语言和社会关系的论断以及意义的功能观被弗斯(Firth)、海姆斯(Hymes)等语言学家们所接受,并且在他们那里得到了详尽的发展。在此基础上,韩礼德(Halliday)将语境知识投射到了到语言系统,即语言的实际结构上。后来,他把语境进一步概念化,并提出了三个变量,分别是"话语范围"(field of discourse,简称语场)、"话语方式"(mode of discourse,简称语式)和"话语基调"(tenor of discourse,简称语旨)。话语范围指实际发生的交际事件,包括谈话的题材以及说话人或作者的活动和经历;话语方式指交际事件中某一语篇的功能,包括交际的媒介和渠道,如口语或书面语,即兴语篇或者事先准备好的语篇,也包括语篇体裁或者修辞方式,如叙述、说教、劝说以及寒暄语等;话语基调指交际者之间的互动角色关系及其相关的社会关系,包括临时性的交流角色关系和长期的社会角色关系。总之,"语场、语式和语旨三者定义了语篇的情景语境"(Halliday & Hasan,1976:22)。

韩礼德(Halliday,1978:144)的又一贡献是区分了语言的三种功能:概念功能(观察者功能)、人际功能(闯入者功能)和语篇功能(相关功能)。

语言的概念功能可以细分为经验功能(experiential)和逻辑功能(logical)。前者与语言的内容有关,它所表征的是说话者对交际环境的反映,关涉的是说话人对外部世界和内心世界的经验。逻辑功能所表达的是"事物之间从经验中间接衍生来的抽象的逻辑关系"(Halliday & Hasan,1976:26)。人际功能所反映的是人与人之间的关系,它关涉的是参与者之间的角色关系、地位和亲疏关系以及角色分配等。语篇功能指的是语言在组织语篇方面的功能,即"使成"功能(enabling),缺少了这一功能,概念功能和人际功能则无法真正得以实现。

在此基础上,韩礼德又研究了语境变量与语义结构之间的对应关系。他发现,当情景语境的三个变量投射到语言上时,语场便影响着说话人对概念意义的选择,语旨影响着说话人对人际意义的选择,而语式则影响着说话人对语篇意义的选择。而这三种意义又分别影响着说话人对词汇－语法的选择。例如,概念意义由及物性系统和词语的经验意义,以及位于不同级阶的逻辑关系来体现;人际意义由语气和情态系统以及词汇的评价意义来体现;语篇意义则由小句的主位结构,信息结构以及各种衔接关系来体现。

2. 及物性

本文将在小句层面上探讨语言的概念意义。换言之,就是研究小句的命题意义,或者说是研究"客观世界里所发生的事情"(what is going on)。在这里,小句所表征的是说话人对客观世界的经验以及内心世界的经验。确切地说,它是对过程的表征。一个小句通常包含三个成分:过程(Process),参与者(Participant)以及与过程有关的环境成分(Circumstance)。其中,过程是小句的核心成分。而及物性系统是语言的一个语义系统,其作用就是通过小句这一结构形式来传递人们的经验意义:把现实世界里所发生的事情分成若干种过程,并指明与各种过程有关的参与者及环境成分。

3. 过程

通常情况下,小句的过程由动词词组来体现。过程是小句的核心成分。根据其在小句中的语义和句法表征,本文将过程分成了五种不同的类型:物质过程(Material Process),归属过程(Ascription Process),心理过程(Mental Process),言语过程(Verbal Process)和关系过程(Relational Process)。

4. 物质过程

先说物质过程。

物质过程所关涉的是"做什么"(即韩礼德所说的"doing")或者"发生了什么"(即韩礼德意义上的"happening")的过程类型。请看下面的例子:

(1) 马在跑。
(2) 马死了。

对句(1),我们可以问"马在做什么?";而对句(2),我们则可以问"发生了什么事?"或者是"马怎么了?"

在这里,"做什么","发生",以及"怎么了"都是用来替代句(1)和句(2)的过程成分的,即代动词(pro-verbs)形式。简单地说,凡是能够用此类代动词来替代的过程都是物质过程。

5. 不同类型的物质过程

首先,来看下面的句子:

(1) a. 他在跑。
　　 b. 他在打我。

在例(1)中，a句只有一个参与者"他"，即动作的执行者，这里称为"动作者"(Actor)。诸如"跑"之类的小句中只有一个内在的参与者，即动作者。韩礼德将此类过程称之为"无指向"物质过程(non-directed)，将含有此种过程的小句称为"描述性"小句(descriptive)，详见韩礼德(1966)。通常情况下，无指向物质过程不能带有其他参与者。试比较：

(2) a. 王平在跑。
    b. *王平在跑操场。

(3) a. 李英在工作。
    b. *李英在工作英语。

在例(1)中，b句涉及了两个参与者，即"他"和"我"。前者是动作的执行者，仍然称作"动作者"；后者则是动作的接受者或称是动作的目标，我们将这一成分称为"目标"(Goal)。诸如"打"之类的过程通常包含两个内在的参与者，此类过程被称为"有指向"物质过程，包含这种过程的小句被称为"有效"小句(effective)(见 Halliday, 1966)。试比较：

(4) a. 王平在打李英。
    b. *王平在打。

(5) a. 王平在找小刀。
    b. *王平在找。

很显然，4b和5b缺少了一个内在的参与者成分，因而是不合语法的。

在汉语中，某些物质过程既可以是"有指向"的，也可以是"无指向"的。例如：

(6) a. 王平在玩玩具。
    b. 王平在玩。

(7) a. 他在笑我。
    b. 他在笑。

回过头来仔细研究上述例句，我们发现，在这些小句中，所有的动作者都位于过程之前的位置上，而所有的目标则出现在过程之后，这一语序不可改变。且看下例：

(8) a. 李英在打王平。
　　b. *李英在打。
(9) a. *小刀在找王平。
　　b. *小刀在找。
(10) a. *玩具在玩王平。
　　b. *玩具在玩。

在(8b),(9a),(9b),(10a)和(10b)中,其目标参与者均出现在了动作者的位置,因而是不合语法的。(8a)虽然合乎语法,但是句子的意义发生了根本性的变化:原来的目标"李英"变成了动作者,原来的动作者"王平"则变成了目标(对比 4a)。所以,此句的意义也由原来的"王平在打李英"变成了本例中的"李英在打王平"。

请看另一组句法结构完全有别于上述小句的例子。

(11) a. 房子卖了。
　　 b. 他卖了房子。
(12) a. 菜切了。
　　 b. 李英切了菜。
(13) a. 衣服洗了。
　　 b. 我们洗了衣服。

在这三组例句中,小句(11a),(12a)和(13a)里都只有一个参与者,而(11b),(12b)和(13b)则包含了两个参与者。从此种意义上说,它们与上面例子中的 6b 和 7b 以及小句 6a 和 7a 相似。例(6)和(7)与(11),(12),(13)之间另一个相似之处是它们既可以出现在"有效"小句中,也可以出现在"描述"小句中。但是,仔细分析,我们发现在例(6)和例(7)中,"有效"小句和"描述"小句的参与者成分均出现在了同一个位置,即动作者的位置;与此相反,例(11),(12)和(13)的情况则有所不同:在描述小句中,参与者成分位于动词之前,在"有效"小句中则位于动词之后。如下例所示:

(7') a. 他在笑我。
　　 b. 他在笑。
(13') a. 我们洗了<u>衣服</u>。
　　　b. <u>衣服</u>洗了。

在本例中,我们可以假定(13'b)的参与者"衣服"与(7'b)中"他"

是根本不同的:"衣服"可以出现在动词之后,因而不是动作者。同理,(13'a)中的"衣服"也不同于(7'a)中的参与者成分"我":"衣服"可以出现在动词之前,因此不是目标。在本文中,我们将这一类成分称为"受事"(Patient),而把"我们"这类参与者成分称为"施动者"(A-gent)。与此相对应,我们把诸如上述例句(7'a),(7'b),(13'a)和(13'b)的过程分别称作"有指向"动作者过程,"无指向"动作者过程,"有指向"受事者过程和"无指向"受事者过程。需要说明的是,这里的动作者是个必具性成分,而目标则是个可选性成分:它可以出现在"有指向"动作者过程中,但不可以出现在"无指向"动作者过程中。另一方面,在"施动者"过程中(包括有指向受事和无指向受事),其"受事"是必需的,而"施动者"则是可选的。

6. 归属过程

先看下面的例子:

(1) a. 他高。

　　b. 常虹很胖。

　　c. 这件事非常重要。

以上例句所表征的不是动作或活动,而只是赋予了其参与者一些属性或特征。我们将这类过程叫做"归属过程"(Ascription)。其中的"他"、"常虹"和"这件事"是过程的"载体"(Carrier)成分。

7. 物质过程与归属过程

本节探讨物质过程和归属过程之间的区别。

如前文所述,物质过程表达的是一个事件或者动作,而归属过程则是赋予参与者一个特定的属性。正因为如此,物质过程可以用"做什么"或者"发生"等形式来提问,但归属过程不同,它的替代动词是"怎么样"。试比较:

(1) a. 马在跑。

　　b. 马在做什么?

　　c. *马(在)怎么样?

(2) a. 房子卖了。
    b. 什么事发生了?
    c. *房子怎么样?
(3) a. 他高。
    b. 他怎么样?
    c. *他做什么?
    d. *什么事发生了?

第二,由于归属过程只是赋予了参与者一个属性,而非动作,所以,它不能用于进行时。通常情况下,归属过程中不包含任何的体标记词;相反,带有动作者的过程或者"有指向"受事过程均可以用于进行时之中,也可以带有体标记,而"无指向"受事过程甚至还可以单独存在。且看下面的例子:

(4) a. *他在高。
    b. 他高。
    c. 马在跑。
    d. *房子卖。

第三,归属过程没有祈使形式,物质过程却可以用在祈使句中。试比较:

(5) a. *(你)高!
    b. (你)跑!
    c. (你)卖!

第四,归属过程可以被"很"、"非常"、"太"、"极端"等副词修饰,而物质过程不可以。试比较:

(6) a. 他很高。
    b *马很跑。
    c *房子很卖了。

最后,物质过程可以是有指向的,也可以是无指向的,而归属过程则只能是无指向的。请看下例:

(7) a. 他高。
    b. *他高墙。

8. 心理过程

心理过程是表达"感觉"(perception),"反应"(reaction)和"认知"(cognition)的过程。换言之,就是表达"看见"(seeing)、"感觉"(feeling)或者"了解"(knowing)的过程类型。心理过程一般有两个内在的参与者。一个出现在动词之前,称为"感知者","反应者"或者"认知者"(本文将其通称为"感知者",Cognizant),另一个则出现在动词之后,所表达的是被主体所感知的现象、引起的反应或认知,我们将其称之为"现象"(Phenomenon)。很显然,"感知者"必须是人或者是具有人的特性的实体。换句话说,它必须具有意识;而现象可以是人,事物,或者是一个事实(此种情况下,它总是以小句的形式出现)。例如:

(1) a. 我看见他在走。
   b. 他听到一个声音。
   c. 小红喜欢鸟。
   d. 我怕他来。
   e. 那姑娘不懂法文。
   f. 老师知道老王不去。
   g. *石头听见一个声音。

在1g中,由于无意识的物体"石头"充当了小句的"感知者",因此是不合语法的。但在下列两种情况下却是合乎语法的。第一,"石头"用作某人的名字或者昵称使用,但此时它已不再是一个无意识的物体了。第二,"石头"被赋予了人的特性,或者说他被拟人化了(personification)。拟人可以出现在某些类型的语篇中,尤以诗歌和儿童故事最为普遍。

9. 物质过程与心理过程之比较

本节将对物质过程和心理过程做综合对比。

首先,如前文所述,物质过程可以通过"做什么"或者"发生了什么"等形式来提问,但是不能用它们对心理过程进行提问。请看下面的例子:

(1) a. 常诚看见一只老虎。
    b. *常诚做什么?
(2) a. 常诚怕老虎。
    b. *什么事发生了?

第二,在心理过程中,位于动词之前的参与者必须是人或者拟人化了的东西,但物质过程则没有这一要求。例如:

(3) a. *这把钥匙恨这把锁。
    b. 这把钥匙开这把锁。

第三,在心理过程中,位于动词之后的参与者可以是事实,这一点与物质过程不同。试比较:

(4) a. 老师知道他懂英语。
    b. *老师教他懂英语。

最后,心理过程不能出现在现在进行时中,物质过程则常用于现在进行时。试比较:

(5) a. 他现在相信你。
    b. *他现在在相信你。
(6) a. *他现在洗衣服。
    b. 他现在在洗衣服。

10. 言语过程

简言之,言语过程是关于"言谈"(saying)的过程。请看下例:

(1) a. 小王问:"你明天来不来?"
    b. 小王说他今天来。

上述两个例子表明,含有言语过程的小句实际上是一个小句复合体(clause complex)。它包含两个独立的句子:言语过程本身所在的小句被称为"投射句"(reporting clause),另一个则是"被投射句"(reported clause)。投射句中的参与者称为"说话者"(Sayer),它位于言语过程之前。

与心理过程中的"感知者"不同,"说话者"可以是人,也可以是其他无意识的物体。例如：

(2) a. 老师说王伟不去北京。
b. 传单说王伟不去北京。

但是，汉语中表达言语过程的动词很少，只有"讲"、"告诉"、"高呼"等少数几个。

11. 关系过程

先看几个关系过程的例子，

(1) a. 他<u>是</u>一个学生。
b. 他<u>是</u>李明。
c. 李斌去年<u>成为</u>一名老师。
d. 陈华<u>有</u>三本书。
e. 程红<u>在</u>教室里。
f. 地图<u>在</u>书架上。

如上所示，关系过程必须包含两个参与者。这一过程所反映的是两个参与者之间处于何种关系：内包（如"是"）、所有（如"有"）或者环境（如"在"）。

关系过程可以分为"识别"(identifying)和"属性"(attributive)两大类型。在识别类关系过程中，两个参与者的位置可以互换。例如：

(2) a. 她是金凤。
b. 金凤是她。
(3) a. 杜丽是我们的老师。
b. 我们的老师是杜丽。
(4) a. 今天是七号。
b. 七号是今天。

在这类关系过程中，位于动词之前的那个参与者称为"被识别者"(Identified)，而出现在动词之后的参与者称为"识别者"(Identifier)。

如前所述，识别类关系过程的两个参与者的位置可以互换，但这会引起它们语义上的变化：位于动词之后的"被识别者"变成了"识别者"，而位于动词之前的"识别者"则变成了"被识别者"。当它们出现

在疑问句环境中,这种变化则更为明显。试比较:

(5) a. 她是谁?

b. 她是金凤。

c. *金凤是她。

(6) a. 金凤是谁?

b. 金凤是她。

c. *她是金凤。

(7) a. 谁是金凤?

b. 她是金凤。

c. *金凤是她。

很显然,小句 5c,6c 和 7c 不能准确地回答小句 5a,6a 和 7a 所提出的问题,因为句中的"被识别者"和"识别者"的角色已经发生了变化。

与识别类关系过程不同,属性类关系过程的两个参与者位置不能互换。如下例所示:

(8) a. 他是一个工人。

b. *一个工人是他。

(9) a. 晁芳有两个妹妹。

b. *两个妹妹有晁芳。

(10) a. 画在墙上。

b. *墙上在画。

属性类关系过程也有两个参与者,其中一个位于动词之前,另一个位于动词之后。前者被称为"载体"(Carrier),后者被称为"属性"(Attribute)。其中,"载体"的功能就是将某些品质或特征赋予或归附到某一实体上。

在汉语中,包括"内包"、"所有"和"环境"在内的三种关系类型都可出现在属性类关系小句中,但唯有"内包"型关系过程能够出现在识别类小句中。请见上文有关例句(2—4)和(8—10)的分析。

其实,"所有"型和"环境"型关系过程中的两个参与者的位置也可以互相交换。请看下例:

(11) a. 我有一本书。

b. 那本书属于我。

15

(12) a. 那本字典在桌子上。
　　 b. 桌子上有一本字典。

从本例可以看出,两个参与者位置的互换引起了某些词汇上的变化,例如,原来的"有"变成了"属于",原来的"在"变成了"有"。据此,我们似乎可以断定"所有"和"环境"类关系过程的两个参与者可以通过词汇手段来实现其位置的互换。但事实并非如此。请看下面的例子:

(13) a. 一本书属于我。
　　 b. 我有那本书。
(14) a. 桌子上有那本字典。
　　 b. 一本字典在桌子上。

很显然,词汇的变化使得小句的意义发生了很大改变。因此,我们可以断言,"所有"和"环境"类关系过程的两个参与者的位置根本不能互换。事实上,上例中的两种小句形式是互补的,它们的分布模式是由该小句的信息结构来决定的。有关这方面的内容,本文不做讨论。

12. "把"字句结构

本节探讨汉语的"把"字句结构。先看下面几个例子,

(1) a. 他卖了房子。
　　b. 他把房子卖了。
(2) a. 常艳洗了衣服。
　　b. 常艳把衣服洗了。

对比上面两组句子,我们可以看出,在 a 句中位于动词之后的参与者,在 b 句中却出现在了动词之前,"把"字之后。我们将"把"及其后面的参与者一起称为"把"字句结构。"把"字句结构只能出现在动词之前。请看下例:

(3) a. *他卖了把房子。
　　b. *常艳洗了把衣服。

其次,只有位于动词之后的"受事"才可以提至动词之前,"把"字

之后。"目标"、"现象"、"行为者"、"识别者"、"属性"等其他参与者则不能做此移动。如下面的例子所示：

(4) a. 王峰烧了信。
    b. 王峰把信烧了。 （受事）
(5) a. 王峰打了我。
    b. *王峰把我打了。 （目标）
(6) a. 王峰喜欢那张画。
    b. *王峰把那张画喜欢。 （现象）
(7) a. 王峰说他不去。
    b. *王峰把他不去说。 （报告）
(8) a. 王峰是那个人。
    b. *王峰把那个人是。 （识别者）
(9) a. 王峰有一张画。
    b. *王峰把一张画有。 （属性）

其次，"把"字句结构只能用来引导有确定所指的"受事"。例如：

(10) a. 他卖了那三本书。
     b. 他把那三本书卖了。
(11) a. 他卖了三本书。
     b. *他把三本书卖了。

但含有修饰语"一"的名词词组常具有定指功能。如，

(12) 我把一个东西丢了。

很显然，这里的"一个东西"是有特指的（至少对于说话人来说）。

另外，"把"字句结构所传递的往往是已知信息（Given Information）。这在"问一答"句中体现的尤为明显。例如：

(13) a. 你的字典在哪儿？
     b. *我卖了我的字典。
     c. 我把字典卖了。

在本例中，b 句之所以不能用来回答 a 句的问题，是因为词组"你的字典"在 a 句中已经是已知信息了，但在 b 句中却又变成了新信息。由于已知信息和新信息所关涉的是语言信息结构中的语篇功能，所以在此不做详细论述。

17

13. 被动句结构

本节探讨汉语的被动句结构。

"被动"(passivity)不是汉语的普遍特征,但汉语中经常使用被动句结构。例如:

(1) a. 她姐姐打了她。
  b. 她被她姐姐打了。

这里的 b 句就是被动句。对比被动句和主动句,我们发现,在被动句中,原来位于动词之后的参与者被前提至小句的句首位置,位于动词之前的那个参与者则被移至了"被"字之后。这就好像告诉我们,汉语的被动句是由主动句衍生而来的。但事实并非如此,因为前置的参与者除了被"主位化"以外,还被说话人认为是"受害者"(sufferer),或者是某些说话人(包括听话人)所不愿意接受的事情。因此,a 句和 b 句不仅语篇意义不同,而且人际意义也不相同。所以说,被动句形式是说话人表述同一事件时所采用的不同方式。

但是,"被"动结构只能引出"动作者"或者"受事"。换句话说,被动句结构只能出现在"有指向"的物质过程中,而不能出现在心理过程、言语过程或者关系过程中。请看下例:

(2) a. 书被我拿了。
  b. 书被我烧了。
  c. *书被我喜欢。
  d. *书不好被我说了。
  e. *书被我有。

由于被动句中的目标或者受事往往被描述为"受害者"或某些令人不快事件的"经受者",所以其过程必须要涉及某些动作或者事件。正因为如此,被动句过程必须使用完成体,而不是进行体。试比较下面两组句子:

(3) a. 我被他打了。
  b. *我在被他打。
(4) a. 房子被他烧了。
  b. *房子在被他烧。

但是，某些动作者过程是不能用在被动句之中的。例如：

(5) a. *书被他找了。
　　b. *我被他追了。

究其原因，是因为诸如"找"和"追"等过程即便用在了完成体中，也不能对目标产生任何影响，因而也不可能引出"受害者"或者变化的承担者。

其次，当"被"字单独出现在句子中时，其动作者或者施动者常常是非定指的。例如：

(6) a. 书被偷了。
　　b. 肉被吃了。

另外，"给"在被动句中也能引出动作者或施动者，但此种情况多用于口语中。例如：

(7) a. 我的字典给小偷偷了。
　　b. 饭给狗吃了。
　　c. 小华给骗了。

14. 复合过程与双参与者

汉语通常把两个过程联结在一起，从而出现了"复合过程"（complex process）的现象。请看下例：

(1) 老太太哭瞎了眼睛。

本例中的"哭瞎"就是一个复合过程。在复合过程里，第二个过程通常是第一个过程的结果，而第一个过程通常是用来指明引起该结果的手段或方式。因此，"哭瞎"就意味着"通过哭的方式而使眼睛变瞎"。

同时，在例(1)中，位于动词之后的参与者"眼睛"承担着两个参与者的功能。一是"哭"这个动作者过程的"目标"，二是无指向受事过程"瞎"的"受事"。该类参与者被称为"双参与者"（double participant），通常出现在"把"字句结构中，例如：

(2) 老太太把眼睛哭瞎了。

事实上,复合过程有多种组合方式,下文将一一进行详细探讨。

14.1 无指向动作者过程+无指向动作者过程

在所有的复合过程中,数这一类的数量最少,但有时的确会出现。且看下例:

(3) 他把我哭笑了。

在例(3)中,"他"是"哭"这一过程的动作者,而"我"却是个"双参与者":一则充当了"哭"的目标,同时还是"笑"这个动作的动作者。但是,此类复合过程中也有无指向参与者的情况。例如:

(4) 他跑哭了。

在本例中,"他"既是"跑"这一过程的动作者,也是"哭"的动作者,因而属于"双参与者"。

14.2 无指向动作者过程+无指向受事过程

与上节14.1所说的复合过程相比,这一类复合过程较为常见。例如:

(5) a. 赵亮走出了汗。
　　 b. 姑娘笑掉了牙。
　　 c. 鸟飞折了翅膀。

在本例中,小句的第一个参与者是第一个过程的动作者,而第二个参与者,即"双参与者"充当了第一个过程的目标,但同时还是第二个过程的受事。

此类复合过程中也有无指向参与者的情况。如下例所示:

(6) a. 他跑丢了。
　　 b. 他哭病了。

这里的"双参与者"也是句中唯一一个参与者:"他"既是第一个过程的动作者,又是第二个过程的受事。

14.3 无指向动作者过程+归属过程

先看一个实例:

(7) a. 她把眼睛哭红了。

    b. 钱菲把嗓子喊痛了。
    c. 他把嘴巴吃馋了。

在这些例句中,第一个参与者充当的是第一个过程的动作者,而第二个参与者既是第一个过程的目标,同时还是第二个过程的载体。

同样,此类复合过程中也有无指向参与者的情况。如:

(8) a. 他走热了。
    b. 鹰飞高了。

如例(8)所示,本句唯一一个参与者,即"双参与者",既是第一个过程的动作者,同时还是第二个过程的载体。

14.4 指向动作者过程＋无指向动作者过程

请看下面的例子:

(9) a. 他把石头推动了。
    b. 他把小孩吓哭了。

在这个复合过程中,第一个参与者"他"充当了第一个过程的动作者,但第二个参与者"石头"和"小孩"同时充当了第一个过程的目标和第二个过程的动作者。

14.5 指向动作者过程＋无指向受事过程

下面的例句均属于这一类复合过程。

(10) a. 汽车把狗撞死了。
    b. 这会把杯子压破。
    c. 吴斌把肉吃完了。

在这里,第一个参与者承担的是第一个过程的参与者,第二个参与者既承担了第一个过程的目标,同时还充当了第二个过程的受事。

14.6 指向动作者过程＋归属过程

先看以下实例:

(11) a. 陈涛把我的脸打青了。
    b. 秦峰把猪喂肥了。
    c. 你把他画高了。

在这些例句中,第一个参与者是第一个过程的动作者,而"双参与者"既充当了第一个过程的目标,还充当了第二个过程的载体。

14.7 指向受事过程＋无指向动作者过程

与14.1的情况相似,该类复合过程的数量也很少。例如:

(12) a. 老工人把机器开动了。
　　　b. 火把孩子烧哭了。

本例中的第一个参与者是第一个过程的施动者,第二个参与者既是第一个过程的受事,同时还是第二个过程的动作者。

14.8 指向受事过程＋无指向受事过程

先看下面的例子:

(13) a. 他把鸡蛋卖光了。
　　　b. 小华把铁板磨穿了。
　　　c. 你会把萝卜拔断。

在这些例句中,第一个参与者所承担的是第一个过程的施动者,而第二个参与者同时承担了两个过程的受事。

14.9 指向受事过程＋归属过程

最后,指向受事过程与归属过程结合在一起,也可以组成复合过程。且看下例:

(14) a. 晓春把你的衣服洗干净了。
　　　b. 火把石头都烧红了。
　　　c. 你先把刀磨快。

在这里,第一个参与者充当了第一个过程的施动者,第二个参与者既充当了第一个过程的受事,同时还充当了第二个过程的载体。

以上我们探讨了9种类型的复合过程。但需要强调的是,尽管复合过程包含两个过程,但其句法功能还和单个的过程一样。它们的主要特点是:在复合过程中,两个过程成分之间不可再插入任何其他成分;二者的顺序不可互换;句中经常包含一个"双参与者"。在句法功能上,复合过程很像是一个受事过程,其"双参与者"就像是一个受事。这一点可以从"双参与者"能够用于"把"字句结构这一事实中找到佐证。此外,所有出现在"有效句"中的"双参与者"("无指向动作者过程"+"无指向动作者过程"的情况除外)均可以用在动词之前,这时的施动者或者动作者往往是不确指的。请看下面的例子:

(15) a. 汗都走出来了。
　　 b. 眼睛哭红了。
　　 c. 小孩吓哭了。
　　 d. 狗撞死了。
　　 e. 我的脸打青了。
　　 f. 机器开动了。
　　 g. 鸡蛋卖光了。
　　 h. 你的衣服洗干净了。

15. 复合过程中的关系过程"成"

其实,内包型关系过程也可以用在复合过程中。其中的一个例子就是"成",它单独出现时可以充当一个关系过程,但不是很常用。如下例所示:

(1) a. 小孩成人了。
　　b. 他成了工程师。

但是,"成"作为复合过程的一个组成部分,它的功能非常活跃:它可以与其他多种过程联合组成复合过程。接下来,我们将一一探讨这些不同的组合形式。

15.1 无指向动作者过程+"成"

此类复合过程非常少见。请看下例:

(2) a. 王丽哭成泪人了。
　　b. 他走成瘸子了。

与前面第14小节所谈的复合过程不同,本例中这两个小句的"双参与者"是第一个参与者(即位于动词之前),而不是第二个参与者(即位于动词之后)。一方面,它充当了第一个过程的动作者,同时还充当了第二个过程的载体,小句的另一个参与者为属性。

15.2 有指向动作者过程＋"成"

此类复合过程也非常罕见。如例(3)所示：

(3) a. 他把我打成瘸子了。
　　b. 他把棍儿踢成了两段。

在这里，两个复合过程都包含三个参与者。第一个参与者为第一个过程的动作者；第二个参与者是个"双参与者"：它既是第一个过程的目标，同时还是第二个过程的载体；第三个参与者为属性。但是，由于属性位于动词之后，所以必需要通过"把"字句结构来引出这个"双参与者"。

15.3 受事过程＋"成"

先看下面的例子：

(4) a. 你把笋子切成片。
　　b. 他把尺子折成了两段。
　　c. 他把骨头烧成了灰。

本例中的三个句子也包含三个参与者：第一个参与者为第一个过程的施动者；第二个参与者为"双参与者"：它既是第一个过程的受事，同时还是第二个过程的载体；第三个参与者是第二个过程的属性。出于同样的原因，这里的"双参与者"也必需要由"把"字句结构来引导。

需要说明的是，由受事过程和"成"一起构成的复合过程，其功能和单个的受事过程一样。换言之，这里的"双参与者"如同受事一样，可以出现在动词之前，但其施动者所指不明确。例如：

(5) a. 笋子切成了片。
　　b. 尺子折成了两段。
　　c. 骨头烧成了灰。

15.4 心理过程＋"成"

心理过程也可以跟"成"结合在一起，形成复合过程。且看下例：

(6) a. 我把那头牛看成了一匹马。

  b. 他把'爸'听成了'妈'。
  c. 我把'你来'听成了'我来'。

  在本例中,第一个参与者为第一个过程的感知者;第二个参与者是个"双参与者":它既充当了第一个过程的现象,又充当了第二个过程的载体;另一个参与者为第二个过程的属性。如前所述,这里的"双参与者"也要通过"把"字结构来引导。

  15.5 归属过程＋"成"

  请看下面的例子:

   (7) a. 李华瘦成一根棍儿了。
    b. 他的头发白成雪了。

  本例中的第一个参与者兼职两个过程的载体,而第二个参与者则为第二个过程的属性。

  15.6 言语过程＋"成"

  先看下面的例句:

   (8) a. 他把'小王去'说成'小黄去'了。
    b. 我把'花红吗'问成了'瓜红吗'。

  在本例中,第一个参与者为第一个过程的说话人;第二个参与者,即第一个转述小句,既是第二个过程的转述内容,同时也是它的载体;第三个参与者,即位于引号里的第二个小句,则是第二个过程的属性。如前所述,由于属性占据了动词之前的位置,因此必需要通过"把"字句结构来引导其双参与者。

16. 复合过程中的关系过程"在"

  除了上面所说的"成"以外,环境类关系过程"在"也可以构成复合过程。主要有两种情况:一种是"在"与无指向动作者过程的结合,另一种是"在"与受事过程的结合。分别举例说明如下。

  16.1 无指向动作者过程＋"在"

  请看下面的例子:

(1) a. 他坐在板凳上。
　　b. 李华站在桌子上。
　　c. 王平躲在床下。

在这些例句中,出现在动词之前的那个参与者就是我们前面所说的"双参与者":它既是第一个过程的动作者,也是第二个过程的载体。出现在动词之后的那个参与者则是第二个过程的属性。之所以出现这样的组合方式,是因为无指向动作者过程具有这种倾向,而它们本身又不能单独出现在日常交际中。如下例所示:

(2) a. *他坐。
　　b. *李华站。
　　c. *王平躲。

上述情况必需要与祈使语气或与进行体后缀"着"一起出现时,方可成立。且看下例。

(3) a. 请坐。
　　b. 他坐着。

在复合过程中,环境类关系过程"在"不仅可以紧跟在无指向动作者过程的后面,而且还可以出现在它的前面。看下面的例子:

(4) a. 他在板凳上坐。
　　b. 李华在桌子前站了两个钟头。
　　c. 王平在窗下躲了一天。

如本例所示,当"在"出现在动词之前时,它就不再是个过程了:其功能是引导一个方位型的环境成分。这一点可以通过"在哪里"这一问句形式来进行验证。例如,我们可以对上面的例(1)进行提问,但例(4)不可以。

由"在"来引导的环境成分还可以与指向动作者过程、心理过程或者言语过程一起组成复合过程。例如:

(5) a. 他在街上打人。
　　b. 我在教室里看见他。
　　c. 李颖在台上说,"我不怕"。

某些无指向动作者过程,如例(1)所示,可以在动词之后直接带一个名词词组。这一点将在后面的"处所范围"一节中(第 23.4 节)单独讨论。

16.2 受事过程＋"在"

请看下面的例子：

  （6）a. 他把铅笔放在桌子上。

    b. 张颖把女孩儿留在了家里。

    c. 他把画挂在墙上。

在这些例句中，第一个参与者为第一个过程的施动者；第二个参与者由"把"字句结构来引导，它既是第一个过程的受事，同时还是第二个过程的载体；另外一个参与者是第二个过程的属性。出于相同的原因，这里的"双参与者"也要通过"把"字句结构得以引导出来。

其实，上面这些复合过程在功能上仍然像单个的受事过程。其双参与者可以出现在动词之前，但此时小句的施动者是不能出现的。如下例所示：

  （7）a. 铅笔放在桌子上。

    b. 女孩儿留在了家里。

    c. 画挂在墙上。

17. 复合过程里的指向动词

汉语里有这样一类词，它们能够用来表达过程的方向或者参与者的位移（displacement）情况。这就是本节所说的"指向动词"（directional verbs）。主要有以下三类：

  （i）来，去

  （ii）上，下，进，出，回，开，起，过

  （iii）上来，上去，下来，下去，进来，出去，回来，起来，过来，过去

很显然，第三类指向动词是由前两类指向动词联合而成的。

首先，指向动词本身可以充当一个小句的过程成分。例如：

  （1）a. 他来了。

    b. 他进门了。

  c. 他出去了。

  但通常情况下,它们是作为复合过程的组成成分出现的。且看下面的例子:

  (2) a. 孙英走出来了。
    b. 迟萍跑回去了。
    c. 我把书买回来了。
    d. 他把铅笔找出来了。
    e. 船沉下去了。
    f. 小偷逃出去了。
    g. 他把纸吞下去了。
    h. 我把字典卖出去了。

  事实上,指向动词通常并不指称实际的方向,它们只是说话人自身对过程的方向或者参与者的位移情况所做的一种主观透视。例如:

  (3) a. 我把书买下了。
    b. 他把我看上了。

在这种情况下,指向动词的功能和无指向受事过程一样。
又如:

  (4) 他把铅笔找出来了。

  在这个复合过程小句里,只有"出"一个动词是指向动词,动词"来"不是指向动词,它是一个独立的过程。

18. 复合过程、嵌入句和分枝句之比较

  先来看下面三个例子:

  (1) a. 他打跑了狗。
    b. 他喜欢打狗。
    c. 他去打狗。

  我们分别把这个三个句子叫做带有复合过程的小句、带有嵌入句(embedded)的小句以及带有分枝句(branched)的小句。在 1a 中,"打跑"是一个复合过程。如前所述,复合过程是由两个过程复合而成的。

其中第一个过程表征的是手段或方法,第二个过程表达的是结果。例句 1b 和 1c 中不存在这种关系。例如,我们不能说"打"这个过程是"喜欢"(见 1b)或者"去"(见 1c)的结果。在(1a)中,"狗"是一个"双参与者":它既是"打"这一过程的目标,同时还是"跑"这一过程的受事。但在 1b 和 1c 中,"狗"仅仅是"打"这一过程的目标,跟第一个过程"喜欢"和"去"没有什么关系。

其次,在 b 句中,"打狗"是一个小句,却被当做了参与者来使用。这类小句被称为"嵌入句"或者"级转位"(rankshifted)小句。具体说来,在 b 句中,"打狗"充当的是小句的现象。这一点可以通过"什么"这一问句形式对"打狗"进行提问来加以验证。但是,对于 a 句的"跑了狗"和 c 句的"打狗"则不能做此提问。试比较:

(2) a. *他打什么?
    b. 他喜欢什么?
    c. *他去什么?

另外,在 b 句中,第二个过程可以带有一个独立的参与者(其位置在动词之前),但这在 a 句和 c 句中是行不通的。试比较:

(3) a. *他打你跑了狗。
    b. 他喜欢你打狗。
    c. *他去你打狗。

在例(1)中,c 句是一个分枝小句,即,一个小句同时带有两个或多个过程,彼此之间独立存在,但两者的参与者相同。主要有两种类型,一种类型是第二个过程陈述第一个过程的目的,如(1c)所示;另一种类型是两个过程的发生具有一定的先后顺序。且看例(4):

(4) 我上完课回家。

篇幅所限,本文对分枝小句的结构不再展开论述。

19. 使役结构

除了上面所谈的几种情况之外,某些动作者过程还可以用在使役结构中(causative construction)。请看下面的例子:

(1) a. 李明在跑马。

b. 老太太在晒太阳。
c. 我在烤火。
d. 他在斗鸡。

这四个小句都有两个参与者,但真正的动作者是位于动词之后的那个,而不是位于动词之前的那个。例(2)更能说明这一点:

(2) a. 马在跑。
b. 太阳晒着老太太。
c. 火烤着我。
d. 鸡在斗。

另一方面,位于动词前的那个参与者,不是动作的执行者,它只是引发了该动作。这类参与者被称为"致使者"(causer),相应地,该类小句被称为"使役句"。由于是致使者引发了某个动作,所以其动作者必定不会自愿地执行该动作。换句话说,动作者的动作完全是在致使者的影响下进行的。从此种意义上来说,使役句中的动作者具有双重功能:它既是个使成者,又是个动作者。我们称之"使成动作者"(effected actor)。

同样,使役小句里的过程也行使着双重功能:它既是个使役过程,同时还是个动作者过程。我们将该类过程称为"使役过程"(causativized)。请看下面的分析:

(3) a. 李明在使马跑。
b. 老太太在让太阳晒。
c. 我在让火烤。
d. 他在叫鸡斗。

像这里的"使"、"让"或者"叫"都属于"使役过程",其功能只是在表达动作者和致使者之间的使役关系而已,别无其它。

但是,当有指向动作者过程用在使役结构中时,其致使者就会充当其暗含的目标(尽管这个目标从来没有明确说明过)。这一点在单个的使役小句里显得更为清楚。请看下例:

(4) a. 老太太让太阳晒她自己。
b. 我让火烤我自己。

需要注意,使役结构没有被动形式。例如:

(5) a. *马在被李明跑。
　　b. *太阳在被老太太晒。
　　c. *火在被我烤。
　　d. *鸡在被他斗。

而且,受动动作者也不能够出现在"把"字句结构中。如:

(6) a. *李明把马跑了。
　　b. *老太太把太阳晒了。
　　c. *我把火烤了。
　　d. *他把鸡斗了。

上例好像是说某些归属过程和受事过程也可以用在使役结构中。如下例所示:

(7) a. 他在热饭。
　　b. 姚琳在烫衣服。
　　c. 他退了票。
　　d. 他在停车。

然而,如果我们对此做进一步的分析,就能够看到本例中的过程与例(1)中那些真正的使役过程之间有很大差别。

首先,位于动词之后的那个参与者可以提至动词之前。这时,它在语义上就像是个受事者,只不过是缺少了动词之前的那个参与者。请看下面的例子。

(8) a. 饭热了。
　　b. 衣服烫了。
　　c. 票退了。
　　d. 车停了。

其次,例(7)中的这些过程均可以出现在被动结构中。例如:

(9) a. 饭被他热了。
　　b. 衣服被姚琳烫了。
　　c. 票被他退了。
　　d. 车被他停了。

第三,在例(7)中,那些位于动词之后的参与者都可以出现在"把"字句结构中。如下例所示:

(10) a. 他把饭热了。
　　 b. 姚琳把衣服烫了。
　　 c. 他把票退了。
　　 d. 他把车停了。

综上可以看出，上述例(7)中的小句都不属于使役结构：小句 7c 和 7d 只是普通的受事者过程；7a 和 7b 则是"受事化了的归属过程"(patientized ascription process)。确切地说，无论是受事者过程，还是受事化了的过程，其施动者都行使了致使者的功能。同时，它还充当了动作者的角色。这就是说，这里的施动者是动作者和致使者两个参与者的重合体(conflated)。具体说来，7a 中的"他"既执行了"加热"这一动作，又造成了"热"这一结果；7b 中的"姚琳"既是"烫"这一动作的执行者，同时也造成了"热"的结果；7c 中的"他"既是"退票"这一动作的执行者，也导致了"退"的结果；7d 中的"他"既行使了"停车"动作本身，同时也造成了"停"的结果。

最后，许多归属过程可以被受事化，其中只有少数具有指向，而大多数受事化了的归属过程都是无指向的。请看下面的例子：

(11) a. 新政策繁荣了经济。
　　 b. 经济繁荣了。
　　 c. 他端正了态度。
　　 d. 他的态度端正了。
　　 e. 树叶红了。
　　 f. 小芳高了。
　　 g. 天气冷了。
　　 h. 房间干净了。
　　 I. 我累了。

可以看出，无指向过程的受事化过程必定伴有完成体的出现。离开了完成体，就不能表达状态变化这一意义，归属过程也不再像是无指向的受事过程了。具体内容，详见下文第 24 节的分析。

20. 位相结构

在汉语里，位相结构(phase structure)是一个非常复杂的现象，很少有人研究。本节也只是做尝试性的探讨。

先看下面几个例子：

(1) a. 我叫你去。
    b. 他托我买书。

上面两个例句都包含两个过程，其中第二个过程从属于第一个过程。两个过程之间是一个参与者，它有两个功能：它既是第一个动作过程的接受者，同时也是第二个动作过程的执行者。我们把这类参与者称作"二重参与者"（dual participant），把发生在同一个小句中的两个过程（其中后一个过程从属于第一个过程），及其所共享的参与者一起称作位相结构。

首先，第二个过程能否在句中出现，完全取决于第一个过程的性质。例如，动词"叫"本身就要求带有第二个过程，而"洗"就没有这个要求。我们把这类能够允许第二个过程单独出现的动词叫做"位相动词"。但是，如果该动词出现在了第二个过程中，这就势必要求引入第三个过程。这就是位相结构的递归性特征（recursive）。请看下例：

(2) a. 我叫你叫他…去。
    b. 他托我托孙颖…买书。
    c. 我请你帮我叫他来。
    d. 我求你别叫他带李彬来。

又如：

(3) a. 这使我很高兴。
    b. 那个小孩讨人喜欢。
    c. 他让雨淋。
    d. 王磊在帮我搬床。
    e. 工人们选他当经理。
    f. 我骂他为贱胎。
    g. 我准许他去工厂。

其次，某些位相结构里的二重参与者可以出现在"把"字句结构中，或者被动句结构中。例如：

(4) a. 我把他骂为贱胎。
    b. 他被我骂为贱胎。

c. 王平把他叫去了。
d. 他被王平叫去了。

需要注意,我们一定不要把例(4)跟前面所说的复合过程混淆起来。两者之间的区别在于其各自的参与者:位相结构的二重参与者要求出现在两个过程之间,但复合过程里的双参与者则没有此要求。

另外,也要将位相结构与心理过程区别开来,后者以嵌入小句来作为自己的现象。详见下例:

(5) a. 我看见他来。
b. 我叫他来。

在 a 句中,"他来"是一个嵌入小句,其功能是充当了心理过程"看见"的现象。"他"只是嵌入小句的参与者,在主句中没有发挥作用。但在 b 句中,"他"具有双重功能,"他来"不是个小句,也没有参与者角色。下例可以清楚地说明这一点。

(6) a. 我看见他来这件事。
b. *我叫他来这件事。

事实上,这一点还可以从"他来"这一事实中得到验证。例如,在 a 句中,"他来"是小句的参与者,因而可以通过"什么"来对其提问;但在 b 句中,"他来"不是嵌入小句,也不是参与者,因而不可以用"什么"进行提问。请看下例:

(7) a. 你看见了什么?
b. *你叫什么?

在 5b 中,第二个过程依附于第一个过程:它只是表明了第一个过程的结果。换言之,"他来"这一结果只是因为"我叫他来"。但在 5a 中,两个过程之间就没有这种依附性:我们不能说"他来"是因为"我看到了他",这个理由显然不够充分。

再者,例(5)中的两个例句还向我们展示了不同类型的被动句结构。如下例所示:

(8) a. 他来这件事被我看见了。
b. 他被我叫来了。
c. *他被我看见来了。
d. *他来这件事被我叫了。

在 8a 中,"他来"是一个嵌入句,起到了参与者的功能,与例(5)中的 a 句相同。但在 8d 中,"他来"不是个参与者(与 5b 的情况相同);另一方面,8b 中的"他"充当了过程"叫"的参与者,而不是"看见"的参与者,这一点可以从 8c 中得到证明。

还有,能否成为位相结构的论元还可以从其能否使用"把"字句这一特征中找到佐证。例如,上面的 5b 可以用在被动句结构中,但 5a 却不可以。请看下面的例(9):

(9) a. *我把他看见来了。
　　 b. 我把他叫来了。

最后,位相结构还要跟另一种结构区分开来。先看一个例子:

(10) 我买了一份报看。

在本例中,"买"和"看"的目标都是"报",其动作者也都是"我"。但是,句子的第二个过程明显不再依附于第一个过程,两个过程之间可能是方法与目的的关系,也可能是方法与时间顺序的关系。本文将其分析为"分枝小句",但它省略了第二个过程的参与者。由于小句复合体和衔接都不是本文研究的范围,故此不再展开。

21. 位相结构中的"有"

从信息的分布情况来看,汉语倾向于把已知信息(given)或"旧"信息安排在动词(即过程)之前,而把"新"信息(new)或未知信息放在动词之后。但是,当负载着新信息的参与者必需出现在动词之前的位置时,这就需要通过"有"这一结构来为其创造条件。请看下面的例子:

(1) a. 那个人来了。
　　 b. 有一个人来了。
　　 c. 那三本书丢了。
　　 d. 有三本书丢了。

从表面上来看,b 和 d 中的"有"像是个位相动词,但它却没有任何概念意义:它只是新信息的标志。这一点可以通过能否增删"有"这个动词而得到证明。如下例所示:

(2) a. *有那个人来了。
　　b. 一个人来了。
　　c. *有那三本书丢了。
　　d. 三本书丢了。

显而易见,这里的 a 句和 c 句由于"有"字的存在,而变得不再合乎语法;b 句和 d 句却因删去了"有"而改变了原来小句的意义。

需要说明的是,"有"可以出现在某些处所或时间的表达式之前,它甚至可以出现在人称代词或某些名词词组的前面。但不管是哪一种情况,上述原则仍然奏效。请看例(3):

(3) a. 房间里有一个人叫张丽。
　　b. *房间里有那个人叫张丽。
　　c. 我有两本书丢了。
　　d. *我有那两本书丢了

由于信息结构不属于及物性系统的研究范围,所以本文不再详细讨论。

22. 受益者

以上我们集中探讨了汉语的基本过程类型及其相关关系。接下来,我们将对这些过程所涉及的参与者(participant)情况进行详细描写和阐述。

所谓参与者,指参与某一过程的人、物或事实。通常情况下,它由名词词组来体现。除了前面所谈到的各种参与者之外,还有两种参与者功能,这就是"受益者"(Beneficiary)和"范围"(Range)。

首先来看受益者。受益者指的是"积极或消极地受益于过程"(Halliday,1967a:53)的参与者类型。它主要出现在物质过程和言语过程中(如划线部分所示)。请看下例:

(1) a. 老师给我们书。
　　b. 周蓉告诉我们她明天去北京。

一般说来,受益者通常会紧跟在过程之后出现,但也有出现在(某些)介词之后的情况。例如:

(2) a. 他送给我一本书。
    b. 他送一本书给我。

根据语义特征,受益者可以分成四类,即"给"(to)、"向"(from)、"为"(for)和"替"(on behalf of)。如下例所示:

(3) a. 吴峰给一本书给我。
    b. 我向陈宇借了一本书。
    c. 他为祖国上前线。
    d. 我替他写信。

有时候,"给"也可以当作"为"或者"替"来使用。且看下例:

(4) a. 我在给病人看病。
    b. 我给他写了两篇作文。

"给"类受益者可以出现在过程和动词后的那个参与者之间。这时的"给"可用可不用,具体依情况而定,如例(1)和例(2)所示。当受益者由"给"来引导时,它还可以出现在动词之后的那个参与者之后,如3a所示。

当受益者由"向"来引导时,它可以出现在动词之前,如前面的3b所示。反之,只能出现在动词之后。请看例(5):

(5) 我借了陈宇一本书。

但是,"为"类和"替"类受益者的使用必需要由介词来引导,尤其是当"替"类受益者出现在动词之前时;"替"类受益者通常出现在动词之前,少数情况下也可以出现在动词之后。且看下例:

(6) a. 他生为祖国,死为人民。
    b. 我上学为人民。

23. 范围

范围(Range)指的是小句中具体说明某一过程本身所延及的成分,如范围(区域),自然结果,或工具等。根据它与过程之间的关系,我们把汉语的范围细分为六类:同源(Cognate)、度量(Measurement)、结果(Result)、处所(Location)、工具(Instrument)和过程(Process)。分别举例说明如下:

23.1 同源范围

同源范围指的是"与过程具有一致意义的功能成分",它只是"过程的名词化","是过程的直接的、本质的延伸",并与过程之间构成一种"相互依存的语义关系"(Halliday,1967a:59)。如下例划线部分所示:

(1) a. 李峰在唱<u>歌</u>。
　　b. 我吃了<u>饭</u>了。
　　c. 小孩在睡<u>觉</u>。
　　d. 别说<u>话</u>。
　　e. 他输了<u>钱</u>。

事实上,"同源"这种说法并不准确,因为上面例句中的名词和动词之间并非是同源的。但二者之间的本质关系还是非常清楚的。例如,"歌"是"唱"的行为称谓,"饭"是"吃"的行为称谓,"觉"是"睡"的行为称谓,"话"是"说"的行为称谓。同样,"钱"是赌博过程中输或赢这一行为进行的媒介。

同源范围通常由名词词组来体现,因而其所指非常宽泛,因为它们仅仅是过程的延伸,是个没有实质性意义的"假"参与者(pseudo)。拿 c 句来说,这里的"饭"指的是"三餐中任何可以吃的东西"。但如果将其换成"米饭",它就不再是同源范围了,而是动作的"受事"了。

另外,同源范围可以带有自己的修饰成分,这时,它的所指就会非常具体了。请看下例:

(2) a. 李峰在唱<u>民歌</u>。
　　b. 我吃了<u>午饭</u>了。
　　c. 小孩在睡<u>午觉</u>。
　　d. 他会说<u>英国话</u>。

最后,同源范围只能出现在无指向动作者过程中。

23.2 度量范围

度量范围是过程延伸的又一种形式。它的功能是使过程得以量化,而这里的量又必须是它的内在价值的一部分。度量范围主要出现于归属过程。请看例(3):

(3) a. 赵勇身高一米七。
    b. 猪重六十公斤。
    c. 这辆汽车值一万元。
    d. 这块地长二十米,宽十五米。

在这些例句中,"一米七"是身高的固有高度范围,"六十公斤"是重量的固有度量范围,"一万元"是该汽车价值的度量范围,而"二十米"和"十五米"则分别是长度和宽度的固有度量范围。我们之所以说这些度量范围是固有的,是因为其它度量是不适合这些过程的。且看下例:

(4) a. *赵勇身高六十公斤。
    b. *猪重三米。
    c. *这块地长二十平方米,宽十五立方米。

至于上面提到的 3c,(归属)过程"值"更要求由"一万元"这样的成分来做其度量范围,否则句子就不合语法了。当然,"值"的同源范围还可以是"钱"。

另外,某些受事或被受事化了的过程也可以带度量范围。请看下面的例子:

(5) a. 表卖了五十元。
    b. 他胖了三公斤。

同样,同源范围有时也可以带度量性的修饰成分。例如:

(6) a. 李峰唱了三支歌。
    b. 我吃了两顿饭了。
    c. 他睡了两个午觉了。

这些例句中的范围显然不是度量范围,而是同源范围的修饰语。又如:

(7) a. 他跳了两跳。
    b. 他看了一看。
    c. 我尝一尝。
    d. 我走一走。

23.3 结果范围

结果范围是使某一过程的本质结果具体化的参与者类型。它仅仅出现于少数受事者过程中。如下例所示：

(8) a. 裤子破了一个<u>洞</u>。
　　b. 墙裂了一条<u>口</u>。
　　c. 岩石开了一条<u>缝</u>。

在这些例句中，"洞"是"破"的自然结果；"口"是"裂"的自然结果；"缝"也是"开"的自然结果。

23.4 处所范围

处所范围是对某一过程的内在地点或位置做出具体描述的参与者。如下面的划线部分所示：

(9) a. 他会泅<u>水</u>。
　　b. 我游<u>长江</u>，你游<u>黄河</u>。
　　c. 我坐<u>车</u>。
　　d. 我们去吃<u>馆子</u>。
　　e. 他走<u>路</u>去。

之所以说这些处所范围是本质的、内在的，是因为它们跟过程之间的紧密关系是显而易见的。在这里，"水"是"泅"这一动作发生的位置之所在；"长江"和"黄河"是"游"的位置所在；"坐车"的意思不是"坐在车里"，而是"坐着车旅游"，"车"和"飞机"、"船"一起都是"坐"和"旅游"的位置所在；"馆子"是"吃"的地方（与"家"相区别）；同样，"路"通常是"走"这一动作所发生的位置。

其实，处所范围与过程之间的这种内在关系还可以从二者能否被"在"这一结构分开的事实中找到依据。试比较：

(10) a. *他会在水里泅。
　　 b. *我在长江游，你在黄河游。
　　 c. 我在车上坐。
　　 d. *我们在馆子吃。
　　 e. *他在路上走去。

很显然，由于"在"的缘故，使得本例中的 a,b,d 三句都变得不合乎语法了。c 句尽管在语法上是合适的,但意义已经完全发生了变化。

有时,尽管位于动词之后的那个参与者指定了过程所发生的地点或位置,但是它们也不是处所范围,而是过程的其它成分,因为它们与过程之间不存在本质的、内在的联系。所以,它们能够从原来的过程中分离出来。例如:

  (11) a. 他去北京。
    b. 他到北京去。
    c. 他上山了。
    d. 他上到山上了。

很明显,a 句中的"北京"和 c 句里的"山"不是范围,而是"去"这一动作的目标。因此,处所范围仅限于带有单一动作者的过程中。

23.5 工具范围

工具范围是使过程或行为得以实施的必要工具。它也仅仅出现于无指向动作者过程中。请看下例:

  (12) a. 他吃大碗。
    b. 我吃筷子。
    c. 他会写钢板。
    d. 他写毛笔。
    e. 他在给我打针。

在这里,"碗"和"筷子"是"吃"这一动作得以实现的必不可少的工具;"钢板"是人们赖以在蜡纸上"写字"的工具;"毛笔"曾经是国人仅有的书写工具;"针"是人们注射时必需使用的工具。对于这一类范围成分,我们通常用动词"用"来进行引导,但此时小句的语序有变化。另外,汉语中只有少数过程可以带有工具范围。

23.6 过程范围

上面所谈及的五种范围类型都是名词性范围或参与者范围,其意义或多或少能够在过程中暗示出来。然而,在很多实例中,"过程仅仅是通过名词词组来表达的,而名词词组本身就是范围,动词无实际意义"(Halliday, *forthcoming*: 86)。这一类范围称为过程范围。请看下面的例子:

(13) a. 他在做买卖。
　　 b. 我在做工。
　　 c. 他常做梦。
　　 d. 我们在搞运动。
　　 e. 他搞生产。
　　 f. 我搞宣传。
　　 g. 小王在干活。
　　 h. 他们干架了。
　　 i. 我们干革命。
　　 j. 他在打鼾。
　　 k. 我打赌。
　　 l. 他们在打足球。

可以看出,过程范围也可以看做是一种同源范围。

24. 受事、施动者、动作者、目标和载体之比较

本节拟比较受事、施动者、动作者、目标和载体等参与者之间的异同。

在本文中,受事指的是经历某种状态变化的参与者。请看下例:

(1) a. 我把房子卖了。
　　 b. 房子卖了。
　　 c. 他打死了人。
　　 d. 人打死了。
　　 e. 病人死了。
　　 f. 花红了。
　　 g. 他把骨头烧成了灰。
　　 h. 蝌蚪变成了青蛙。

上面的划线部分都是受事,因为它们都经历了某种状态的变化。具体说来,在 a 和 b 中,"卖"这一过程使得"房子"的所有权发生了变化;在 c 和 d 中,由于"打"的缘故,"人"经历了从"生"到"死"这一状态的变化;同样的变化也发生在 e 句中;在 f 中,"花儿"经历了由"不红"到"红"的变化过程;在 g 中,由于"烧"这一行为的原因,使得"骨头"也

经历了从"骨"到"灰"的变化过程;而在 h 中,"蝌蚪"也经历了从"蝌蚪"到"青蛙"的变化过程。

正是由于"状态变化"这个语义特征,才使得受事跟动作者、目标、载体或其它任何参与者区别开来。也正是出于这个原因,我们通常用"怎么了"这一形式对小句中的受事进行提问,但对其它参与者,则不可说"怎么了"。且看下面的例子:

(2) a. 我把猪打死了。
　　 b. 猪丢了。
　　 c. 猪病了。
　　 d. 猪肥了。
　　 e. 他把猪烧成灰了。
　　 f. 猪变成狗了。
　　 g. 猪怎么了?
(3) a. 猪尿了。(动作者)
　　 b. 猪咬了人。(动作者)
　　 c. 他在找猪。(目标)
　　 d. *猪怎么了。
(4) a. 猪肥。(载体)
　　 b. *猪怎么了?

由于都可以出现在动词之后,所以,受事跟目标两个参与者之间非常相似。但事实上,二者之间大相径庭。通常情况下,目标所标明的是过程的目的或终点,受事则是指那些在过程中被处理或被转移的事物。我们可以处理或转移受事本身,或者通过受事对其他事物行使某种动作或行为,但对目标不可以这样做。正因为如此,受事可以出现在"把"字句结构中,目标却不可以。对此,前文已有论述。又如:

(5) a. 我把书烧了。
　　 b. 他把猪卖了。
　　 c. *他把书找了。
　　 d. *他把猪打了。

上面我们提到,受事是受事者过程中的一个必要成分,但目标却是动作者过程中的可选成分;当施动者指代不明时,受事可以出现在动词之前,但目标只能出现在动词之后。

最后，我们对受事可以通过"怎么了"这一形式进行提问，如例（2）所示，但不可以对目标做此提问，详见 3c 和 3d。又如：

(6) a. 我打了狗。
　　b. 他在看狗。
　　c. *狗怎么了？

由于两者均能出现在动词之前，无指向动作者过程的动作者与无指向受事者过程的受事者也很相似。两者的区别在于是否是某一动作的执行者。另一方面，受事通常要经历某些状态的变化，但动作者不会。因此，我们对动作者可以用"做/干什么"来进行提问，而只能用"怎么了"对受事者进行提问。请看下面的例子：

(7) a. 他笑了。
　　b. 他做什么了？
　　c. *他怎么了？
　　d. 他死了。
　　e. *他做了什么？
　　f. 他怎么了？

再者，有指向过程的动作者在功能上很像是施动者，因为二者都可以出现在动词之前，都可以用"做什么"来进行提问。其实，动作者本身就是个施动者（如前文所述）。两者的区别在于施动者还是个"致使者"。此外，施动者在受事者过程中是一个可选成分，也就是说，只有当出现在有指向过程中时，受事才是个必选成分。但是，动作者在动作者过程中却是个必要成分，它可以把目标当作可选性参与者。

再来看一看载体这个参与者。载体带有属性关系过程所提供的属性，并把它赋予或者归附到关系过程身上。它与动作者之间的区别在于它不是动作的执行者，不能被"做什么"这一形式所替代；它与受事的区别在于它本身不经历任何状态的变化，因此不能被"怎么了"这一形式所替代。但却可以出现在诸如"怎么样"之类的问句中，这使得它有别于动作者和受事。看下面的例子：

(8) a. 他高。
　　b. 他有五本书。
　　c. 他怎么样？
　　d. *他做什么？

e. *他怎么了？

(9) a. 他在跑。

b. 他死了。

c. *他怎么样？

25．受动受事和使成受事

本节我们来探讨两种受事者类型。先看下面的例子：

(1) a. 他烧了一封<u>信</u>。

b. 他写了一封<u>信</u>。

c. 他们开了<u>门</u>。

d. 他们开了<u>井</u>

这些例句中划线部分的参与者都是受事者，但 a 和 c 中的受事明显有别于 b 和 d 中的受事。说的具体些，在 a 和 c 中，"信"和"门"这两个事物原本就存在，它们不是过程的衍生物，但因过程而发生了某些变化。换言之，它们的意思是"某人对其做了什么"或"通过它对其它事物做了什么"。相反，b 和 d 中的"信"和"井"则是由于过程的原因而被创造出来的：它们之前是不存在的。据此，我们把前面一种受事称为"受动受事"(affected)，而把后一种叫做"使成受事"(effected)。使成受事也经历了某种状态的变化，是因为"创造"本身就涉及了从"无"状态到"有"状态的变化。使成受事的论元就是个受事，因为它可以出现在"把"字句结构中，或者位于动词之前，但缺少明确的施动者。请看下例：

(2) a. 他把那封信写了。

b. 他们把那口井开了。

c. 信写了。

d. 井开了

但是，对使成受事却不能用"怎么了"来进行提问。例如：

(3) a. *信怎么了？

b. *井怎么了？

之所以如此，是因为例(3)中的问题本身就预设了受事先于过程

而存在的事实,但使成受事(如例 2 所示)则没有这种预设。又如:

(4) a. 他们盖了一栋<u>房子</u>。
    b. 农民们挖了一座<u>水库</u>。
    c. 他在墙上打了一个<u>洞</u>。
    d. 工人们在河上建了一座<u>桥</u>。
    e. 她今天缝了两件<u>衣服</u>。
    f. 他做了一个<u>玩具</u>。

26. 句式过程及其参与者

让我们先从一组例子说起。

(1) a. 书丢了。
    b. 他丢了书。
    c. 人死了。
    d. 村子里死了人。

从表面上来看,本例中的"丢"和"死"只是两个普通的受事过程,其中,"书"和"人"分别是它们的受事,而"他"和"村子里"分别是二者的施动者。然而,仔细观察,我们发现,"他"和"村子里"根本不是过程的施动者。因为我们不可以说"他"就是"丢"这一动作的执行者或者是"丢"的致使者;同样,"村子里"也不是"死"这一动作的执行者或者"死"的致使者。这一点可以通过它们不能使用"把"字句、被动句或者使役动词这些特征来加以验证。请看例(2):

(2) a. *他把书丢了。
    b. *书被他丢了。
    c. *他使书丢了。
    d. *村子里把人死了。
    e. *人被村子里死了。
    f. *村子里使人死了。

这里的 a 句和 b 句可以认为是合乎语法的,但"丢"的原义已经发生了变化:不再表示"丢"的结果,而是表达"扔掉"或"丢掉"的动作本身,俨然变成了另一个过程。

事实上,例(1)中没有发生任何的动作或行为,它们都是无指向受事者过程,需要受事来充当其唯一的参与者,如 1a 和 1c 所示,而 1b 和 1d 所反映出来的问题则是如何解释句中的第二个参与者。

在 1b 和 1d 中,我们假设"他"和"村子里"都是受事者,而"丢了书"和"死了人"都是嵌入句,它们的功能相当于一个无指向受事者过程,所描述的是"受事者身上发生了什么事情"。"书"和"人"是嵌入小句的受事,它们从动词之前的位置移到了动词之后。原因主要有两个:一是因为小句的句首位置早已被高一级的受事(higher patient)所占据;第二,新信息的身份又要求它必需出现在动词之后的位置上。其中,后一条原因可以通过"旧信息不能出现在动词之后的位置"这一原则得到验证,如下面的例(3)所示;同时,负载着新信息的受事者是可以出现在动词之后的,如例(4)所示。

(3) a. *他丢了那本书。
b. *村子里死了那个人。
(4) a. 来了一个人。
b. 死了一条狗。

另外,负载新信息的低一级受事可以出现在动词之前的位置,但此时需要由新信息的标志词"有"来引导(前面 21 节已有论述)。请看下例:

(5) a. 他有一本书丢了。
b. 村子里有人死了。

如前所述,"他"和"村子里"(见 1b 和 1d)均被看做是受事,而"丢了书"和"死了人"都被认为是嵌入句,相当于一个无指向受事过程。这一观点可以从各自的替代词中找到答案。例如,后者可以被"怎么了"或"发生"等代动词形式所替代,但前者只能用"怎么了"来进行替代。请看下面的例子:

(6) a. 他丢了书。
b. 他怎么了?
c. 什么事发生了?
d. 村子里死了人。
e. 村子里怎么了?
f. 什么事发生了?

但是,只有当小句用来表达诸如"出现"(appearance)或"消失"

(disappearance)之类的意义时,我们才说该过程是一个句式受事过程。此类过程只是无指向受事者过程中的一个小部分,它们要么出现在完成体之中,要么出现在无指向复合过程中,后者以指向动词作为其重要的组成部分。又如:

(7) a. 王冕七岁死了父亲。

b. 外面走进来一个人。

c. 昨天来了九个人。

d. 他的脸上出现了皱纹。

e. 农场跑了三头牛。

事实上,一个小句不仅可以起到受事过程的作用,还可以起到归属过程的功能。详见下例:

(8) a. 他头痛。

b. 教室里坐着一个人。

在这里,"头痛"和"坐着一个人"都是个小句,它们在功能上相当于一个归属过程。我们可以用"怎么样"这一形式对它们进行提问;"他"和"教室里"则是小句的载体,因为它们只能被"…怎么样"所替代。请看例(9):

(9) a. 他怎么样?

b. 教室里怎么样?

27. 句式过程中的受事/载体与属有格

从上一节(即 26)的讨论中,我们似乎可以下这样的结论,受事和载体都是属有格(possessive)名词词组的不同形式,而带有句式过程的小句都是简单句,其中没有涉及任何嵌入成分。例如,(1)中的句子均可以改写成例(2)。

(1) a. 他丢了书。

b. 村子里死了人。

c. 他头痛。

d. 教室里坐着一个人。

(2) a. 他的书丢了。

  b. 村子里的人死了。
  c. 他的头痛。
  d. 教室里的那个人坐着。

  然而,上面的观点是站不住脚的,理由如下。第一,如果我们用"……怎么了"和"……怎么样"分别对上述受事和载体进行提问,我们得到的答案分别是"他","村子里","他","教室里"(见例1)和"书","人","头","人"(见例2)。这就说明例(1)例(2)具有不同的受事和载体。

  第二,副词的出现表明了两组句子在结构上大有不同。请看下面的例子:

  (3) a. 他又丢了书。
   b. 他的书又丢了。
   c. 村子里又死了人。
   d. *村子里的那个人又死了。
   e. 他又头痛了。
   f. 他头又痛了。
   g. 他的头又痛了。
   h. 教室里又坐着一个人。
   i. 教室里的那个人又坐着。

  很明显,上述句子的意思是不同的。具体说来,a,c 和 h 三句意味着过程中所涉及到的是另外一本书或另外一个人;相反,在 b,d 和 i 句中,过程中所关涉的是同一本书或者同一个人。

  同时,像"又"这样的副词只能紧跟在过程之前出现。当它出现在名词词组和动词词组之前时(如 e 句所示),表明名词词组可以跟动词词组一起来充当小句的过程。在 1c 中,副词"又"可以出现在两个位置,这就意味着该小句拥有两个过程类型:一个是主要小句的过程,另一个则是嵌入小句的过程。

  当我们将 1c 和另外一个带有属有格名词词组的小句进行比较时,上述问题就会变得更清楚。请看下例:

  (4) a. 他头痛。
   b. 他(的)脚痛。
   c. 他又头痛了。

  d. *他又脚痛了。
  e. 他头又痛了。
  f. 他脚又痛了。
  g. 他还头痛吗？
  h. *他还脚痛吗？
  i. 他头还痛吗？
  j. 他脚还痛吗？

  在这里,尽管"他的脚痛"可以说成是"他脚痛",但与"他头痛"之间差别很大。前者只包含一个过程,后者则包含两个过程,如例(4)所示。这就说明,"他脚痛"中的"他"只是属有格"他的"一种变体形式;但是,在"他头痛"中,"他"却是小句过程的受事,因而不能把属有格"他的"当作自己的变体形式。

  第三,某些属有结构没有与自己相对应的非属有格结构。例如：

  (5) a. 小孩的曾祖父二十年前死了。
    b. *小孩二十年前死了曾祖父。

  同样,某些句式过程中的受事或者载体也没有自己的属有格结构。请看下例：

  (6) a. 家里死了父亲。
    b. *家里的父亲死了。

  在这里,6b之所以不成立,是因为它预设着这样一个命题,即"家外至少还有一个父亲"。

28. 受事、目标和范围之比较

  本节主要探讨受事、目标和范围三个参与者之间的关系和区别。

  如前所述,范围指的是过程本身所暗含的参与者成分,这是它区别于受事或目标的主要特征。正因为如此,范围与过程之间是不可分离的,但受事或目标却可以与过程分开。三者之间的区别如下。

  首先,在被动句中,受事或目标可以前置,但范围不能。且看下例：

  (1) a. 衣服被洗了。

b. 狗被打了。

c. *话被说了。

第二,受事或目标能够出现在"假分裂句"结构中,但范围不能。例如:

(2) a. 他洗的是衣服。

b. 他打的是狗。

c. *他说的是话。

第三,受事或目标能够出现在"把"字句结构中,但范围不能。请看下例:

(3) a. 我把衣服洗了。

b. 他把门打破了一个洞。

c. *我把歌唱了。

d. *他把洞打破了。

e. 门把洞破了。

最后,当施动者不明确时,受事能够出现在动词之前的位置,但范围不能。

(4) a. 衣服洗了。

b. 杯子破了。

c. *法国话说了。

d. *洞破了。

29. 总结

下表总结了汉语的过程类型(这里不包括复合过程)及其所涉及的参与者数目和类型。其中,下划线部分指的是必具性参与者,其他的是可选性参与者,符号"/"的意思是"在一组参与者中,只能选择其一"。

过程类型及其参与者

过程类型 参与者	动作者过程		受事者过程		归属过程	心理过程	言语过程	关系过程	
	有指向	无指向	有指向	无指向				属性类	识别类
参与者1	动作者	动作者	施事	受事	载体	感知者	说话人	载体	被识别者
参与者2	目标	同源范围/处所范围/工具范围/过程范围/受益者	受事	度量范围/结果范围/受益者	度量范围	现象	受益者	属性	识别者
参与者3	受益者	受益者	受益者						

注：如果一个无指向动作者过程已经选择了受益者作为它的第二个参与者，就不能再选择另外一个受益者了。

附录　英文原文[①]

Transitivity in Chinese

Long, Rijin

A Thesis Submitted in Partial Requirement for
the Degree of M. A. (Honours) in Applied Linguistics
University of Sydney

March 1981

---

① 正文中出现"[ ]"及其数码的地方,系原文某页结束;如[23],即原文第23页到此结束。

Contents

Preface

Notations

1. Functional Theory of Language
2. Transitivity
3. Processes
4. Material Process
5. Different Types of Material Processes
6. Ascription Process
7. Material Process vs. Ascription Process
8. Mental Process
9. Material Process and Mental Process Compared
10. Verbal Process
11. Relational Process
12. 'Ba' Construction
13. Passive Construction
14. Complex Process and Double Participant
    - 14.1. Non-directed Actor Process plus Non-directed Actor Process
    - 14.2. Non-directed Actor Process plus Non-directed Patient Process
    - 14.3. Non-directed Actor Process plus Ascription Process
    - 14.4. Directed Actor Process plus Non-directed Actor Process
    - 14.5. Directed Actor Process plus Non-directed Patient Process
    - 14.6. Directed Actor Process plus Ascription Process
    - 14.7. Directed Patient Process plus Non-directed Actor Process
    - 14.8. Directed Patient Process plus Non-directed Patient Process
    - 14.9. Directed Patient Process plus Ascription Process
15. Relational Process 'Cheng' in a Complex Process
    - 15.1. Non-directed Actor Process plus 'Cheng'
    - 15.2. Directed Actor Process plus 'Cheng'

15.3. Patient Process plus 'Cheng'
15.4. Mental Process plus 'Cheng'
15.5. Ascription Process plus 'Cheng'
15.6. Verbal Process plus 'Cheng'
16. Relational Process 'Zai' in a Complex Process
    16.1. Non-directed Actor Process plus 'Zai'
    16.2. Patient Process plus 'Zai'
17. Directional Verbs in a Complex Process
18. Complex Process, Embedded Clause and Branched Clause Compared
19. Causative Construction
20. Phase Structure
21. 'You' in Phase Structure
22. Beneficiary
23. Range
    23.1. Cognate Range
    23.2. Measurement Range
    23.3. Result Range
    23.4. Location Range
    23.5. Instrument Range
    23.6. Process Range
24. Patient, Agent, Actor, Goal and Carrier Compared
25. Affected Patient and Effected Patient
26. Clausal Processes and Their Participants
27. Patient or Carrier of a Clausal Process vs. Possessive Case
28. Patient, Goal and Range Compared
29. A Brief Summary
Bibliography

Preface

This thesis is an attempt at applying Professor M. A. K. Halliday's functional theory of language to Chinese. The area chosen for the study is transitivity.

Transitivity has as the object of study the processes themselves in the clause, the participants in them, and the circumstances associated with them; but only the former two will constitute the scope of this thesis.

Many of the notions in this thesis are borrowed from Professor Halliday, e. g. : Material Process, Mental Process, Verbal Process, Relational Process, Cognizant, Phenomenon, Sayer, Report, Identifier, Identified, Carrier, Attribute, Beneficiary, Range, and so on. Some terms are coined by me for the analysis of Chinese, e. g. : Actor Process, Patient Process, Ascription Process, Measurement Range, Location Range, Result Range, Instrument Range, Complex Process, Double Participant, and so on. Some terms are borrowed but used in a different way so as to have a different coverage, e. g. : Actor, Goal, Patient and so on.

I would like to express specially my gratitude to my teachers and supervisors Professor Halliday and Dr. J. R. Martin. Without their patient and enlightening instruction in the previous two years and the generous and untiring guidance and assistance throughout the entire dissertation, it would have been totally impossible for me to write this thesis. [1]

Notations

f. p.	forepositioning particle
i. a.	inchoative aspect
i. p.	interrogative particle
m.	measure word
m. s.	modifier suffix
n. p	nominalizing particle
p. a.	perfective aspect
pl.	plural suffix
p. p.	progressive particle
p. s.	progressive suffix
*	ungrammatical clause
.../...	... or ...

Capitalization is used in this thesis to mark the names of the functions in the clause, e. g. : Actor, Goal, Agent, Patient, Carrier, etc.

Each example clause in this thesis is given in three lines: the first line is the original Chinese clause; the second line is a literal translation of the words in the Chinese clause done by me; the third line, i. e. the line in the brackets, is my English translation of the Chinese clause.

All the Chinese words in this thesis are spelt according to the 'Pinyin' system (the system used officially in China to Romanize the Chinese language). [2]

1. Functional Theory of Language

The functional linguists argue that language is fashioned by what language has to do and meaning is simply, function in context. The argument was first put forward by Malinowski. While doing anthropological fieldwork in the Trobriand Islands, Malinowski found out that the Trobrianders used language to organize fishing expeditions. He also discovered the impossibility of translating terms and texts from the language of one culture to that of another. This could not be explained if language was supposed to-be a self-contained system. Malinowski's explanation was that language is far from being self-contained; it is evolved in response to the specific demands of the society and so its nature and use reflect specific characteristics of that society. As rightly stated by Malinowski, "utterance and situation are bound up inextricably with each other and the context of situation is indispensable for the understanding of the words" (Malinowski, 1923, p. 307). In other words, language develops from the particular needs and activity of 'social man' in his community. Therefore, the meaning of an utterance can only be assessed in the 'context of situation' in particular and 'context of culture' in general. Malinowski distinguishes between 'context of situation' and 'context of culture'. By 'context of situation', he means what is actuallygoing on at the time, or the situation in which language is actualized. By 'context of culture', he means the social system with the speaker himself in the middle of it. According to Malinowski, "the meaning of a word must be always gathered, not from a passive contemplation of this word, but from an analysis of its functions, with reference [3] to the given culture" (Malinowski, 1923, p. 309). The three major functions of language which he identified in one Trobriand society are the pragmatic function, the magical function and the narrative function.

Malinowski's view of the relation between language and society and his definition of meaning as function in context were accepted and subsequently elaborated by Firth, and by a number of other linguists such as Hymes.

However it was M. A. K. Halliday who mapped the features of the situation onto the linguistic system, the actual structure of language.

Halliday proposed 'field', 'mode' and 'tenor' as three components of the 'context of situation'. "The field is the total event in which the text is functioning, together with the purposive activity of the speaker or writer; it thus includes the subject-matter as one element of it. The mode is the function of the text in the event, including therefore both the channel taken by the language—spoken or written, extempore or prepared—and its genre, or rhetorical mode, as narrative, didactic, persuasive, 'phatic communion' and so on. The tenor refers. to the type of role interaction, the set of relevant social relations, permanent or temporary, among the participants involved. Field, mode and tenor collectively define the context of situation of a text." (Halliday & Hasan, 1976, p. 22)

Halliday divides the semantics of language into three functional components:

  ideational   (observer function)
  interpersonal (intruder function) [4]
  textual   (relevance function)

The ideational function of language can be subdivided into two: experiential and logical. The experiential function relates to the content of what is said. It is the representation of the speaker's reflection on the environment, his experience of the external world of phenomena and the internal world of his own consciousness. The logical function is the expression of "the abstract logical relations which derive only indirectly from experience" (Halliday & Hasan, 1976, p. 26).

The interpersonal function is a matter of role relationship. It is concerned with both the speaker's participation in the speech situation and his assignment of speech roles to the other participants.

The textual function makes what the speaker says operational in the context. It is an enabling function, without which the ideational and interpersonal functions cannot be put into effect.

When the features of the context of situation are projected onto language, the field tends to determine the selection of ideational meanings; the tenor tends to determine the selection of interpersonal meanings; and the mode tends to determine the selection of textual meanings.

When the three components of semantics are in turn realized at the lexico-grammatical level, the ideational meaning tends to be realized in the transitivity system of the clause and the lexical meaning of the words (experiential), and the logical relations at all ranks (logical). The interpersonal meaning tends to be realized through the system of [5] mood and modality in the clause and the attitudinal meaning of the words. The textual meaning tends ko be realized through the thematic structure in the clause, the information structure in the tone group and cohesion above the clause.

2. Transitivity

In this thesis the clause is going to be analysed from the point of view of its organization as a representation of experiential meaning, or, in other words, the meaning in the sense of content or 'what is going on'. The clause here is treated as a representation of experience, the experience that lies around the speaker or inside him; and more particularly, as a representation of processes. Here the component parts of the clause are the Process, the Participants and the Circumstances, with the Process as the centre of the clause. Transitivity is the linguistic system which conveys experiential meaning through a structure consisting of Processes, the Participants therein, and the Circumstances associated with them.

3. Processes

A process is typically realized by a verbal group in the clause. The process is the centre of the clause. In this thesis processes are divided into five major types according to their different semantic and syntactic manifestations in the clause. They are Material Processes, Ascription Processes, Mental Processes, Verbal Processes and Relational Processes. [6]

4. Material Processes

Material processes are processes of action or event, i. e. of the 'zuo shenme' ('doing') or 'fashengle shenme' ('happening') type.

Let us examine the following clauses:

(1) a. Ma zai pao.
    horse p. p. run
    (The horse is running.)

  b. Ma sile.
    horse die - p. a.
    (The horse has died.)

If we ask a question about the verb in a., it will be

  c. Ma zai zuo shenme?
    horse p. p. do what
    (What is the horse doing?)

A question asking about the verb in b. would be

  d. Shenme shi fashengle?
    what thing happen - p. a.
    (What has happened?)

or e. Ma zenmele?
    horse how - p. a.

(What has happened to the horse?)

'Zuo shenme', 'fasheng' and 'zenmele' in Clauses c. , d. , and e. are used as substitutive verbs (pro-verbs) for the processes in a. and b. Processes which have such pro-verbs are categorized as Material Processes in this thesis. [7]

5. Different Types of Material Processes

Let us first look at the following clauses:

(1) a. Ta zai pao.
   He p. p. run
   (He is running.)
   b. Ta zai da wo.
   he p. p. beat me
   (He is beating me.)

Clause a. has only one participant 'ta' (he) involved in the process, i.e. the performer of the action, which will be referred to henceforth as the 'Actor'. Processes like 'pao' (run) in a. have only one inherent participant, the Actor, involved in them. Such processes will be referred to as 'non-directed' (Halliday, 1966) material processes. Clauses with such processes will be referred to as 'descriptive' (Halliday, 1966) clauses. A non-directed process normally cannot take a second participant. See examples in (2) below.

(2) a. Wang Ping zai pao.
   Wang Ping p. p. run
   (Wang Ping is running.)
   b. *Wang Ping zai pao caochang.
   Wang Ping p. p. run playground
   (*Wang Ping is running the playground.)
   c. Li Ying zai gongzuo.
   Li Ying p. p. work.
   (Li Ying is working.)

d. * Li Ying zai gongzuo Yingyu.

Li Ying p. p. work English

(* Li Ying is working English.) [8]

In Clause (1) b., there are two participants involved in the process, i.e. 'ta' (he) and 'wo' (me). The former is the performer of the action and will still be named 'Actor'. The latter is the receiver, or the destination, of the action. We will name such a participant 'Goal'. Processes like 'da' (beat) in (1) b. take two intrinsic participants. Such processes will be referred to as 'directed' (Halliday, 1966) material processes. Clauses with such processes will be referred to as 'effective' (Halliday, 1966) clauses. More examples are given in (3) below.

(3) a. Wang Ping zai da Li Ying.

Wang Ping p. p. beat Li Ying

(Wang Ping is beating Li Ying.)

b. * Wang Ping zai da.

Wang Ping p. p. beat

(* Wang Ping is beating.)

c. Wang Ping zai zhao xiaodao.

Wang Ping p. p. look-for knife

(Wang Ping is looking for the knife.)

d. * Wang Ping zai zhao.

Wang Ping p. p. look-for

(* Wang Ping is looking for.)

Clauses b. and d. are ungrammatical because one of the intrinsic participants is missing.

Certain material processes in Chinese can be both directed and non-directed. See the following examples in (4):

(4) a. Wang Ping zai wan wanju.

Wang Ping p. p. play toy

(Wang Ping is playing with the toy.) [9]

b. Wang Ping zai wan.

Wang Ping p. p. play

(Wang Ping is playing.)

c. Ta zai xiao wo.

he p. p. laugh me

(He is laughing at me.)

d. Ta zai xiao.

he p. p. laugh

(He is laughing.)

If we examine the clauses given so far in this chapter, we will notice that all the Actors occur before the processes, while all the Goals occur after the processes. The word order cannot be changed. See the following examples:

(5) a. Li Ying zai da Wang Ping.

Li Ying p. p. beat Wang Ping

(Li Ying is beating Wang Ping.)

b. *Li Ying zai da.

Li Ying p. p. beat

(*Li Ying is beating.)

c. *Xiaodao zai zhao Wang Ping.

knife p. p. look-for Wang Ping

(*The knife is looking for Wang Ping.)

d. *Xiaodao zai zhao.

knife p. p. look-for

(*The knife is looking for.)

e. *Wanju zai wan Wang Ping.

toy p. p. play Wang Ping

(*The toy is playing with Wang Ping.) [10]

f. *Wanju zai wan.

toy p. p. play

(*The toy is playing.)

Clauses b., c., d., e., and f. are all ungrammatical because the Goal occupies the position of the Actor. Clause a. is a grammatical clause, but the meaning of it changes completely. The orginal

Goal 'Li Ying' becomes the Actor, while the original Actor becomes the Goal (cf. Clause (3) a.). So instead of the original meaning of 'Wang Ping is beating Li Ying', the changed clause means 'Li Ying is beating Wang Ping'.

Now let us examine another group of processes which have quite different syntactic behaviours.

(6) a. Fangzi maile.

   house sell - p. a.

   (The house has been sold.)

   b. Ta maile fangzi.

   he sell - p. a. house

   (He has sold the house.)

   c. Cai qiele.

   vegetable cut - p. a.

   (The vegetable has been cut.)

   d. Li Ying qiele cai.

   Li Ying cut - p. a. vegetable

   (Li Ying has cut the vegetable.)

   e. Yifu xile.

   clothes wash - p. a.

   (The clothes have been washed.) [11]

   f. Women xile yifu.

   we wash p. a. clothes

   (We have washed the clothes.)

Among the six clauses given in (6) above, a., c. and e. have only one participant each involved in the process; b., d. and f. have two participants each involved in the process. In this respect, they are similar to Clauses (4) b., (4) d. and (4) a., (4) c. Another similarity between (4) and (6) is that one participant is present in both the effective and descriptive clauses. However a close examination shows that the participant which is present in both the effective and descriptive clauses in (4) remains in the same position, i.e. preverbally as the Actor, while its counterpart in (6) occurs pre-verbally in descriptive clauses but post-verbally in effective clauses. The following diagram shows the difference:

  (4′) c. <u>Ta</u> zai xiao wo.
    d. <u>Ta</u> zai xiao.
  (6′) f. Women xile <u>yifu</u>.
    e. <u>Yifu</u> xile.

We may postulate that 'yifu' in (6) e. is definitely different from 'ta' in (4) d. It is not an Actor since it can occur post-verbally. Similarly 'yifu' in (6) f. is definitely different from 'wo' in (4) c. It is not the Goal since it can occupy the pre-verbal position. In this thesis we will name such a participant 'Patient'. We will name a participant such as 'women' in (6) f. 'Agent' and we will refer to processes such as those in (4) c., (4) d., (6) f. and (6) e. respectively, as Directed Actor Process, Non-Directed [12] Actor Process, Directed Patient Process and Non-Directed Patient Process. What is inherent in an actor process is that it requires an obligatory Actor. Goal here is an optional participant. It is present in directed actor processes but absent in non-directed actor processes. On the other hand, the presence of a Patient is obligatory in a patient process. Agent, as an optional participant, is present in the directed patient process but absent in the non-directed patient process.

6. Ascription Process

Look at the following clauses:

  (1) a. Ta gao.
     he tall
     (He is tall.)
    b. Chang Hong hen pang.
     Chang Hong very fat
     (Chang Hong is very fat.)
    c. Zhejian shi feichang zhongyao.

this - m. business very important.

(This is very important.)

There is no action involved in the processes in the above clauses. Those Processes only ascribe a certain feature to their participants. We will call such processes 'Ascription Processes'. The participant in such processes will be referred to as the 'Carrier'. [13]

7. Material Process vs. Ascription Process

As stated before, a material process expresses an action or event, whereas an ascription process attributes a certain feature to its Participant. Precisely for this reason a material process has 'zuo shenme' (do what) or 'fasheng' (happen) as its pro-verb form, an ascription process cannot take such a pro-verb form. It takes 'zenmeyang' (how) instead. See the following clauses:

(1) a. Ma zai pao.

horse p. p. run

(The horse is running.)

b. Ma zai zuo shenme?

horse p. p. do what

(What is the horse doing?)

c. Ma (zai) zenmeyang?

horse (p. p.) how

(*How is the horse?)

(2) a. Fangzi maile.

house sell - p. a.

(The house has been sold.)

b. Shenme shi fashengle?

what thing happen - p. a.

(What has happened?)

c. *Fangzi zenmeyang?

house how

(*How is the house?)

(3) a. Ta gao.

   he tall

   (He is tall.) [14]

b. Ta zenmeyang?

   he how

   (How is he?)

c. *Ta zuo shenme?

   he do what

   (*What does he do?)

d. *Shenme shi fashengle?

   what thing happen - p. a.

   (*What has happened?)

Since an ascription process only assigns a certain feature to its participant and, therefore, is not an action, it cannot take the progressive particle. It typically stands by itself without any aspect marker, whereas an actor or directed patient process can take the progressive particle or an aspect marker, and a non-directed patient process cannot even stand by itself without an aspect marker. Examples are given in (4) below:

(4) a. *Ta zai gao.

   he p. p. tall

   (*He is talling.)

b. Ta gao.

   he tall

   (He is tall.)

c. Ma zai pao.

   horse p. p. run

   (The horse is running.)

d. *Fangzi mai.

   house sell

   (*The house sells.) [15]

An ascription process does not have an imperative form, while a material process can appear in the imperative. See examples in (5):

(5) a. *(Ni) Gao!

　　　(you) tall

　　　(*Tall!)

　　b. (Ni) Pao!

　　　(you) run

　　　(Run!)

　　c. (Ni) Mai!

　　　(you) sell

　　　(Sell it!)

An ascription process can be modified by 'hen' (very), 'feichang' (very), 'tai' (very, too), 'jiduan' (extremely), etc., while a material process cannot. See the following examples:

(6) a. Ta hen gao.

　　　he very tall

　　　(He is very tall.)

　　b. *Ma hen pao.

　　　horse very run

　　　(*The horse very runs.)

　　c. *Fangzi hen maile.

　　　house very sell - p. a.

　　　(*The house has been very sold.)

Lastly, material processes can be directed and non-directed, but ascription processes can only be non-directed. Examples are given in (7) below:

(7) a. Ta gao. [16]

　　　he tall

　　　(He is tall.)

　　b. *Ta gao qiang.

　　　he tall wall

　　　(*He talls the wall.)

8. Mental Process

Mental processes are processes of perception, reaction and cog-nition, i e. processes of the 'seeing', 'feeling' and 'knowing' type. A mental process has two inherent participants in it. The participant which occurs in the pre-verbal position is the perceiver, reactor or cog-nizer. It will be referred to as the 'Cognizant'. The participant occupying the post-verbal position is what is perceived, reacted upon or cognized. We will call it the 'Phenomenon'. A Cognizant must be human or human-like. In other words, it must be what is endowed with consciousness. A Phenomenon can be a person, a thing, or a fact which always takes the form of a clause. The underlined proces-ses in (1) below are all mental processes.

(1) a. Wo kanjian ta zai zou.
   I see he p. p. walk
   (I saw that he was walking.)

b. Ta tingdao yige shengyin.
   he hear one-m. voice
   (He heard a voice.)

c. Xiao Hong xihuan niao.
   Little Hong like bird
   (Little Hong likes birds.) [17]

d. Wo pa ta lai.
   I fear he come
   (I fear that he will come.)

e. Nei guniang bu dong Fawen.
   that girl not understand French
   (That girl does not understand French.)

f. Laoshi zhidao Lao Wang bu qu.
   teacher know Old Wang not go
   (The teacher knows that Old Wang is not going.)

g. *Shitou tingjian yige shengyin.

stone hear one-m. voice

(*The stone heard a voice.)

Clause g. is ungrammatical owing to the fact that an unconscious object occurs as the Cognizant. Such a clause can be grammatical under two circumstances. First, when 'Shitou' is the name or nickname of a person, but then it is no longer an unconscious object but a human being. Secondly, when it is given a human nature, or in other words when it is personified. Humanization, or personification appears in certain types of texts. It is most common in poetry and children's stories.

9. Material Process and Mental Process Compared

As stated before, a material process has a pro-verb form 'zuo shenme' (do what) or 'fasheng' (happen), but a mental process does not have such a pro-verb form. Look at the following clauses:
[18]

    (1) a. Chang Cheng kanjian yizhi laohu.

        Chang Cheng see one-m. tiger

        (Chang Cheng saw a tiger.)

      b. *Chang Cheng zuo shenme?

        Chang Cheng do what?

        (*What did Chang Cheng do?)

      c. Chang Cheng pa laohu.

        Chang Cheng fear tiger

        (Chang Cheng is afraid of tigers.)

      d. *Shenme shi fasheng le?

        what thing happen - p. a.

        (*What happened?)

The pre-verbal participant of a mental process must be human or human-like, whereas its counterpart in a material process can be an unconscious being. See the examples in (2) below:

(2) a. *Zheba yaoshi hen zheba suo.
　　　this-m. key hate this-m. lock
　　　(*This key hates this lock.)
　　b. Zheba yaoshi kai zheba suo.
　　　this-m. key open this-m. lock
　　　(This key opens this lock.)

The post-verbal participant of a mental process can be a fact, but its counterpart in a material process cannot. Examples are given in (3) below:

(3) a. Laoshi zhidao ta dong Yingyu.
　　　teacher know he understand English
　　　(The teacher knows that he understands English.)
　　b. *Laoshi jiao ta dong Yingyu. [19]
　　　teacher teach he understand English
　　　(*The teacher teaches he understands English.)

Mental processes cannot be used in the progressive, whereas material processes normally take a progressive particle when the time reference is to the present.

(4) a. Ta xianzai xiangxin ni.
　　　he now believe you
　　　(He believes you now.)
　　b. *Ta xianzai zai xiangxin ni.
　　　he now p.p. believe you
　　　(*He is believing you now.)
　　c. *Ta xianzai xi yifu.
　　　he now wash clothes
　　　(*He washes clothes now.)
　　d. Ta xianzai zai xi yifu.
　　　he now p.p. wash clothes
　　　(He is washing clothes now.)

10. Verbal Process

Verbal processes are processes of 'saying'. The underlined processes in (1) below are verbal processes.

(1) a. Xiao Wang <u>wen</u>: "Ni mingtian lai bu lai?"
Little Wang asked: "You tomorrow come not come?"
(Little Wang asked: "Are you coming tomorrow?")

b. Xiao Wang <u>shuo</u> ta jintian lai.
Little Wang say he today come
(Little Wang said he would come today.)

From the above two clauses we can see that a clause containing a verbal process is in fact a clause complex. It [20] contains two independent clauses. The clause containing the verbal process will be referred to as the 'Reporting Clause', the other will be called the 'Report Clause'. The participant in the reporting clause will be named 'Sayer'. It occurs in the pre-verbal position.

Unlike the Cognizant which must be human or human-like, a Sayer can be either a human being or an unconscious being. Look at the following examples:

(2) a. Laoshi shuo Wang Wei bu qu Beijing.
teacher say Wang Wei not go Beijing
(The teacher said that Wang Wei would not go to Beijing.)

b. Chuandan shuo Wang Wei bu qu Beijing.
leaflet say Wang Wei not go Beijing
(The leaflet said that Wang Wei would not go to Beijing.)

There are only a small number of verbal processes in Chinese, Other verbal processes are 'jiang' (say), 'gaosu' (tell), 'gaohu' (shout), etc.

11. Relational Process

The processes in the following clauses are all relational processes:

(1) a. Ta shi yige xuesheng.
he be one-m. student
(He is a student.)

b. Ta shi Li Ming.
he be Li Ming
(He is Li Ming.) [21]

c. Li Bin qunian chengwei yiming jiaoshi.
Li Bin last-year become one-m. teacher
(Li Bin became a teacher last year.)

d. Chen Hua you sanben shu.
Chen Hua have three-m. book
(Chen Hua has three books.)

e. Cheng Hong zai jiaoshili.
Cheng Hong at classroom-inside
(Cheng Hong is in the classroom.)

f. Ditu zai shujiashang.
map at bookshelf-top
(The map is on the bookshelve.)

A relational process must have two participants involved in it. The process simply signifies some kind of relationship existing between the two participants, either of equation ('shi' (be)), possession ('you' (have)), or location ('zai' (at)).

Relational processes can be divided into two major types: identifying and attributive. In an identifying relational process the two participants can be reversed. See the following examples:

(2) a. Ta shi Jin Feng.
she be Jin Feng

(She is Jin Feng.)
b. Jin Feng shi ta.
   Jin Feng be she
   (Jin Feng is she.)
c. Du Li shi womende laoshi.
   Du Li be we-m.s. teacher
   (Du Li is our teacher.) [22]
d. Womende laoshi shi Du Li.
   we-m.s. teacher be Du Li
   (Our teacher is Du Li.)
e. Jintian shi qihao.
   today be seventh
   (Today is the seventh.)
f. Qihao shi jintian.
   seventh be today
   (The seventh is today.)

The participant which occurs at the pre-verbal position will be called the 'Identified'. The other, i.e. the one which occupies the post-verbal position, will be referred to as the 'Identifier'.

As stated before the two participants in an identifying relational process are reversible. However, once reversed, their functions in the clause will change, i.e. the identified becomes the Identifier when it occurs post-verbally, and the Identifier becomes the Identified when it is shifted to the pre-verbal position. The point becomes clearer when an identifying relational clause is put into a question-answer context. See the following examples:

(3) a. Ta shi shui?
       she be who
       (Who is she?)
   b. Ta shi Jin Feng.
       she be Jin Feng
       (She is Jin Feng.)
   c. *Jin Feng shi ta.

Jin Feng be she

(Jin Feng is she.) [23]

(4) a. Jin Feng shi shui?

Jin Feng be who

(Who is Jin Feng?)

b. Jin Feng shi ta.

Jin Feng be she

(Jin Feng is she.)

c. * Ta shi Jin Feng.

she be Jin Feng

(She is Jin Feng.)

(5) a. Shui shi Jin Feng?

who be Jin Feng

(Who is Jin Feng?)

b. Ta shi Jin Feng.

she be Jin Feng

(She is Jin Feng.)

c. * Jin Feng shi ta.

Jin Feng be she

(Jin Feng is she.)

Clauses (3) c., (4) c. and (5) c cannot be grammatical answers to (3) a., (4) a. and (5) a. because the roles of the Identified and Identifier are changed.

An attributive relational process is different from an identifying one in that its two participants are not reversible. Examples are given in (6) below:

(6) a. Ta shi yige gongren.

he be one-m. worker

(He is a worker.)

b. * Yige gongren shi ta.

one. m worker is he

(* A worker is he.) [24]

c. Chao Fang you liangge meimei.

　　　　Chao Fang have two. m younger-sister

　　　　(Chao Fang has two younger sisters.)

　　d. *Liangge meimei you Chao Fang.

　　　　two-m. younger-sister have Chao Fang

　　　　(*Two younger sisters have Chao Fang.)

　　e. Hua zai qiangshang.

　　　　picture at wall-top

　　　　(The picture is on the wall.)

　　f. *Qiangshang zai hua.

　　　　wall-top at picture

　　　　(On the wall is the picture.)

　　In an attributive relational process, the post-verbal participant simply attributes a certain feature to the pre-verbal participant. We will call the former the 'Attribute', and the latter the 'Carrier' since it is just the bearer of the feature given by the Attribute.

　　While processes of equation, possession and location can all appear in an attributive relational clause, only those of equation can occur in an identifying clause, as is exemplified in (2) and (6).

　　The participants in relational processes of possession and location do occur in reversed order. Look at the clauses in (7) below:

　(7) a. Wo you yiben shu.

　　　　I have one-m. book

　　　　(I have a book.)

　　b. Naben shu shuyu wo.

　　　　that-m. book belong-to me

　　　　(That book belongs to me.) [25]

　　c. Naben zidian zai zhuozishang.

　　　　that-m. dictionary at desk-top

　　　　(That dictionary is on the desk.)

　　d. Zhuozishang you yiben zidian.

　　　　desk-top have one-m. dictionary

　　　　(There is a dictionary on the desk.)

　　From the above clauses we can see that there is lexical change involved when the two participants are reversed, i. e. 'you' into 'shuyu', and 'zai' into 'you'. It seems that a rule can be generalized that the word order of the two participants in a relational process of possession or location can be reversed through a lexical suppletion of the process. However this is not the case at all. See the following examples:

  (8) a. Yiben shu shuyu wo.
    one-m. book belong-to me
    (One of the books belongs to me.)
   b. Wo you naben shu.
    I have that-m. book
    (I have a copy of that book.)
   c. Zhuozishang you naben zidian.
    desk-top have that-m. dictionary
    (There is a copy of that dictionary on the desk.)
   d. Yiben zidian zai zhuozishang.
    one-m. dictionary at desk-top
    (One of the dictionaries is on the desk.)

From the above examples we can see that the meaning of the clause changes considerably after the lexical suppletion is applied. Therefore we may draw the conclusion that the two [26] participants in the relational process of possession or location are not reversible at all. The two forms of the processes are in complementary distribution. The distribution pattern is governed by the information structure, which is outside the scope of this thesis and so will not be elaborated upon here.

12. 'Ba' Construction

Let us first examine the following clauses:

  (1) a. Ta maile fangzi.
    he sell-p. a. house

(He sold the house.)
b. Ta ba fangzi maile.
he f. p. house sell-p. a.
(He sold the house.)
c. Chang Yan xile yifu.
Chang Yan wash-p. a. clothes
(Chang Yan washed the clothes.)
d. Chang Yan ba yifu xile.
Chang Yan f. p. clothes wash-p. a.
(Chang Yan washed the clothes.)

If we make a comparison between a., c. and b., d., we can see theft the post-verbal participant in the former appears pre-verbally in the latter, preceded by the fore-positioning particle 'ba'. We will call 'ba' and the participant which fellows it immediately the 'ba construction'. In Chinese the 'ba' construction only occurs pre-verbally as can be seen from the examples in (2). [27]

(2) a. * Ta maile ba fangzi.
he sell - p. a. f. p. house
(He sold the house.)
b. * Chang Yan xile ba yifu.
Chang Yan wash-p. a. f. p. clothes
(Chang Yan washed the clothes.)

Only post-verbal patients can be brought to the pre-verbal position by 'ba' as is shown in (3).

(3) a. Wang Feng shaole xin.
Wang Feng burn-p. a. letter
(Wang Feng burnt the letter.)
b. Wang Feng ba xin shaole.   (Patient)
Wang Feng f. p. letter burn-p. a.
(Wang Feng burnt the letter.)
c. Wang Feng dale wo.
Wang Feng beat-p. a. me

(Wang Feng beat me.)

d. *Wang Feng ba wo dale.　　　(Goal)
Wang Feng f. p. me beat-p. a.
(Wang Feng beat me.)

e. Wang Feng xihuan nazhang hua.
Wang Feng like that-m. picture
(Wang Feng likes that picture.)

f. *Wang Feng ba nazhang hua xihuan. (Phenomenon)
Wang Feng f. p. that-m. picture like
(Wang Feng likes that picture.)

g. Wang Feng shuo tabu qu.
Wang Feng say he not go
(Wang Feng said that he wouldn't go.) [28]

h. *Wang Feng ba tabu qu shuo. (Report)
Wang Feng f. p. he not go say
(Wang Feng said that he wouldn't go.)

i. Wang Feng shi nage ren.
Wang Feng be that-m. person
(Wang Feng is that person.)

j. *Wang Feng ba nage ren shi.　　(Identifier)
Wang Feng f. p. that-m. person be
(Wang Feng is that person.)

k. Wang Feng you yizhang hua.
Wang Feng have one-m. picture
(Wang Feng has a picture.)

l. *Wang Feng ba yizhang hua you. (Attribute)
Wang Feng f. p. one-m. picture have
(Wang Feng has a picture.)

'Ba' only introduces Patients with specific reference. See the following clauses:

(4) a. Ta maile na sanben shu.
he sell-p. a. that three-m. book
(He sold those three books.)

b. Ta ba na sanben shu maile.

　　　he f. p. that three-m. book sell-p. a.

　　　(He sold those three books.)

　　c. Ta maile sanben shu.

　　　he sell-p. a. three-m. book

　　　(He sold three books.)

　　d. * Ta ba sanben shu maile.

　　　he f. p. three-m. book sell-p. a.

　　　(He sold three books.) [29]

Note that the nominal group with 'yi' (one) as its modifier has specific reference in the following clause.

　　(5) Wo ba yige dongxi diule.

　　　I f. p. one-m. thing lose-p. a.

　　　(I lost something.)

In (5) 'yige dongxi' (something) has a specific reference at least to the speaker.

The function of 'ba' is to introduce Given Information as can be seen in the question-answer sequence in (6).

　　(6) a. Nide zidian zai nar?

　　　　you-m. s. dictionary at where

　　　　(Where is your dictionary?)

　　　b. * Wo maile wode zidian.

　　　　I sell-p. a. I-m. s. dictionary.

　　　　(I have sold my dictionary.)

　　　c. Wo ba zidian maile.

　　　　I f. p. dictionary sell-p. a.

　　　　(I have sold my dictionary.)

Clause b. cannot serve as an answer to Clause a. because 'nide zidian' (your dictionary) is already treated as Given in a., yet it appears as New in b.

Given and New are textual functions in the system of the information structure of language and so will not be further elaborated upon here. [30]

13. Passive Construction

Passivity is not a common feature in Chinese, but passive construction does occur in Chinese from time to time. Look at the following clauses:

  (1) a. Ta jiejie dale ta.
     she elder-sister beat-p. a. her
    (Her elder sister beat her.)
   b. Ta bei ta jiejie dale.
     she by she elder-sister beat-p. a.
    (She was beaten by her elder sister.)

Clause b. above is in the passive. If we make a comparison between the passive and the active constructions, we will see that in the passive clause the post-verbal participant is put to the front position of the clause and the pre-verbal participant is introduced by 'bei' (by). The 'bei' group precedes the process and follows the forepositioned post-verbal participant. This seems to give the impression that the passive construction in Chinese is derived from the active. However it is not so. Besides being thematized, the forepositioned participant is also depicted by the speaker as a 'sufferer' or something subjected to a change which is undesirable either to the speaker or to the hearer. So Clause a. and Clause b. above have not only different textual meanings but also different interpersonal meanings. Passivization is a different way in which the speaker gives his subjective rendering of the same event.

'Bei' (by) only introduces Actor and Agent. In other words 'bei' construction only appears in directed material processes. Look at the following examples: [31]

  (2) a. Shu bei wo nale.   (actor process)
    book by me take-p. a.

(The book has been taken by me.)
    b. Shu bei wo shaole.   (patient process)

       book by me burn-p. a.

       (The book has been burnt by me.)

    c. *Shu bei wo xihuan.   (mental process)

       book by me like

       (*The book is liked by me.)

    d. *Shu bu hao bei wo shuole. (verbal process)

       book not good by me say-p. a.

       (That the book was not good was said by me.)

    e. *Shu bei wo you.   (relational process)

       book by me have

       (The book is owned by me.)

Since the Goal or Patient in the passive clause is depicted as a sufferer or an undergoer of some undesirable change, the process of the clause must depict some action or event which has taken place. Therefore the process in a passive clause must be in the perfective aspect. The progressive particle can never occur in a passive clause. This is made clear by the examples in (3) below:

    (3) a. Wo bei ta dale.

         I by him beat-p. a.

         (I have been beaten by him.)

      b. *Wo zai bei ta da.

         I p. p. by him beat

         (I am being beaten by him.) [32]

      c. Fangzi bei ta shaole.

         house by him burn-p. a.

         (The house has bean burnt by him.)

      d. *Fangzi zai bei ta shao.

         house p. p. by him burn

         (The house is being burnt by him.)

Certain actor processes cannot appear in the passive construction. See the following examples:

(4) a. *Shu bei ta zhaole.

　　　book by him look-for-p. a.

　　　(*The book was looked for by him.)

　　b. Wo bei ta zhuile.

　　　I by him chase-p. a.

　　　(I have been chased by him.)

The reason for this is that processes like 'zhao' (look for) and 'zhui' (chase) do not produce any effect on the Goal even when they are in the perfective aspect, and hence cannot be used to predicate a sufferer or the undergoer of a change.

The Actor or Agent may not be specified in the passive construction. Then 'bei' will stand alone by itself. Sometimes it is even difficult to specify the Actor or Agent. Loot at the clauses in (5):

(5) a. Shu bei toule.

　　　book by steal-p. a.

　　　(The book has been stolen.)

　　b. Rou bei chile.

　　　meat by eat-p. a.

　　　(The meat has been eaten.) [33]

Another word which can introduce Actor or Agent in a passive construction is 'gei'. 'Gei' is used in colloquial speech. Examples are given in (6):

(6) a. Wode zidian gei xiaotou toule.

　　　I-m. s. dictionary by thief steal-p. a.

　　　(My dictionary was stolen by a thief.)

　　b. Fan gei gou chile.

　　　rice by dog eat-p. a.

　　　(The rice has been eaten by the dog.)

　　c. Xiao Hua gei pianle.

　　　Little Hua by cheat-p. a.

　　　(Little Hua was cheated.)

14. Complex Process and Double Participant

It is a common phenomenon in Chinese for two processes to join together to function as one process. Such a process will be referred to in this thesis as a complex process. Look at the following example:

(1) Lao taitai kuxiale yanjing.
old lady cry-blind-p. a. eye
(The old lady has cried her eyes blind.)

'Kuxia' in (1) is a complex process. In a complex process, the second process typically states the result of the first process, and the first process specifies the means to achieve the result expressed by the second process. So 'kuxia' means 'to make ... blind through crying' or 'to cry as to make ... blind'.

The post-verbal participant in (1), i. e. 'yanjing' (eye) has two participant functions. First it is the Goal of [34] the actor process 'ku' (cry). Secondly it is the Patient of the non-directed patient process 'xia' (become blind). Such a participant will be referred to as a double participant in this thesis.

A double participant more commonly occurs in the 'ba' construction. See the example in (2).

(2) Lao taitai ba yanjing kuxiale.
old lady f. p. eye cry-blind-p. a.
(The old lady cried her eyes blind.)

There are different combinations of processes into a complex process. Each type will be dealt with separately in the following sections.

14.1. Non-directed Actor Process plus Non-directed Actor Process

This is a very rare type, but it does occur sometimes. Look at the example in (3) below:

> (3) Ta ba wo kuxiaole.
> he f. p. me cry-laugh-p. a.
> (He cried in such a funny way that I laughed.)

In (3), 'ta' (he) is the Actor of the first process 'ku' (cry). 'Wo' (me) is the double participant. It is the Goal of the first process 'ku' (cry) and at the same time the Actor of the second process 'xiao' (laugh).

Some complex processes of this type are non-directed, e. g.:

> (4) Ta paokule.
> he run-cry-p. a.
> (He shed tears as a result of the running.) [35]

Here the double participant is the Actor of both the first and the second processes in the complex process.

14.2. Non-directed Actor Process plus Non-directed Patient Process

This is a much more common type than that in 14.1.
Look at the following examples:

> (5) a. Zhao Liang zouchule han.
> Zhao Liang walk-come-out-p. a. sweat
> (Zhao Liang walked so much that he sweated.)
> b. Guniang xiaodiaole ya.
> girl laugh-fall-p. a. tooth
> (The girl was so amused that she laughed her tooth off.)
> c. Niao feishele chibang.
> bird fly-break-p. a. wing
> (The bird flew so hard that its wings broke.)

Here the first participant in the clause is the Actor of the first process. The second, i.e. the double participant, is the Goal of the first process and at the same time the Patient of the second process.

Complex processes of this type can also be non-directed, e. g. :

(6) a. Ta paodiule.

he run-lose-p. a.

(He got lost from the others.)

b. Ta kubingle.

he cry-ill-p. a.

(He cried himself sick.) [36]

Here the double participant is the only participant involved in the complex process. It is the Actor of the first process and the Patient of the second one.

14.3 Non-directed Actor Process plus Ascription Process

Look at the following clauses in (7):

(7) a. Ta ba yanjing kuhongle.

she f. p. eye cry-red-p. a.

(She cried her eyes red.)

b. Qian Fei ba sangzi hantongle.

Qian Fei f. p. throat shout-aching-p. a.

(Qian Fei shouted so much that his throat ached.)

c. Ta ba zuiba chichanle.

he f. p. mouth eat-gluttonous

(He has eaten his mouth gluttonous. [He has eaten so much good food that he has become a glutton.])

In the above clauses the first participant is the Actor of the first process. The second participant is the Goal of the first process and meanwhile the Carrier of the second process.

Complex processes of this type can also be non-directed, e. g. :

(8) a. Ta zourele.

he walk-hot-p. a.

(He felt hot through walking.)

b. Ying feigaole.

eagle fly-high-p. a. [37]

(The eagle has flown high up.)

The only participant in the clause here, the double participant, is the Actor of the first process and the Carrier of the second process.

14.4. Directed Actor Process plus Non-directed Actor Process

The complex processes in the clauses in (9) below belong to this type.

(9) a. Ta ba shitou tuidongle.
   he f. p. stone push-move-p. a.
   (He pushed the stone with such strength that it moved.)
   b. Ta ba xiaohai xiakule.
   he f. p. child frighten-cry-p. a.
   (He frightened the child into crying.)

The first participant in the above clauses is the Actor of the first process in the complex process. The second participant is the Goal of the first process and the Actor of the second.

14.5 Directed Actor Process plus Non-directed Patient Process

All the processes below fall into this category.

(10) a. Qiche ba gou zhuangsile.
   car f. p. dog bump-die-p. a.
   (The car bumped into the dog and killed it.)
   b. Zhe hui ba beizi yapo.
   this will f. p. cup press-break
   (This will crush the cup.) [38]
   c. Wu Bin ba rou chiwanle.
   Wu Bin f. p. meat eat-finish-p. a.
   (Wu Bin ate all the meat.)

The first participant in the above clauses is the Actor of the first process. The second participant is the Patient of the second process as well as the Goal of the first.

14.6 Directed Actor Process plus Ascription Process

Look at the following clauses:

 (11) a. Chen Tao ba wode lian daqingle.
    Chen Tao f. p. I-m. s. face beat-bruised-p. a.
    (Chen Tao hit me in the face and bruised it.)
  b. Qin Feng ba zhu weifeile.
    Qin Feng f. p. pig feed-fat-p. a.
    (Qin Feng fed the pig so well that it has become fat.)
  c. Ni ba ta huagaole.
    you f. p. him paint-tall-p. a.
    (You painted him tall.)

The first participant in the above clauses is the Actor of the first process in the complex process. The second participant is the Goal of the first process and the Carrier of the second. [39]

14.7. Directed Patient Process plus Non-directed Actor Process

This is a very rare type. Examples are given in (12) below:

 (12) a. Lao gongren ba jiqi kaidongle.
    old worker f. p. machine start-move-p. a.
    (The old worker started the machine.)
  b. Huo ba haizi shaokule.
    fire f. p. child burn-cry-p. a.
    (The fire burnt the child so that it cried.)

Here the first participant is the Agent of the first process in the complex process. The second participant is the Actor of the second process and at the same time the Patient of the first one.

14.8. Directed Patient Process plus Non-directed Patient Process

Look at the following examples:

 (13) a. Ta ba jidan maiguangle.

he f. p. chicken-egg sell-finish-p. a.

(He has sold all the eggs.)

b. Xiao Hua ba tieban mochuanle.

Xiao Hua f. p. iron-plate grind-through-p. a.

(Xiao Hua ground a hole in the iron plate.)

c. Ni hui ba luobo baduan.

you will f. p. turnip extract-snap

(You will break the turnip [if you pull at it like that].)

In the clauses above the first participant is the Agent of the first process. The second participant is both [40] the Patient of the first process and that of the second.

14.9. Directed Patient Process plus Ascription Process

All the complex processes in the following clauses belong to this type.

(14) a. Xiao Chun ba nide yifu xiganjingle.

Xiao Chun f. p. you-m. s. clothes wash-clean-p. a.

(Xiao Chun washed your clothes clean.)

b. Huo ba shitou dou shaohongle.

fire f. p. stone even burn-red-p. a.

(The fire burnt even the stones red.)

c. Ni xian ba dao mokuai.

you first f. p. knife grind-sharp

([you] Sharpen the knife first.)

The first participant in the above clauses is the Agent of the first process. The second participant is the Patient of the first process and the Carrier of the second.

It should be stressed that although a complex process consists of two processes it behaves like a single process. Nothing can be inserted between the two component processes. Their order cannot be changed. Besides there is always a double participant accompanying the complex process.

A complex process behaves more or lees like a patient process, and the double participant behaves like a Patient. This can be seen from the fact that the double participant can occur pre-verbally in the 'ba' construction. Moreover all the double participants in the effective clauses above in this chapter except that in 14.1 can occur pre-verbally [41] with the Agent or Actor unspecified, Examples are given in (15) below:

(15) a. Han zouchulaile.

    sweat walk-come-out-p. a.

    (Sweat came out through walking.)

b. Yanjing kuhongle.

    eye cry-red-p. a.

    (The eyes became red through crying.)

c. Xiaohair xiakule.

    child frighten-cry-p. a.

    (The child was frightened so that it cried.)

d. Gou zhuangsile.

    dog bump-die-p. a.

    (The dog was bumped into and got killed.)

e. Wode lian daqingle.

    I-m. s. face beat-bruised-p. a.

    (My face was hit and bruised.)

f. Jiqi kaidongle.

    machine start-move-p. a.

    (The machine was started.)

g. Jidan maiguangle.

    chicken-egg sell-finish-p. a.

    (The eggs were all sold out.)

h. Nide yifu xiganjingle.

    you-m. s. clothes wash-clean-p. a.

    (Your clothes were washed clean.) [42]

15. Relational Process 'Cheng' in a Complex Process

A relational process of equation can also take part in a complex process. The one which has such a function is 'cheng' (become). 'Cheng' can function alone as a relational process although it is not very common. Examples of it are given in (1) below:

(1) a. Xiao hair cheng ren le.
   child become man i. a.
   (The child has become a man.)
   b. Ta chengle gongchengshi.
   he become-p. a. engineer
   (He became an engineer.)

However as a constituent part of a complex process, 'cheng' is very active. It combines with many types of processes. In the following part of this chapter we will deal with the different combinations one by one.

15.1. Non-directed Actor Process plus 'Cheng'

This is a very rare type. Examples of it are given in (2) below:

(2) a. Wang Li kucheng leirenr le.
   Wang Li cry-become tear-person i. a.
   (Wang Li is all tears.)
   b. Ta zoucheng quezi le.
   he walk-become cripple i. a.
   (He walked so much that he has become crippled.)

The clauses above are different from the previous ones in 14. in that the first participant, i. e. the pre-verbal one instead of the second participant, i. e. the post-verbal [43] one is the double participant in the clause. The double participant here is the Actor of the first process and the Carrier in the second process with the second participant being the Attribute.

15.2. Directed Actor Process plus 'Cheng'

This is also a very rare type. Examples of it are given in (3) below:

(3) a. Ta ba wo dacheng quezi le.

he f. p. me beat-become cripple i. a.

(He beat and crippled me.)

b. Ta ba gunr tichengle liang duan.

he f. p. stick kick-become-p. a. two section

(He gave the stick a kick and broke it in two.)

In the above clauses, there are three participants taking part in the complex process. The first participant is the Actor of the first process. The second participant is the double participant. It is the Goal of the first process and the Carrier in the second one. The third participant is the Attribute here since the Attribute occupies the post-verbal position, it is compulsory for the double participant to be introduced by the forepositioning particle 'ba'.

15.3. Patient Process plus 'Cheng'

Look at the clauses in (4) below:

(4) a. Ni ba sunzi qiecheng pian.

you f. p. bamboo-shoot cut-become slice

([you] Cut the bamboo shoot into slices.) [44]

b. Ta ba chizi zhechengle liang duan.

be f. p. ruler break-become-p. a. two section

(He broke the ruler in two.)

c. Ta ba gutou shaochengle hui.

he f. p. bone burn-become ash

(He burnt the bones to ashes.)

In the above clauses there are also three participants taking part in the complex process. The first one is the Agent of the first process. The second one, i. e. the double participant, is the Patient of the first process and the Carrier in the second process. The third one is the Attribute in the second process.

For the same reason stated in 15.2., i.e. there is already a post-verbal participant, the double participant has to be introduced pre-verbally by the forepositioning particle 'ba'.

A complex process of the patient-process-plus-'cheng' type still behaves like a Patient process. In other words, the double participant may occur pre-verbally just like a Patient with the Agent unspecified. Examples are given in (5) below:

(5) a. Sunzi qiecheng pian.
bamboo-shoot cut-become slice
(The bamboo shoot should be cut into slices.)

b. Chizi zhechengle liang duan.
ruler break-become two section
(The ruler broke into two.)

c. Gutou shaochengle hui.
bone burn-become-p.a. ash
(The bones were burnt to ashes.) [45]

15.4. Mental process plus 'Cheng'

Mental processes can also form complex processes with 'cheng' as can be seen from the following examples:

(6) a. Wo ba natou niu kanchengle yipi ma.
I f.p. that-m. ox see-become-p.a. one-m. horse
(I mistook that ox for a horse.)

b. Ta ba 'ba' tingchengle 'ma'.
he f.p. 'ba' hear-become-p.a. 'ma'
(He misheard 'ba' as 'ma'.)

c. Wo ba 'Ni lai' lijiechengle 'Wo lai'.
I f.p. 'You come' understand-become-p.a. 'I come'
(I misunderstood 'You come' as 'I come'.)

In the above clauses, the first participant is the Cognizant of the first process. The second participant, i. e. the double participant, is the Phenomenon of the first process and the Carrier in the second process. The third participant is the Attribute in the second process.

For the same reason stated in 15.2. and 15.3., the double participant has to be introduced pre-verbally by 'ba'.

15.5. Ascription Process plus 'Cheng'

Look at the following examples:

 (7) a. Li Hua shoucheng yigen gunr le.
   Li Hua thin-become one-m. stick i. a.
   (Li Hua has become as thin as a stick.) [46]
  b. Tade toufa baicheng xue le.
   he-m. s. hair white-become snow i. a.
   (His hair has become as white as snow.)

In the above clauses the first participant is the Carrier of both the first process and the second process. The second participant is the Attribute in the second process.

15.6. Verbal Process plus 'Cheng'

Look at the following examples:

 (8) a. Ta ba 'Xiao Wang qu' shuocheng 'Xiao Huang qu' le.
   he f. p. 'Xiao Wang go' say-become 'Xiao Huang go' i. a.
   (He made a mistake and said 'Let Xiao Huang go' instead of 'Let Xiao Wang go'.)
  b. Wo ba 'Hua hong ma?' wenchengle 'Gua hong ma?'
   I f. p. 'flower red i. p.' ask-become-p. a. 'pumpkin red i. p.'
   (I made a mistake and asked 'Is the pumpkin red?' instead of 'Is the flower red?')

In the above clauses, the first participant is the sayer of the first process. The second participant, i.e. the first Report clause, is the Report as well as the Carrier in the second process. The third participant, i.e. the second clause in the quotation marks, is the Attribute in the second process.

For the same reason as is stated in the previous sections, it is compulsory for the double participant to be introduced pre-verbally by 'ba'. [47]

16. Relational Process 'Zai' in a Complex Process

Besides 'cheng' (become), the relational process of location 'zai' can also take part in a complex process. Two types of processes can combine with 'zai' to form a complex process. They are non-directed actor processes and patient processes. We will discuss them separately in the following sections.

16.1. Non-directed Actor Processes plus 'Zai'

Look at following clauses:

 (1) a. Ta zuozai bandengshang.
   he sit-at bench-top
   (Ha sits on the bench.)
  b. Li Hua zhanzai zhuoziqian.
   Li Hua stand-at table-front
   (Li Hua stands in front of the table.)
  c. Wang Ping duozai chuangxia.
   Wang Ping hide-at bed-under
   (Wang Ping hides under the bed.)

In the clauses above, the first participant, i.e. the pre-verbal one, is the double participant. It is the Actor of the first process in the complex process and at the same time the Carrier in the second process. The second participant, i.e. the post-verbal one, is the Attribute in the second process.

It is an inherent feature of the non-directed actor processes like those in the clauses above to work together with the relational process of location 'zai' to form complex processes. They do not normally stand by [48] themselves in a clause as is shown by examples in (2) below:

> (2) a. * Ta zuo.
> he sit
> (He sits.)
> b. * Li Hua zhan.
> Li Hua stand
> (Li Hua stands.)
> c. * Wang Ping duo.
> Wang Ping hide
> (Wang Ping hides.)

Those processes standing alone without 'zai' can be grammatical only when they are in the imperative mood or occur with the progressive suffix 'zhe'. See the following examples.

> (3) a. Qing zuo.
> please sit
> (Please be seated.)
> b. Ta zuozhe.
> he sit-p. s.
> (He is sitting.)

Besides occurring immediately after a non-directed actor process forming a complex process together with it, 'zai' can also appear before it. Look at the following examples:

> (4) a. Ta zai bandengshang zuo.
> he at bench-top sit
> (He'll sit on the bench.)
> b. Li Hua zai zhuoziqian zhanle liangge zhongtou.
> Li Hua at table-front stand-p. a. two-m. hour
> (Li Hua stood in front of the table for two hours.)
> [49]

       c. Wang Ping zai chuangxia duole yi tian.

          Wang Ping at bed-under hide-p. a. one day

          (Wang Ping hid under the bed for a whole day.)

However, when occurring pre-verbally, 'zai' is no longer a process in the clause. It introduces a circumstantial element of location. This can be proved by the fact that while the question '... zai nali?' (Where is/are/am ...?) can be asked about the clauses in (1), it can never be asked about the clauses in (4).

The circumstantial element introduced by 'zai' can also occur with a directed actor process, a mental process or a verbal process. Examples are given in (5) below:

   (5) a. Ta zai jieshang da ren.

        he at street-top beat person

        (He beat people in the streets.)

      b. Wo zai jiaoshili kanjian ta.

        I at classroom-inside see him

        (I saw him in the classroom.)

      c. Li Ying zai taishang shuo: "Wo bu pa."

        Li Ying at platform-top say: "I am not afraid."

        (Li Ying said on the platform: "I am not afraid.")

Some of the non-directed actor processes like those in (1) can take a post-verbal nominal group directly without functioning together with 'zai'. Such a phenomenon will be discussed later in 23.4 <u>Location Range</u>. [50]

16.2   Patient Process plus 'Zai'

All the processes in the following clauses belong to this type.

   (6) a. Ta ba qianbi fangzai zhuozishang.

        he f. p. pencil put-at desk-top

        (He put the pencil on the desk.)

      b. Zhang Ying ba nühair liuzaile jiali.

        Zhang Ying f. p. female-child leave-at home-inside

(Zhang Ying left her daughter at home.)

 c. Ta ba hua guazai qiangshang.

  he f. p. painting hang-at wahl-top

  (He hung the painting on the wall.)

In the clauses above the first participant is the Agent of the first process in the complex process. The second participant, i.e. the one introduced by 'ba' is the Patient of the first process and the Carrier in the second process. The third participant is the Attribute in the second process.

The double participant has to be introduced pre-verbally by 'ba' for the same reason as is stated in 15.2.

The complex process here still behaves like a patient process. The double participant may occur as the pre-verbal participant when the Agent is not present in the clause. Examples are given in (7) below:

 (7) a. Qianbi fangzai zhuozishang.

   pencil put-at desk-top

   (The pencil was put on the desk.)

  b. Nuhair liuzaile jiali.

   female-child leave-at-p. a. home-inside

   (The daughter was left at home.) [51]

  c. Hua guazai qiangshang.

   painting hang-at wall-top

   (The painting was hung on the wall.)

17. Directional Verbs in a Complex Process

There are a whole set of verbs in Chinese which express the direction of a process or the displacement of a participant. These verbs will be referred to as 'directional verbs' in this thesis. Directional verbs can be divided into three groups:

 a. 'lai' (come), 'qu' (go);

b. 'shang' (up), 'xia' (down), 'jin' (in), 'chu' (out), 'hui' (back), 'kai' (away), 'qi' (up), 'guo' (past, over);

c. 'shanglai' (come up), 'shangqu' (go up). 'xialai' (come down), 'xiaqu' (go down), 'jinlai' (come in), 'chuqu' (go out), 'huilai' (come back), 'qilai' (up), 'guolai' (come over), 'guoqu' (go over), etc.

As can be seen from the examples above, those in c. are formed through different combinations of the directional verbs in b. and those in a. .

The directional verbs can function alone as the process in a clause. Examples are given in (1) below:

(1) a. Ta laile.

he come-p. a.

(He has come.)

b. Ta jin men le.

He in door i. a.

(He has entered the door.) [52]

c. Ta chuqule.

he go-out-p. a.

(He has gone out.)

More often they are used as a component part of a complex process. See the following examples:

(2) a. Sun Ying zouchulaile.

Sun Ying walk-out-come-p. a.

(Sun Ying has come out.)

b. Chi Ping paohuiqule.

Chi Ping run-back-go-p. a.

(Chi Ping has run back.)

c. Wo ba shu maihuilaile.

I f. p. book buy-back-come-p. a.

(I have bought the book and brought it back.)

    d. Ta ba qianbi zhaochulaile.

       he f. p. pencil look-for out-come-p. a.

       (He has found the pencil.)

    e. Chuan chenxiaqule.

       ship sink-down-go-p. a.

       (The ship has sunk.)

    f. Xiaotou taochuqule.

       thief escape-out-go-p. a.

       (The thief has escaped.)

    g. Ta ba zhi tunxiaqule.

       he f. p. paper swallow-down-go-p. a.

       (He has swallowed the paper.)

    h. Wo ba zidian maichuqule.

       I f. p. dictionary sell-out-go-p. a.

       (I have sold the dictionary.) [53]

Very often the directional verbs do not express the actual direction at all. They are just the speaker's subjective rendering of the direction of the process or the displacement of a participant. Examples are given in (3) below:

    (3) a. Wo ba shu maixiale.

       I f. p. book buy-down-p. a.

       (I bought the book.)

    b. Ta ba wo kanshangle.

       he f. p. me look-up-p. a.

       (He picked me out.)

Directional verbs behave like non-directed patient processes in a complex process.

Note that in (4) only 'chu' (out) will be regarded as a directional verb taking part in a complex process. 'Lai' (come) is a separate process.

    (4) Ta zhaochu qianbi lai le.

he look-for-out pencil come i. a.

(He has found a pencil.)

18. Complex Process, Embedded Clause and Branched Clause Compared

Let us examine the following three clauses:

(1) a. Ta dapaole gou.

　　　he beat-run-away-p. a. dog

　　　(He beat the dog away.)

　b. Ta xihuan da gou.

　　　he like beat dog

　　　(He likes to beat dogs.) [54]

　c. Ta qu da gou.

　　　he go beat dog

　　　(He went to beat the dog.)

We call Clauses a., b. and c. a clause with a complex process, a clause with an embedded clause and a branched clause respectively.

'Dapao' in (1) a. is a complex process. As stated before, a complex process is one which is formed through combining two processes together with the former stating the means and the latter specifying the result. Such a relationship does not exist in b. and c. We cannot say beating is the result of liking or going. 'Gou' (dog) in a. is a double participant. It is the Goal of 'da (beat) and the Patient of 'pao' (run away). Yet 'gou' (dog) in b. and c. only participates in the second process 'da' (beat). It has nothing to do with the first process.

'Da gou' (beat dog) in Clause b. is a clause functioning as a participant. We will call such a clause an embedded or rankshifted clause. In b. the embedded clause functions as the phenomenon. This can be proved by the fact that we can use 'shenme' (what) to substitute 'da gou' in b. in a question but we cannot use 'shenme' (what) to substitute 'paole gou' or 'da gou' in a. or c. in a question. See examples in (2) below:

(2) a. * Ta da shenme?

he beat what

(* What did he beat?) [55]

b. Ta xihuan shenme?

he like what

(What does he like?)

c. * Ta qu shenme?

he go what

(* What did he go?)

Besides, the second process in (1) b. can have a separate pre-verbal participant which is simply impossible in a. and c. See (3) below:

(3) a. * Ta da ni paole gou.

he beat you run-away-p. a. dog

(* He beat you run away the dog.)

b. Ta xihuan ni da gou.

he like you beat dog

(He'd like you to beat the dog.)

c. * Ta qu ni da gou.

he go you beat dog

(* He went you to beat the dog.)

Clause c. is a branched clause, i. e. a clause with two or more processes existing independently of each other and sharing the same pre-verbal participant. There are two major types of branched clause structures in Chinese: 1) the second process states the purpose of the first process as in (1) c.; 2) the two processes take place one after another in sequence as in (4) below:

(4) Wo shangwan ke hui jia.

I attend-finish lecture return home

(I'll go home after I finish the lecture.) [56]

Owing to the limited scope of this thesis, the branched clause structure will not be discussed in detail here.

19. Causative Construction

Some actor processes can be used causatively. Look at the following examples:

(1) a. Li Ming zai pao ma.
　　　Li Ming p. p. run horse
　　　(Li Ming is exercising the horse.)
　　b. Laotaitai zai shai taiyang.
　　　old-lady p. p. bathe sun
　　　(The old lady is bathing in the sun.)
　　c. Wo zai kao huo.
　　　I p. p. toast fire
　　　(I am warming myself before the fire.)
　　d. Ta zai dou ji.
　　　he p. p. fight chicken
　　　(He is fighting his cock with another.)

In the clauses cited above, the post-verbal participant instead of the pre-verbal one is the Actor of the process. This is made clear in (2) below:

(2) a. Ma zai pao.
　　　horse p. p. run
　　　(The horse is running.)
　　b. Taiyang shaizhe laotaitai.
　　　sun bathe-p. s. old-lady
　　　(The sun is shining on the old lady.) [57]
　　c. Huo kaozhe wo.
　　　fire toast-p. a. me
　　　(The fire is warming me.)
　　d. Ji zai dou.

chicken p. p. fight

(The cocks are fighting.)

The pre-verbal participant in (1), on the other hand, is not the performer of the action. It simply causes the action to occur. Such a participant will be named the 'causer'. Clauses like those in (1) will be referred to as 'causative clauses'.

Since a Causer causes an action to take place, the Actor cannot be the voluntary performer of the action. It only performs the action because it is made to do so by the Causer. In this sense, the Actor in a causative clause has a double function. It is the effected as well as the Actor. We will call such a double participant the 'Effected Actor'.

Correspondingly the process in a causative clause also performs a double function. Such a process will be referred to as a 'Causativized Process'. A causativized process plays in the clause the function of a causative process as well as an actor process as can be seen from the paraphrased versions of the clauses in (1) which are given in (3) below:

(3) a. Li Ming zai shi ma pao.

　　　Li Ming p. p. cause horse run

　　　(Li Ming is making the horse run.)

　b. Laotaitai zai rang taiyang shai.

　　　old-lady p. p. let sun shine

　　　(The old lady is letting the sun shine on her.) [58]

　c. Wo zai rang huo kao.

　　　I p. p. let fire toast

　　　(I am letting the fire warm me.)

　d. Ta zai jiao ji dou.

　　　he p. p. make chicken fight

　　　(He is making the cocks fight.)

Processes like 'shi' (cause), 'rang' (let) and 'jiao' (make) in (3) are called 'Causative Processes'. A causative process simply expresses a causative relationship. Besides this, it has no other function at all.

When a directed actor process is causativized, it has the Causer as its implied Goal although the Goal is never specified. This can be made explicit in a clause which has a separate causative process. See examples in (4) below:

(4) a. Laotaitai rang taiyang shai taziji.
old-lady let sun shine herself
(The old lady let the sun shine on herself.)
b. Wo rang huo kao woziji.
I let fire toast myself
(I let the fire warm me.)

A causativised process cannot appear in a passive construction. This is exemplified by the ungrammaticality of the clauses in (5) below:

(5) a. *Ma zai bei Li Ming pao.
horse p.p. by Li Ming run
(*The horse is being run by Li Ming.)
b. *Taiyang zai bei laotaitai shai.
sun p.p. by old-lady shine
(*The sun is being shone by the old lady.) [59]
c. *Huo zai bei wo kao.
fire p.p. by me toast
(*The fire is being warmed by me.)
d. *Ji zai bei ta dou.
chicken p.p. by him fight
(*The cocks were fought by him.)

The Effected Actor cannot occur in the 'ba' construction. See the following ungrammatical clauses:

(6) a. *Li Ming ba ma paole.
Li Ming f.p. horse run-p.a.
(Li Ming has exercised the horse.)
b. *Laotaitai ba taiyang shaile.

old-lady f. p. sun shine-p. a.

(* The old lady has shone the sun.)

c. *Wo ba huo kaole.

I f. p. fire toast-p. a.

(* I have warmed the fire.)

d. *Ta ba ji doule.

he f. p. chicken fight-p. a.

(* He has fought the cocks.)

It seems that certain ascription processes and patient processes can also be causativized. Look at the clauses in (7):

(7) a. Ta zai re fan.

he p. p. hot rice

(He is heating the rice.)

b. Yao Lin zai tang yifu.

Yao Lin p. p. burning-hot clothes

(Yao Lin is ironing the clothes.) [60]

c. Ta tuile piao.

he retreat-p. a. ticket

(He has returned the ticket.)

d. Ta zai ting che.

he p. p. stop car

(He is stopping [parking] the car.)

However a careful examination will reveal that the processes in (7) behave differently from the causativized processes in (1).

First, the post-verbal participants in the processes in (7) above can be put to the pre-verbal position, just as a Patient, with the pre-verbal participants unspecified. See examples in (8) below:

(8) a. Fan rele.

rice hot-p. a.

(The rice has been heated.)

b. Yifu tangle.

clothes burning-hot-p. a.

(The clothes have been ironed.)
c. Piao tuile.
ticket retreat-p. a.
(The ticket has been returned.)
d. Che tingle.
car stop-p. a.
(The car has stopped.)

Secondly, processes in (7) can all appear in the passive construction. Look at the examples in (9) below:

(9) a. Fan bei ta rele.
rice by him hot-p. a.
(The rice has been heated by him.) [61]
b. Yifu bei Yao Lin tangle.
clothes by Yao Lin burning-hot-p. a.
(The clothes have been ironed by Yao Lin.)
c. Piao bei ta tuile.
ticket by him retreat-p. a.
(The ticket has been returned by him.)
d. Che bei ta tingle.
car by him stop-p. a.
(The car was stopped by him.)

Thirdly, the post-verbal participants in the clauses in (7) can all appear in the 'ba' construction. Examples are given in (10) below:

(10) a. Ta ba fan rele.
he f. p. rice hot-p. a.
(He heated the rice.)
b. Yao Lin ba yifu tangle.
Yao Lin f. p. clothes burning-hot-p. a.
(Yao Lin has ironed the clothes.)
c. Ta ba piao tuile.
he f. p. ticket retreat-p. a.
(He returned the ticket.)

  d. Ta ba che tingle.

   he f. p. car stop-p. a.

   (He stopped the car.)

  Therefore we may postulate that the processes in (7) are different from those in (1). They are not causativized processes. The processes in (7) c. and d. are ordinary patient processes. Those in (7) a. and b. will be referred to in this thesis as 'patientized ascription processes'. [62]

  Definitely the Agent in a patient or patientized process plays the role of the Causer, but it has another function besides that, i. e. the Actor. An Agent is in fact a conflated function of an Actor and a Causer. So the Agent 'ta' in (7) a. did the action of heating as well as caused the rice to be hot. The Agent 'Yao Lin' in (7) b. performed the action of heating as well as caused the clothes to be hot (ironing). The Agent 'ta' in (7) c. performed the action of returning the ticket as well as caused the ticket to be returned. The Agent 'ta' in (7) d. performed the action of stopping the car and at the same time caused the car to stop.

  Many of the ascription processes can be patientized, but only a small number of them can be directed. Most of the patientized ascription processes are non-directed. More examples of patientized ascription processes are given in (11) below:

  (11) a. Xin zhengce fanrongle jingji.

    new policy flourishing-p. a. economy

    (The new policy caused the economy to flourish.)

   b. Jingji fanrongle.

    economy flourishing-p. a.

    (The economy flourished.)

   c. Ta duanzhengle taidu.

    he correct-p. a. attitude

    (He corrected his attitude.)

   d. Tade taidu duazhengle.

    he-m. s. attitude correct-p. a.

(His attitude has been corrected.) [63]

e. Shuye hongle.
   tree-leaf red-p. a.
   (The leaves have turned red.)
f. Xiao Fang gaole.
   Little Fang tall-p. a.
   (Little Fang has grown taller.)
g. Tianqi lengle.
   weather cold-p. a.
   (The weather has become cold.)
h. Fangjian ganjingle.
   room clean-p. a.
   (The room has been cleaned.)
i. Wo leile.
   I tired-p. a.
   (I have become tired.)

In the patientization of the non-directed processes, the perfective aspect is indispensable. Without it, the idea of a change of state cannot be expressed and then the ascription process would not behave like a non-directed patient process. (See Chapter 24.)

20. Phase Structure

Phase structure is a complicated phenomenon In Chinese and an area very little researched upon. The present chapter is only an attempt to discuss it briefly.

Let us first examine the following clauses:

(1) a. Wo jiao ni qu.
       I ask you go
       (I ask you to go.) [64]
    b. Ta tuo wo mai shu.
       he entrust me buy book
       (He asked me to buy books for him.)

There are two processes in each of the above two clauses with the second dependent on the first. There is a participant between the two processes which has two functions in the clause. In the above clauses, it is the receiver of the action of the first process and at the same time the performer of the action of the second. We will call such a participant a 'dual participant'. We will refer to the two processes occurring in the same clause with the latter dependent on the former and sharing a dual participant as the phase structure.

The possibility of the occurrence of a second process depends entirely on whether the first process permits it or not, For instance, 'jiao' (ask) requires a second process while 'xi' (wash) simply does not allow it. We will call these verbs which allow a second verb to occur dependently after it 'phase verbs'. If a phase verb is selected as the second process, a third process may be introduced into the phase structure, so phase structure can be recursive. Look at the following examples:

(2) a. Wo jiao ni jiao ta ... qu.
   I ask you ask him ... go
   (I ask you to ask him ... to go.)
   b. Ta tuo wo tuo Sun Ying ... mai shu.
   he entrust me entrust Sun Ying ... buy book
   (He asked me to ask Sun Ying ... to buy books for him.) [65]
   c. Wo qing ni bang wo jiao ta lai.
   I ask you help me ask him come
   (I ask you to help me ask him to come.)
   d. Wo qiu ni bie jiao ta dai Li Bin lai.
   I beg you don't ask him bring Li Bin come
   (I beg you not to ask him to bring Li Bin here.)

More examples of phase structure are given in (3) below:

(3) a. Zhe shi wo hengaoxing.
   this make me very glad
   (This makes me very glad.)

b. Nage xiaohair tao ren xihuan.

　　that-m. child invite person like

　　(That child is likable.)

c. Ta rang yu lin.

　　he let rain pour

　　(He let the rain pour on him.)

d. Wang Lei zai bang wo ban chuang.

　　Wang Lei p. p. help me move bed

　　(Wang Lei is helping me move the bed.)

e. Gongrenmen xuan ta dang jingli.

　　worker-p. s. elect him be manager

　　(The workers elected him the manager.)

f. Wo ma ta wei jiantai.

　　I curse him be bastard

　　(I cursed him for a bastard.)

g. Wo zhunxu ta qu gongchang.

　　I permit him go factory

　　(I permit him to go to the factory.) [66]

The dual participant in some phase structures can occur in the 'ba' construction or pre-verbally in a passive clause. See the examples in (4) below:

(4) a. Wo ba ta ma wei jiantai.

　　　I f. p. him curse be bastard

　　　(I curse him for a bastard.)

b. Ta bei wo ma wei jiantai.

　　he by me curse be bastard

　　(He was cursed as a bastard by me.)

c. Wang Ping ba ta jiao qule.

　　Wang Ping f. p. him ask go-p. a.

　　(Wang Ping called him away.)

d. Ta bei Wang Ping jiao qule.

　　he by Wang Ping ask go-p. a.

　　(He was called away by Wang Ping.)

The clauses in (4) must not be confused with clauses with a complex process. The two are different in that the dual participant in a phase structure always has the potential to occur between the two processes while the double participant in a complex process does not.

A phase structure should also be distinguished from a mental process having an embedded clause as its Phenomenon. Let us examine the following clauses carefully:

  (5) a. Wo kanjian ta lai.
    I see he come
    (I saw that he came.)
   b. Wo jiaota lai.
    I ask him come
    (I ask him to come.) [67]

In Clause a. 'ta lai' is an embedded clause functioning as the Phenomenon of the mental process 'kanjian'. 'Ta' is only a participant in the embedded clause. It has no function in the main clause. While in Clause b., 'Ta' has a dual function and 'ta lai' is not a clause functioning as one participant at all. This is made clear by (6).

  (6) a. Wo kanjian ta lai zhejian shi.
    I see he come this-m. matter
    (I saw that he came.)
   b. *Wo jiao ta lai zhejian shi.
    I ask he come this-m. matter
    (*I ask that he comes.)

The above point is also proved by the fact that 'ta lai' as a clause functioning as one participant in a., can be substituted by 'shenme' (what) in a question; while 'ta lai', not being an embedded clause functioning as one participant, cannot. See (7) below:

  (7) a. Ni kanjianle shenme?
    you see-p. a. what
    (What did you see?)

b. * Ni jiao shenme?

you ask what

(* What did you ask?)

In Clause (5) b., the second process is dependent on the first. It exists only as a result of the first process. In other words, he should come only because I ask him to come. Yet in Clause (5) a., there is no such a dependency. We cannot say he came because I saw him. [68]

The two clauses in (5) also display different patterns of passivization. See examples in (8) below:

(8) a. Ta lai zhejian shi bei wo kanjianle.

he come this-m. matter by me see-p. a.

(That he came was seen by me.)

b. Ta bei wo jiao laile.

he by me ask come-p. a.

(He was called here by me.)

c. * Ta bei wo kanjian laile.

he by me see come-p. a.

(* He was seen come by me.)

d. * Ta lai zhejian shi bei wo jiaole.

he come this-m. matter by me ask-p. a.

(* That he came was asked by me.)

Clause (8) a. shows that 'ta lai' is an embedded clause functioning aa a participant in (5) a., while Clause (8) d. shows that 'ta lai' is not a participant in (5) b. On the other hand, Clause (8) b. shows that 'ta' is a participant in the process 'jiao', while 'ta' is proved by (8) c. as not being one in 'kanjian'.

The argument is further backed up by the possibility of the 'ba' construction in (5) b. and the impossibility of it in (5) a. See (9) below:

(9) a. * Wo ba ta kanjian laile.

I f. p. him see come-p. a.

(I saw him come.)

    b. Wo ba ta jiao laile.

       I f. p. him ask come-p. a.

       (I have called him here.) [69]

There is another structure which should be distinguished from a phase structure. Look at the following clause:

    (10) Wo maile yifen bao kan.

        I buy-p. a. one. m newspaper read.

        (I bought a newspaper to read.)

In Clause (10) both 'mai' (buy) and 'kan' (read) have 'bao' (newspaper) as their Goal and 'wo' (I) as their Actor. The second process is independent instead of dependent on the first process. The relationship between the two is either that of means and purpose or a sequence of time. We will analyse such a clause as a branched clause with the post-verbal participant of the second process omitted. As a detailed discussion on clause complex and cohesion is beyond the scope of this thesis, the argument will not be pursued further.

21. 'You' in Phase Structure

There is a very strong tendency in Chinese for the Given to appear pre-verbally and the New to occur post-verbally. When a participant conveying New information has to appear in the pre-verbal position, 'you' (have) is introduced before the participant to create a post-verbal position for the New information. Look at the following clauses:

    (1) a. Nage ren laile.

        that-m. person come-p. a.

        (That man has come.)

       b. You yige ren laile.

        have one-m. person come-p. a.

        (A man has come.) [70]

  c. Na sanben shu diule.

   that three-m. book lose-p. a.

   (Those three books have been lost.)

  d. You sanben shu diule.

   have three-m. book lose-p. a.

   (Three books have been lost.)

Superficially 'you' in b. and d. looks like a phase verb, but actually it does not have any ideational function. It just serves as a marker for the New. This is further proved by the impossibility of deleting 'you' in b. and d. or adding 'you' in a. and c. See the examples in (2) below:

  (2) a. * You nage ren laile.

    have that-m. person come-p. a.

    (That man has come.)

   b. Yige ren laile.

    one-m. person come-p. a.

    (One of the persons came.)

   c. * You na sanben shu diule.

    have that three-m. book lose-p. a.

    (Those three books have been lost.)

   d. Sanben shu diule.

    three-m. book lose-p. a.

    (Three of the books have been lost.)

From the above examples, we can see that the addition of 'you' in a. and c. results in ungrammaticality, and the deletion of 'you' in b. and d. changes the meaning of the original clauses. [71]

  'You' can be preceded by an expression of place or time. It can even be preceded by a personal pronoun or some other nominal group. But the above principle still prevails. See examples in (3) below:

  (3) a. Fangjianli you yige ren jiao Zhang Li.

    room-inside have one-m. person call Zhang Li

(There is a man in the room called Zhang Li.)
b. *Fangjianli you nage ren jiao Zhang Li.
room-inside have that-m. person call Zhang Li
(*There is that man in the room called Zhang Li.)
c. Wo you liangben shu diule.
I have two-m. book lose-p. a.
(Two of my books have been lost.)
d. *Wo you na liangben shu diule.
I have that two-m. book lose-p. a.
(*I have the two books lost.)

As information structure is outside the system of transitivity, the issue will not be elaborated further.

22. Beneficiary

So far we have been chiefly concentrating on the process. In the following part of this thesis, we are going to elaborate more on the participants.

A participant is a person, a thing or a fact which participates in the process. It is typically realized by a nominal group in the clause. [72]

In the previous chapters we have introduced quite a few participants. There are two more participants which have not yet appeared so far, i.e. the Beneficiary and the Range. The Beneficiary will be discussed in this chapter and the Range will be dealt with in the next.

The Beneficiary is the participant 'which benefits from the process expressed in the clause' either positively or negatively (Halliday, 1967a, p. 53). The Beneficiary occurs in material and verbal processes. 'Women' (us) is the Beneficiary in the clauses in (1) below:

(1) a. Laoshi gei women shu.
teacher gives us book

(The teacher gives us books.)
  b. Zhou Rong gaosu women ta mingtian qu Beijing.
   Zhou Rong tell us she tomorrow go-to Beijing
   (Zhou Rong told us that she would go to Beijing tomorrow.)

The Beneficiary often occurs immediately after the process before the other post-verbal participant. Besides appearing directly in the clause, it can also be introduced by a preposition. See examples in (2) below:

  (2) a. Ta song gei wo yiben shu.
    he give to me one-m. book
    (He gave me a book.)
   b. Ta song yiben shu gei wo.
    he give one-m. book to me
    (He gave a book to me.) [73]

Semantically Beneficiaries fall into four sub-categories, i. e. 'to', 'from', 'for' and 'on behalf of'. Typically they take the prepositions 'gei', 'xiang', 'wei' and 'ti' respectively. Examples are given in (3) below:

  (3) a. Wu Feng gei yiben shu gei wo.
    Wu Feng give one-m. book to me
    (Wu Feng gave a book to me.)
   b. Wo xiang Chen Yu jiele yiben shu.
    I from Chen Yu borrow-p. a. one-m. book
    (I borrowed a book from Chen Yu.)
   c. Ta wei zuguo shang qianxian.
    he for motherland go-up battle front
    (He went to the battle front for his motherland.)
   d. Wo ti ta xie xin.
    I on-behalf-of him write letter
    (I'll write a letter for [on behalf of] him.)

'Gei' (to) can also be used in the sense of 'for' and 'on behalf of'. Look at the following examples:

 (4) a. Wo zai gei bingren kan bing.

   I p. p. for patient look illness

   (I am treating my patient.)

  b. Wo gei ta xiele liangpian zuowen.

   I on-behalf-of him write-p. a. two-m. composition

   (I write two compositions for [on behalf of] him.)

Beneficiaries of the 'to' type can occur between the process and the post-verbal participant either with or without 'gei' (to) as can be seen from the examples in (1) [74] and (2). They can also appear after the post-verbal participant when introduced by 'gei' as is exemplified by (3) a.

Beneficiaries of the 'from' type appear pre-verbally when they are introduced by 'xiang' (See (3) b.), but post-verbally before the other post-verbal participant when they are not accompanied by 'xiang' as is exemplified in (5) below:

 (5) Wo jiele Chen Yu yiben shu.

  I borrow-p. a. Chen Yu one-m. book

  (I borrowed a book from Chen Yu.)

Beneficiaries of the 'for' and 'on behalf of' types have to be introduced by a preposition. It is compulsory for those of the 'on behalf of' type to appear pre-verbally. Those of the 'for' type normally occur pre-verbally. Only under rare circumstances can they occupy the post-verbal position. Examples are given in (6) below:

 (6) a. Ta sheng wei zuguo, si wei renmin.

   he live for motherland, die for people

   (He lived for the motherland and died for the people.)

  b. Wo shang xue wei renmin.

   I attend school for people

   (I attend school for the people.)

23. Range

A Range is a participant in a process that specifies what is intrinsically implied in the process, such as its range or scope, its natural result, the intrinsic instrument used in it, and so on. Thus the sole function of a Range is to add specifications to what is inherent in the process in question. [75]

According to the different kinds of specifications added to the process, Ranges are categorized into six sub-types in this thesis, namely: Cognate Range, Measurement Range, Result Range, Location Range, Instrument Range and Process Range. Each of the six will be dealt with separately in the following sections of this chapter.

23.1 Cognate Range

A Cognate Range is a Range which "is co-extensive with", and "is indeed merely a nominalization of, the process". It is best thought of as an "'extension inherent in the process' leading to a mutual expectancy of collocation" (Halliday, 1967a, p. 59) between itself and the process in question. Examples of Cognate Ranges are given in (1) below:

(1) a. Li Feng zai chang ge.
　　　 Li Feng p. p. sing song
　　　 (Li Feng is singing a song.)
　　b. Wo chile fan le.
　　　 I eat-p. a. meal i. a.
　　　 (I have had my meal.)
　　c. Xiaohair zai shui-jiao.
　　　 child p. p. sleep-sleep
　　　 (The child is sleeping.)
　　d. Bie shuo-hua.
　　　 don't speak-speech
　　　 (Don't speak.)

e. Ta shule qian.

   he lose (in gambling)-p. a. money

   (He lost in a gamble.) [76]

Cognate here is only a borrowed term. Actually the nouns and the verbs in the above clauses are not cognates. However the inherent relationship between the noun and the verb is very clear. 'Ge' (song) is a piece of singing; 'fan' (meal or food) is what is eaten at three meals; 'jiao' (sleep) is the nominal form of 'shui' (to sleep); 'hua' (speech) is what is spoken; and 'qian' (money) is what is lost or won at gambling.

A Cognate Range is generally a nominal group having a very general reference. This is determined by its nature of just being an extension of the process, a pseudo participant which does not have much substantial meaning. Take Clause c. for example. The Cognate Range 'fan' means 'anything which is eaten at a meal'. When it has a specific reference meaning 'rice', it will no longer be a Cognate Range, but a Patient instead.

Sometimes a Cognate Range takes a modifier. Then it will have a more specific referent pointing to a sub-class of the original Range. See the following examples:

(2) a. Li Feng zai chang min-ge.

   Li Feng p. p. sing folk-song

   (Li Feng is singing a folk song.)

   b. Wo chile wu-fan le.

   I eat-p. a. noon-meal i. a.

   (I have had my lunch.)

   c. Xiaohair zai shui wu-jiao.

   child p. p. sleep noon-sleep

   (The child is having a mid-day nap.) [77]

   d. Ta hui shuo Yingguo hua.

   he can speak English-country speech

   (He can speak English.)

Cognate Ranges only occur in non-directed actor processes.

23.2 Measurement Range

A Measurement Range is another type of extension of the process. It specifies the quantity of a process which has such type of quantity as part of its inherent value. Measurement Ranges chiefly occur in ascription processes. Clauses in (3) below all have a Measurement Range.

(3) a. Zhao Yong shen gao yi mi qi.
  Zhao Yong body tall one metre seven
  (Zhao Yong is one hundred and seventy centimeters tall.)
 b. Zhu zhong liushi gongjin.
  pig heavy sixty kilogram
  (The pig weighs sixty kilograms.)
 c. Zheliang qiche zhi yi-wan yuan.
  this-m. car worth ten-thousand yuan
  (This car is worth ten thousand yuan.)
 d. Zhekuai di chang ershi mi, kuan shiwu mi.
  this-m. land long twenty metre, wide fifteen metre
  (This piece of land is twenty metres long and fifteen metres wide.)

In the clauses above, 'yi mi qi' (one hundred and seventy centimetres) is an inherent measurement of tallness; [78] 'liushi gongjin' (sixty kilograms) is an inherent measurement of weight; 'ershi mi' (twenty metres) and 'shiwu mi' (fifteen metres) are inherent measurements of length and width. We say that they are inherent because other types of measurements just do not fit into those processes at all. Look at the following ungrammatical clauses in (4):

(4) a. *Zhao Yong shen gao liushi gongjin.
  Zhao Yong body tall sixty kilogram
  (*Zhao Yong is sixty kilograms tall.)
 b. *Zhu zhong san mi.
  pig heavy three metre

(* The pig weighs three metres.)

    c. * Zhekuai di chang ershi pingfangmi, kuan shiwu lifangmi.

       this-m. land long twenty square metre, wide fifteen cubic metre

       (* This piece of land is twenty square metres long and fifteen cubic metres wide.)

As for Clause (3) c., it is even compulsory for the ascription process 'zhi' (worth) to take a Measurement Range like 'yi-wan yuan' (ten thousand yuan) in it; otherwise the clause will be ungrammatical. ('Zhi' (worth) can also take 'qian' (money) as its Cognate Range.)

Some patient or patientized processes can also take a Measurement Range. See the following examples:

    (5) a. Biao maile <u>wushi yuan</u>.

       watch sell-p. a. fifty yuan

       (The watch was sold for fifty yuan.) [79]

    b. Ta pangle <u>san gongjin</u>.

       he fat-p. a. three kilogram

       (He has gained three kilograms.)

Cognate Ranges sometimes take measurement modifiers. Look at the following clauses:

    (6) a. Li Feng changle <u>sanzhi ge</u>.

       Li Feng sing-p. a. three-m. song

       (Li Feng sang three songs.)

    b. Wo chile <u>liangdun fan</u> le.

       I eat-p. a. two-m. meal i. a.

       (I have had two meals.)

    c. Ta shuile <u>liangge wu-jiao</u> le.

       he sleep-p. a. two-m. noon-sleep i. a.

       (He has had two naps.)

The Ranges in the above clauses will not be treated as Measurement Ranges but Cognate Ranges with modifiers.

The Ranges in the clauses in (7) below are also Cognate Ranges with modifiers.

(7) a. Ta tiaole <u>liang tiao</u>.
    he jump-p. a. two jump
    (He jumped two jumps.)

b. Ta kanle <u>yi kan</u>.
   he look-p. a. one look
   (He took a look.)

c. Wo chang <u>yi chang</u>.
   I taste one taste
   (I'll have a taste.)

d. Wo zou <u>yi zou</u>.
   I walk one walk
   (I'm walking a walk.) [80]

23.3 Result Range

A Result Range is a participant which specifies the intrinsic result of a process. It occurs only in a very small number of patient processes. All the clauses in (8) below have a Result Range in them.

(6) a. Kuzi pole yige <u>dong</u>.
    trousers break-p. a. one-m. hole
    (The trousers got a hole in them.)

b. Qiang liele yitiao <u>kou</u>.
   wall crack-p. a. one-m. gap
   (The wall has got a crack in it.)

c. Yanshi kaile yitiao <u>feng</u>.
   rock open-p. a. one-m. crack
   (A crack appeared in the rock.)

In the above clauses, 'dong' (hole) is the natural result of 'po' (to break); 'kou' (crack) is the natural result of 'lie' (to crack); and 'feng' (crack) is the natural result of 'kai' (to crack).

23.4 Location Range

A Location Range is a participant which specifies the inherent location or place where a process takes place. Look at the following examples:

(9) a. Ta hui qiu-shui.
   he can swim-water
   (He can swim.)

b. Wo you Changjiang, ni you Huanghe.
   I swim the-Yangtze, you swim the-Yellow-River
   (I swim in the Yangtze and you swim in the Yellow River.) [81]

c. Wo zuo che.
   I sit vehicle
   (I'll take the bus/train.)

d. Women qu chi guanzi.
   we go eat restaurant
   (We'll go and eat in a restaurant.)

e. Ta zou-lu qu.
   he walk-road go
   (He'll go there on foot.)

The intrinsic nature of the relation between the process and the Location Range in the above clauses is obvious: 'shui' (water) specifies the only place where one can swim; the Yangtze and the Yellow River are only specific areas of water in which one can swim; 'zuo che' does not really mean 'to sit in a vehicle'. It means 'to sit in and travel by a vehicle'. 'Che' (vehicle) together with 'feiji' (airplane) and 'chuan' (ship) are the only places in which one can sit and travel; 'guanzi' (restaurant) is the only place in which one can eat if one is going to eat away from one's home; and 'lu' (road) is the only place on which one normally walks.

The intrinsic nature of the Location Range is also proved by the impossibility of separating them from the processes by 'zai' (at).

See the following examples:

  (10) a. * Ta hui zai shuili you.
     he can at water-inside swim
     (* He can swim in water.) [82]
   b. * Wo zai Changjiang you, ni zai Huanghe you.
     I at the-Yangtze Swim, you at the-Yellow-River swim
     (I swim in the Yangtze and you swim in the Yellow River.)
   c. Wo zai cheshang zuo.
     I at vehicle-top sit
     (I'll sit in the bus.)
   d. * Women zai guanzi chi.
     we at restaurant eat
     (We'll eat at a restaurant.)
   e. * Ta zai lushang zou qu.
     he at road-top walk go
     (He'll walk on the road and go there.)

  Clauses a., b., d., and e. all become ungrammatical when 'zai' is introduced. Clause c. is still a grammatical clause, but the meaning has changed completely.

  Note that the post-verbal participants in the clauses in (11) below are not Location Ranges although they specify a place or a location. The reason is that they do not specify the location or place where a process intrinsically takes place. They can be separated from the process.

  (11) a. Ta qu Beijing.
     he go Beijing
     (He is going to Beijing.)
   b. Ta dao Beijing qu.
     he to Beijing go
     (He is going to Beijing.) [83]
   c. Ta shang shan le.

he up mountain i. a.

(He has gone up the mountain.)

d. Ta shang-dao shan-shang le.

he upto mountain-top i. a.

(He has gone up the mountain.)

'Beijing' (Peking) and 'shan' (mountain) in a. and c. are Goals instead of Location Ranges.

Location Ranges only occur in a small number of non-directed actor processes.

23.5 Instrument Range

An Instrument Range is a participant which specifies the intrinsic instrument with which the action of a process is performed. An Instrument Range can only occur in a non-directed actor process. All the pest-verbal participants in the clauses in (12) below are Instrument Ranges.

(12) a. Ta chi da wan.

he eat big bowl

(He eats with a big bowl.)

b. Wo chi kuaizi.

I eat chopstick

(I eat with chopsticks.)

c. Ta hui xie gangban.

he can write steel-stencil-board

(He can write with a steel-stencil-board.)

d. Ta xie mao-bi.

he write hair-pen

(He writes with a brush.) [84]

e. Ta zai gei wo da-zhen.

he p. p. for me inject-needle

(He is giving me an injection.)

The intrinsic relation between the instrument and the action is obvious in the above clauses: 'wan' (bowl) and 'kuaizi' (chopsticks) are the indispensable instruments with which the Chinese people eat at meals; 'gangban' (steel stencil board) is the only instrument with which one can write on a stencil; 'maobi' (brush) used to be the sole instrument to write with in China; and 'zhen' (needle) is the sole instrument with which an injection can be given.

Normally the semantic notion of an instrument has to be expressed by the verb 'yong' (to use). Only very few processes in Chinese can take an Instrument Range.

23.6 Process Range

All the five types of Ranges discussed so far are nominal or participant Ranges, the meanings of which are more or less inherently implied in the processes in which they are functioning as participants. Yet in many other instances, 'the nature of the process is expressed only by a nominal group functioning as Range, the verb being one of a small set whose meaning is so general that it signals no more than the fact that some process or other is being referred to' (Halliday, forthcoming, p. 86). We will refer to such a Range as a Process Range. Examples of Process Ranges are given in (13) below: [85]

    (13) a. Ta zai zuo mai-mai.
       he p. p. do buy-sell
       (He is doing business.)
      b. Wo zai zuo gong.
       I p. p. do work
       (I am working.)
      c. Ta chang zuo meng.
       he often do dream
       (He often dreams.)
      d. Women zai gao yundong.
       we p. p. do movement
       (We are carrying on a movement.)
      e. Ta gao shengchan.

he do production

(He is engaged in production.)

f. Wo gao xuanchuan.

I do propaganda

(I do propaganda work.)

g. Xiao Wang zai gan huo.

Little Wang p. p. do work.

(Little Wang is working.)

h. Tamen gan-jia le.

they do-quarrel/fight i. a.

(They have quarreled/come to blows.)

i. Women gan geming.

We do revolution

(We make revolution.)

j. Ta zai da-han.

he p. p. do-snore

(He is snoring.) [86]

k. Wo da-du.

I do-bet

(I bet [on it].)

l. Tamen zai da zuqiu.

they p. p. do soccer

(They are playing soccer.)

A Process Range can be regarded as a type of Cognate Range.

24. Patient, Agent, Actor, Goal and Carrier Compared

The term Patient in this thesis is used to refer to a participant which undergoes a change of state in the process. Look at the following examples:

(1) a. Wo ba fangzi maile.

I f. p. house sell-p. a.

(I sold the house.)

b. <u>Fangzi</u> maile.

   house sell-p. a.

   (The house was sold.)

c. Ta dasile <u>ren</u>.

   he beat-die-p. a. person

   (He beat a man to death.)

d. <u>Ren</u> dasile.

   person beat-die-p. a.

   (The man was beaten to death.)

e. <u>Bingren</u> sile.

   patient die-p. a.

   (The patient died.) [87]

f. <u>Hua</u> hongle.

   flower red-p. a.

   (The flowers have become red.)

g. Ta ba <u>gutou</u> shaochengle hui.

   he f. p. bone burn-become-p. a. ash

   (He burnt the bones to ashes.)

h. <u>Kedou</u> bianchengle qingwa.

   Tadpole change-become-p. a. frog

   (The tadpoles have become frogs.)

The underlined participants in the above clauses are all Patients because they all undergo a change of state in the process they take part in. 'Fangzi' (house) in (1) a. and b. has its ownership changed in the process 'mai' (sell). 'Ren' (person) in (1) c. and d. changes from the state of being alive to the state of being dead in the process 'dasi' (beat to death). 'Bingren' (patient) in (1) e. goes through the same change of state in the process 'si' (die). 'Hua' in (1) f. changes from the state of not being red to the state of being red in the process 'hongle' (become red). 'Gutou' (bone) in (1) g. changes from bones into ashes in the process 'shaocheng' (burn into). 'Kedou' (tadpole) in (1) h. changes from tadpoles into frogs in the process 'biancheng' (become).

It is exactly this semantic notion of change of state which differentiates a Patient from an Actor, a Goal, a Carrier, or any other participant. Precisely because of this, a Patient in a clause can always be picked out by the question '... zenmele?' (What [has] happened to ... ?) which asks about a change of state, while the other participants [88] cannot. Look at the following examples:

(2) a. Wo ba zhu dasile.
   I f. p. pig beat-die-p. a.
   (I beat the pig to death.)

b. Zhu diule.
   Pig lose-p. a.
   (The pig was lost.)

c. Zhu bingle.
   Pig ill-p. a.
   (The pig fell ill.)

d. Zhu feile.
   Pig fat-p. a.
   (The pig has grown fat.)

e. Ta ba zhu shaocheng hui le.
   He f. p. pig burn-become ash i. a.
   (He has burnt the pig to ashes.)

f. Zhu biancheng gou le.
   Pig change-become dog i. a.
   (The pig has become a dog.)

g. Zhu zenmele?
   Pig how-p. a.
   (What happened to the pig?)

(3) a. Zhu niaole.   (Actor)
   Pig urinate-p. a.
   (The pig has urinated.)

b. Zhu yaole ren.   (Actor)
   pig bite-p. a. person
   (The pig has bitten people.) [89]

c. Ta zai zhao zhu. (Goal)

he p. p. look-for pig

   (He is looking for the pig.)

d. *Zhu zenmele?

   pig how-p. a.

   (*What happened to the pig?)

(4) a. Zhu fei. (Carrier)

   pig fat

   (The pig is fat.)

b. *Zhu zenmele?

   pig how-p. a.

   (*What happened to the pig?)

A Patient is similar to a Goal in that both can occur in the post-verbal position. However the two are very different from each other. A Goal specifies the goal or terminal point of a process while a Patient is something which is disposed of in a process. We can do something to or with a Patient. but not a Goal. Precisely because of this, a Patient can occur in the 'ba' construction which is a structure expressing the idea of disposal but a Goal cannot. Some examples illustrating this have been given in the chapter on 'ba' construction. More examples will be given in (5) below:

(5) a. Wo ba shu shaole.

   I f. p. book burn-p. a.

   (I burnt the book.)

b. Ta ba zhu maile.

   he f. p. pig sell-p. a.

   (He sold the pig.) [90]

c. *Wo ba shu zhaole.

   I f. p- book look-for-p. a.

   (I looked for the book)

d. *Ta ba zhu dale.

   he f. p. pig beat-p. a.

   (He beat the pig.)

As mentioned earlier, the Patient is the obligatory participant in a patient process while the Goal is an optional participant in an actor process. The Patient can occur pre-verbally with the Agent unspecified but the Goal cannot occupy the pre-verbal position.

Lastly the Patient can be picked out from a clause by the question '... zenmele?' as can be seen from examples in (2) but the Goal cannot as can be seen from (3) c. and d. More examples are given in (6) to illustrate this.

(6) a. Wo dale gou.

   I beat-p. a. dog

   (I beat the dog.)

b. Ta zai kan gou.

   he p. p. look-at dog

   (He is looking at the dog.)

c. Gou zenmele?

   dog how-p. a.

   (*What happened to the dog?)

The Actor of a non-directed actor process is similar to the Patient of a non-directed patient process in [91] that both occur pre-verbally. The two are different in that the Actor is the performer of the action in the process while the Patient is not. On the other hand the Patient undergoes a change of state in the process but the Actor does not. Therefore only the Actor can be picked out from a clause by '... zuo/gan shenme?' (... do what?), whereas on the other hand only the Patient can be picked out by '... zenmele?' (What happened to...?) See examples in (7) below:

(7) a. Ta xiaole.

   he laugh-p. a.

   (He laughed.)

b. Ta zuo shenme le?

   he do what i. a.

   (What did he do?)

c. *Ta zenmele?

   he how-p. a.

   (*What happened to him?)

d. Ta sile.

he die-p. a.

(He died.)

e. *Ta zuole shenme?

he do-p. a. what

(*What did he do?)

f. Ta zenmele?

he how-p. a.

(What happened to him?) [92]

The Actor of a directed process is very similar to the Agent in that both occur pre-verbally and both can be picked out by '... zuo shenme?' (... do what?) The Agent is in fact an Actor as pointed out before. What distinguishes the Agent from the Actor is that the Agent is at the same time a Causer. Besides, the Agent is an optional participant which occurs in a patient process, i. e. a process which has a Patient as its obligatory participant only when it is directed; while the Actor is the obligatory participant in an actor process which may have a Goal as its optional participant.

A Carrier is the participant which carries the feature given by the ascription process or the attribute in a relational process. It is different from an Actor in that it is not the performer of an action and so cannot be picked out by '... zuo shenme?' (... do what?) It is different from a Patient in that it does not go through a change of state in the process and so cannot be picked out by '... zenmele?' (What happened to...?) On the other hand it can appear in the question '... zenmeyang?' (How is...?) which singles it out from an Actor or a Patient. Look at the following clauses:

(8) a. Ta gao.

he tall

(He is tall.)

b. Ta you wuben shu.

he have five-m. book

(He has five books.) [93]

c. Ta zenmeyang?

he how

(How is he?)

  d. *Ta zuo shenme?

   he do what

   (*What does he do?)

  e. *Ta zenmele?

   he how-p. a.

   (*What has happened to him?)

(9) a. Ta zai pao.

   he p. p. run

   (He is running.)

  b. Ta sile.

   he die-p. a.

   (He has died.)

  c. *Ta zenmeyang?

   he how

   (*How is he?)

25. Affected Patient and Effected Patient

Let us first examine the following clauses:

(1) a. Ta shaole yifeng xin.

   he burn-p. a. one-m. letter

   (He has burnt a letter.)

  b. Ta xiele yifeng xin.

   he write-p. a. one-m. letter

   (He has written a letter.) [94]

  c. Tamen kaile men.

   they open-p. a. door

   (They have opened the door.)

  d. Tamen kaile jing.

   they open-p. a. well

   (They have dug a well.)

The underlined participants in the above clauses are all Patients, yet those in a. and c. are somewhat different from those in b. and d.

'Xin' (letter) in a. and 'men' (door) in c. already existed before the processes started. They are things which were disposed of in the process. In other words somebody did something to or with them. 'Xin' (letter) in b. and 'jing' (well) in d., on the other hand, were created in the processes. They did not exist before the processes. We will refer to the former as 'Affected Patients' and the latter as 'Effected Patients'. We can say that an Effected Patient also goes through a change of state in the process since creation can be regarded as a change of state from non-existence to existence. The argument of an Effected Patient being a Patient at all is backed up by the fact that it can appear in the 'ba' construction or occur pre-verbally with the Agent unspecified. See the examples in (2) below:

(2) a. Ta ba nafeng xin xiele.
   he f. p. that-m. letter write-p. a.
   (He has written the letter.)

b. Tamen ba nakou jing kaile.
   they f. p. that-m. well open-p. a.
   (They have dug the well.) [95]

c. Xin xiele.
   letter write-p. a.
   (The letter has been written.)

d. Jing kaile.
   well open-p. a.
   (The well has been dug.)

However an Effected Patient can never be picked out by the question '...zenmele?' (What happened to...?) So the questions in (3) below cannot serve as appropriate questions for (2).

(3) a. *Xin zenmele?
   letter how-p. a.
   (*What happened to the letter?)

b. *Jing zenmele?
   well how-p. a.
   (*What happened to the well?)

The reason for this is that the questions in (3) presuppose the existence of the Patient before the process while an Effected Patient such as those in (2) does not exist before the process.

More examples of Effected Patients are given in (4) below:

(4) a. Tamen gaile yidong <u>fangzi</u>.
   they build-p. a. one-m. house
   (They built a house.)

b. Nongminmen wale yizuo <u>shuiku</u>.
   peasant-pl. dig-p. a. one-m. reservoir
   (The peasants dug a reservoir.) [96]

c. Ta zai qiangshang dale yige <u>dong</u>.
   he at wall-top strike-p. a. one-m. hole
   (He made a hole in the wall.)

d. Gongrenmen zai heshang jianle yizuo <u>qiao</u>.
   worker-pl. at river-top construct-p. a. one-m. bridge
   (The workers built a bridge across the river.)

e. Ta jintian fengle liangjian <u>yifu</u>.
   she today sew-p. a. two-m. coat
   (She has sewn two coats today.)

f. Ta zuole yige <u>wanju</u>.
   he make one-m. toy
   (He made a toy.)

26. Clausal Processes and Their Participants

Let us first look at the following clauses:

(1) a. Shu diule.
   book lose-p. a.
   (The book was lost.)

b. Ta diule shu.
   he lose-p. a. book
   (He lost a book.)

c. Ren sile.

person die-p. a.

(The man died.)

d. Cunzili sile ren.

village-inside die-p. a. person

(A man died in the village.) [97]

Superficially 'diu' (lose) and 'si' (die) in the above clauses are just ordinary patient processes with 'shu' (book) and 'ren' (person) being the Patients, and 'ta' (he) and 'cunzili' (village-inside) being the Agents respectively. However a closer examination will reveal that 'ta' (he) and 'cunzili' (village-inside) are not Agents at all. We cannot say that 'ta' (he) performed the action of losing or caused the book to be lost. Similarly we cannot say that 'cunzili' (village-inside) performed the action of dying or caused the man to die. The above point is proved by the impossibility of the 'ba' construction, the passive construction or a causative verb in the clauses in (1) above. Examples are given in (2) below:

(2) a. * Ta ba shu diule.

he f. p. book lose-p. a.

(He lost the book.)

b. * Shu bei ta diule.

book by him lose-p. a.

(The book was lost by him.)

c. * Ta shi shu diule.

he cause book lose-p. a.

(* He caused the book to be lost.)

d. * Cunzili ba ren sile.

village-inside f. p. person die-p. a.

(* The village died the man.)

e. * Ren bei cunzili sile.

person by village-inside die-p. a.

(* The man was died by the village.) [98]

f. * Cunzili shi ren sile.

village-inside cause person die-p. a.

(* The village caused the man to die.)

Clauses a. and b. above can be grammatical but then the process 'diu' in them would mean 'to threw away' instead of 'to lose' and it would be a different process altogether.

In fact there is no action involved in the two processes in (1) at all. They are both inherently non-directed patient processes which require a Patient as their only participant as can be seen in Clauses (1) a. and c. The problem posed by Clauses (1) b. and d. is how to account for the presence of a second participant in the clause.

We postulate that 'ta' (he) and 'cunzili' (village-inside) in (1) b. and d. are Patients, while 'diule shu' (lose-p. a. book) and 'sile ren' (die-p. a. person) are embedded clauses functioning as non-directed patient processes depicting what happened to the Patients. 'Shu' (book) and 'ren' (person) are Patients in the embedded clauses which are shifted from the pre-verbal position to the post-verbal position for two reasons: 1) the clause initial position is already occupied by the Higher Patient; 2) their post-verbal position is necessitated by the fact of their being New Information. The latter point is proved by the impossibility of Given Information occurring in the post-verbal position as is shown in (3) below, and the possibility of a Patient carrying New Information appearing in the post-verbal position in a clause which has only one Patient in it as is shown in (4) below. [99]

(3) a. * Ta diule naben shu.
he lose-p. a. that-m. book
(He lost that book.)

b. * Cunzili sile nage ren.
village-inside die-p. a. that-m. person
(That man died in the village.)

(4) a. Laile yige ren.
come-p. a. one-m. person
(A man comes.)

b. Sile liangtiao gou.
die-p. a. two-m. dog
(Two dogs died.)

The Lower Patient carrying New Information can occur pre-verbally, but then it has to be introduced by the New Information marker 'you' (have) as mentioned in Chapter 21. See examples in (5) below:

(5) a. Ta you yiben shu diule.
he have one-m. book lose-p. a.
(A book of his got lost.)

b. Cunzili you ren sile.
village-inside have person die-p. a.
(Someone died in the village.)

The argument that 'ta' (he) and 'cunzili' (village-inside) in (1) b. and d. are Patients, and 'diule shu' (lose-p. a. book) and 'sile ren' (die-p. a. person) are embedded clauses functioning as non-directed patient processes is backed up by the fact that the latter can be substituted by the pro-verbal form 'zenmele' (how-p. a.) or 'fasheng' (happen), and the former can be picked out by the question '... zenmele?' (What happened to ...?) Look at the examples in (6) below:

(6) a. Ta diule shu.
he lose-p. a. book
(He lost a book.)

b. Ta zenmele?
he how-p. a.
(What happened to him?)

c. Shenme shi fashengle?
what thing happen-p. a.
(What has happened?)

d. Cunzili sile ren.
village-inside die-p. a. person
(A man died in the village.)

e. Cunzili zenmele?
village-inside how-p. a.
(What happened in the village?)

f. Shenme shi fashengle?
what thing happen-p. a.
(What has happened?)

Only a clause with a process which expresses appearance or disappearance can function as a clausal patient process. A process of appearance or disappearance is one of a small number of non-directed patient processes in the perfective aspect or non-directed complex processes which have a directional verb as their component part. More examples of clausal patient processes are given in (7) below:

(7) a. Wang Mian qisui sile fuqin.

　　　Wang Mian seven-years-old die-p. a. father

　　　(Wang Mian lost his father when he was seven.)
　　　[101]

　b. Waimian zoujinlai yige ren.

　　　outside walk-in-come one-m. person

　　　(A man came in from outside.)

　c. Zuotian laile jiuge ren.

　　　yesterday come-p. a. nine person

　　　(Yesterday nine people came.)

　d. Tade lianshang chuxianle zhouwen.

　　　he-m. s. face-top appear-p. a. wrinkles

　　　(Wrinkles appeared on his face.)

　e. Nongchang paole santou niu.

　　　farm run-away-p. a. three-m. oxen

　　　(Three oxen ran away from the farm.)

A clause can function not only as a patient process but also as an ascription process. Look at the following examples:

(8) a. Ta tou tong.

　　　he head ache

　　　(He has a headache.)

　b. Jiaoshili zuozhe yige ren.

　　　classroom-inside sit-p. s. one-m. person

　　　(There is a man sitting in the classroom.)

The status of 'tou tong' (head ache) and 'zuozhe yige ren' (sit-p. s. a man) being clauses functioning as ascription processes can be proved by the fact that they can be substituted by 'zenmeyang' (how) in a question. The status of 'ta' (he) and 'jiaoshili' (classroom-inside) being Carriers is made clear by the possibility of picking them out in the question '... zenmeyang?' (How is ...?) Look at the examples in (9) below: [102]

(9) a. Ta zenmeyang?
he how
(How is he?)
b. Jiaoshili zenmeyang?
classroom-inside how
(What's happening in the classroom?)

27. Patient or Carrier of a Clausal Process vs. Possessive Case

It seems that we can argue that the Patients and Carriers in the clauses in 26. are variant forms of nominal groups in the possessive case, the clauses with a clausal process are simply simple clauses with no embedding in them at all, and the clauses in (1) below can be rewritten into clauses in (2) below.

(1) a. Ta diule shu.
he lose-p. a. book
(He lost a book.)
b. Cunzili sile ren.
village-inside die-p. a. person
(A man died in the village.)
c. Ta tou tong.
he head ache
(He has a headache.)
d. Jiaoshili zuozhe yige ren.
classroom-inside sit-p. s. one-m. person
(There is a man sitting in the classroom.)
(2) a. Tade shu diule.
he-m. s. book lose-p. a.

　　　　(His book was lost.) [103]

　　b. Cunzilide ren sile.

　　　　village-inside-m. s. person die-p. a.

　　　　(The man in the village died.)

　　c. Tade tou tong.

　　　　he-m. s. head ache

　　　　(His head is aching.)

　　d. Jiaoshilide nage ren zuozhe.

　　　　classroom-inside-m. s. that-m. person sit-p. s.

　　　　(The man in the classroom is sitting.)

However, the above argument cannot stand. The reasons are as follows:

Firstly, if we used the questions '... zenmele?' (What happened to...?) and '... zenmeyang?' (How is...?) to pick out the Patients and the Carriers from the above clauses, we will pick out 'ta' (he), 'cunzili' (village-inside), 'ta' (he) and 'jiaoshili' (classroom-inside) in (1) but 'shu' (book), 'ren' (person), 'tou' (head) and 'ren' (person) in (2). This proves that the clauses in (1) and those in (2) have different Patients or Carriers in them.

Secondly, the occurrence of adverbs reveals that the structures of the two sets of clauses are drastically different. Look at the following clauses:

(3) a. Ta you diule shu.

　　　　he again lose-p. a. book

　　　　(He lost a book again.)

　　b. Tade shu you diule.

　　　　he-m. s. book again lose-p. a.

　　　　(His book was lost again.) [104]

　　c. Cunzili you sile ren.

　　　　village-inside again die-p. a. person

　　　　(Another man died in the village.)

　　d. *Cunzilide nage ren you sile.

viliage-inside-m. s. that-m. person again die-p. a.

(* The man in the village died again.)

e. Ta you tou tong le.

he again head ache i. a.

(He has a headache again.)

f. Ta tou you tongle.

he head again ache-p. a.

(He has a headache again.)

g. Tade tou you tongle.

he-m. s. head again ache-p. a.

(His head is aching again.)

h. Jiaoshili you zuozhe yige ren.

classroom-inside again sit-p. s. one-m. person

(There is a man sitting in the classroom again.)

i. Jiaoshilide nage ren you zuozhe.

classroom-inside-m. s. that-m. person again sit-p. s.

(That man in the classroom is again in a sitting position.)

The difference in meaning in the above clauses is obvious. Clauses a., c. and h. imply that a different book or man takes part in the processes whereas in Clauses b., d. and i. the same book or man takes part in the process for [105] a second time.

Adverbs like 'you' (again) only occur immediately before the process. The presence of an adverb before a nominal group and a verbal group in Clause e. shows that the nominal group and the verbal group are functioning together as a process. The two possible positions of the adverb 'you' (again) in (1) c. also prove that there are two processes in the clause: a process in the clause and a process in the embedded clause within the clause.

The point becomes clearer if we compare Clause (1) c. with another clause which has a nominal group in the possessive case. Look at the clauses in (4) below:

(4) a. Ta tou tong.

he head ache

(He has a headache.)

b. Ta (de) jiao tong.

he ('s) foot ache

(His foot aches.)

c. Ta you tou tong le.

he again head ache i. a.

(He has a headache again.)

d. *Ta you jiao tong le.

he again foot ache i. a.

(His foot is aching again.)

e. Ta tou you tongle.

he bead again ache-p. a.

(He has a headache again.)

f. Ta jiao you tongle.

he foot again ache-p. a.

(His foot is aching again.) [106]

g. Ta hai tou tong ma?

he still head ache i. p.

(Does he still have a headache?)

h. *Ta hai jiao tong ma?

he still foot ache i. p.

(Is his foot still aching?)

i. Ta tou hai tong ma?

he head still ache i. p.

(Does he still have a headache?)

j. Ta jiao hai tong ma?

he foot still ache i. p.

(Is his foot still aching?)

Although 'Tade jiao tong' (his foot ache) can appear as 'Ta jiao tong' (he foot ache), it is vastly different from 'Ta tou tong' (he head ache). The former has only one process in it while the latter has two processes in it, as can be seen from (4) above. This

145

shows that 'ta' (he) in 'Ta jiao tong' (he foot ache) is only a variant form of 'tade' (his), while 'ta' (he) in 'Ta tou tong' (he head ache) is the Patient of the clausal process which cannot take 'tade' (his) as its variant form.

Thirdly, some possessive structures do not have non-possessive counterparts, e. g. :

 (5) a. Xiaohaide zengzufu ershinianqian sile.
  little-child-m. s. great-grandfather twenty-years-ago die-p. a.
  (The child's great grandfather died twenty years ago.) [107]
 b. * Xiaohai ershinianqian sile zengzufu.
  little-child twenty-years-ago die-p. a. great-grandfather
  (* The child had his great grandfather died twenty years ago.)

Similarly some Patients or Carriers of clausal processes do not have possessive counterparts, e. g. :

 (6) a. Jiali sile fuqin.
  home-inside die-p. a. father
  (Father died at home.)
 b. * Jialide fuqin sile.
  home-m. a. father die-p. a.
  (* The father at home died.)

Clause (6) b. cannot stand because it suggests that there was at least one more father outside the home.

28. Patient, Goal and Range Compared

What differentiates a Range from a Patient or a Goal is that a Range is something which is inherently implied in the process, whereas a Patient or a Goal does not have such a quality. Precisely because of this a Range cannot be separated from the process, whereas a Patient or a Goal can. 'Look at the following examples.

Firstly, while a Patient or a Goal can be forepositioned in a passive clause, a Range cannot, e. g.：

(1) a. Yifu bei xile.

clothes by wash-p. a.

(The clothes were washed.) [108]

b. Gou bei dale.

dog by beat-p. a.

(The dog was beaten.)

c. * Hua bei shuole.

speech by speak-p. a.

(* The speech was spoken.)

Secondly, while a Patient or a Goal can occur in the 'pseudo-cleft' construction, a Range cannot, e. g.：

(2) a. Ta xi de shi yifu.

he wash n. p. be clothes

(What he washed were clothes.)

b. Ta da de shi gou.

he beat n. p. be dog

(What he beat was a dog.)

c. * Ta shuo de shi hua.

he speak n. p. be speech

(* What he spoke was speech.)

Thirdly, while a Patient can occur in the 'ba' construction, a Range cannot, e. g.：

(3) a. Wo ba yifu xile.

I f. p. clothes wash-p. a.

(I washed the clothes.)

b. Ta ba men dapole yige dong.

he f. p. door strike-break-p. a. one-m. hole

(He struck at the door and made a hole in it.)

c. * Wo ba ge changle.

   I f. p. song sing-p. a.

   (I sang the song.) [109]

d. * Ta ba dong dapole.

   he f. p. hole strike-break-p. a.

   (* He struck at and broke the hole.)

e. * Men ba dong pole.

   door f. p. hole break-p. a.

   (* The door broke the hole.)

Fourthly, while a Patient can occur pre-verbally with the Agent unspecified, a Range cannot, e. g. :

(4) a. Yifu xile.

   clothes wash-p. a.

   (The clothes have been washed.)

b. Beizi pole.

   cup break-p. a.

   (The cup has broken.)

c. * Faguo hua shuole.

   France-country speech speak-p. a.

   (* French has been spoken.)

d. * Dong pole.

   hole break-p. a.

   (* The hole broke.)

29. A Brief Summary

The following table is a brief summary of the process types and the participants involved in them (complex processes not included). Those underlined are obligatory participants, the others are optional ones. '.../...' is read as 'or'. It indicates that only one of the listed participants can be selected. [110]

Process Types and Participants in Them

Process Type \ Participants	Actor Process		Patient Process		Ascription	Mental	Verbal	Relational Process	
	Directed	Non-directed	Directed	Non-directed	Process	Process	Process	Attributive	Identifying
Participant 1	Actor	Actor	Agent	Patient	Carrier	Cognizant	Sayer	Carrier	Identified
Participant 2	Goal	Cognate Range/ Location Range/ Instrument Range/ Process Range/ Beneficiary	Patient	Measurement Range/ Result Range/ Beneficiary	Measurement Range	Phenomenon	Beneficiary	Attribute	Identifier
Participant 3	Beneficiary	Beneficiary	Beneficiary						

Note: If a non-directed actor process has already selected a Beneficiary as its second participant, it cannot take another Beneficiary. [111]

Bibliography

Anderson, John M. (1977), <u>On Case Grammar</u>, Croom Helm Humanities Press, London.

Beijing Daxue Zhongwen Xi Hanyu Jiaoyanshi (1973), <u>Yufa Xiuci</u>, Shangwu Yinshuguan, Beijing.

Beijing Shifan Daxue Zhongwen Xi Yuyan Jiaoyanshi, (1979), <u>Xiandai Hanyu Yufa Zhishi</u>, Beijing Chubanshe, Beijing.

Berry, Margaret (1975), <u>Introduction to Systemic Linguistics-1 Structures and Systems</u>, B. T. Batsford, London.

─────────── (1977), <u>An Introduction to Systemic Linguistics-2 Levels and Links</u>, B. T. Batsford, London.

Catford, J. C. (1965), <u>A Linguistic Theory of Translation</u>. Oxford University Press, London.

Chao, Yuen Ren (1968), <u>A Grammar of Spoken Chinese</u>, University of California Press, Berkeley and Los Angeles.

Chen, Wangdao (1978), <u>Wenfa Jianlun</u>. Shanghai Jiaoyu Chubanshe, Shanghai.

Ding, Shengshu (1979), <u>Xiandai Hanyu Yufa Jianghua</u>, Compiled by <u>Zhongguo Yuwen</u> Zazhi She, Shangwu Yinshuguan, Beijing.

Dobson, W. A. C. H. (1974), <u>A Dictionary of the Chinese Particles</u>, University of Toronto Press, Toronto and Buffalo.

Fillmore, Charles (1968), <u>The Casa for Case</u>, in Bach, Emmon and Robert Harms (Eds.) (1968), <u>Universals in Linguistic Theory</u>, Holt, Rinehart, and Winston, New York.

Firth, J. R. (1957), <u>Papers in Linguistics 1934—1951</u>, Oxford University Press, London.

─────────── (1966), <u>The Tongues of Men and Speech</u>, Oxford University Press, London.

─────────── (1968), <u>Selected Papers of J. R. Firth, 1952—59</u>, edited by F. R. Palmer, Longman's Linguistics Library, London. [112]

Gao, Mingkai (1948), <u>Hanyu Yufa Lun</u>, Kaiming Shudian, Shanghai.

Gregory, M. & Carroll, S. (1978), <u>Language and Situation: Language Varieties and Their Social Contexts</u>, Routledge & Kegan Paul, London.

Guo, Shaoyu (1979), <u>Hanyu Yufa Xiuci Xintan</u>, Shangwu Yinshuguan, Beijing.

Halliday, M. A. K. (1956), <u>Grammatical Categories in Modern Chinese</u>, in Transactions of the Philolological Society 1956, pp. 177—224.

_____(1965), Types of Structure, Nuffield Programme in Linguistics and English Teaching Working Paper No. 1.

_____(1967a), Notes on Transitivity and Theme in English, Part I, in Journal of Linguistics, 3.1: 37—81.

_____(1967b), Part II, in Journal of Linguistics, 3.2: 199—244.

_____(1967c), Some Aspects of the Thematic Organization of the English Clause, Memorandum RM-5224-PR, the RAND Corporation, Santa Monica, California.

_____(1968), Structure, to appear in Halliday, M. A. K. & J. R. Martin (eds.) Readings in Systemic Linguistics, Batsford, London.

_____(1968), Notes on Transitivity and Theme in English, Part III, in Journal of Linguistics, 4.2: 179—215.

_____(1970), A Course in Spoken English: Intonation, Oxford University Press, London.

_____(1970), Language Structure and Language Function, in John Lyons (ed.) New Horizons in Linguistics, Penguin Books.

_____(1973), Explorations in the Functions of Language, Edward Arnold, London.

_____(1974), Language and Social Man, Longman (Schools Council Programme in Linguistics and English Teaching, Papers, Series II, 3), London. [113]

Halliday, M. A. K. (1975), Learning How to Mean: Explorations in the Development of Language, Edward Arnold, London.

_____(1976), Halliday: System and Function in Language, edited by Kress, G. R., Oxford University Press, London.

_____(1977a), Text as Semantic Choice in Social Contexts, in Teun A. Van Dijk & Janos Petofi (eds.), Grammars and Descriptions, Walter de Gruyter, Berlin.

_____(1977b), Modes of Meaning and Modes of Expression: Types of Grammatical Structure, and Their Determination by Different Semantic Functions, in Allerton, D. J., Edward Carney & David Holdcroft (eds.), Function and Context in Linguistic Analysis: Essays Offered to William Haas, pp. 57—79, Cambridge University Press, 1979, Cambridge.

_____(1977c), Language as Code and language as Behaviour: A Systemic-Functional Interpretation of the Nature and Ontogenesis of Dialogue, to appear in S. M. Lamb & A. Makkai (eds.), Semiotics of Culture and Language.

_____ (1978), Language as Social Semiotic: Towards a General Sociolinguistic Theory, Edward Arnold, London.

_____ (forthcoming), A Short Introduction to Functional Grammar.

Halliday, M. A. K. & Hasan, R. (1976), Cohesion in English, Longman, London.

Halliday, M. A. K. & McIntosh, A. & Strevens, P. (1964), The Linguistic Sciences and Language Teaching, Longman, London.

Halliday, M. A. K. & Poole, M. E. (1978), Notes on Talking Shop: Demands on Language, Film Australia, Lindfield, N. S. W.

Hu, Yushu (1979), Xiandai Hanyu, Shanghai Jiaoyu Chubanshe, Shanghai.

Huazhong Shifan Xueyuan Zhongwen Xi Xiandai Hanyu Jiaoyanshi (1973), Xiandai Hanyu Cihui Zhishi, Hubei Renmin Chubanshe, Wuhan. [114]

Langendoen, D. T. (1968), The London School of Linguistics: A Study of the Linguistic Theories of B. Malinowski and J. R. Firth, The M. I. T. Press, Cambridge, Massachusetts.

Li, Charles, N. (ed.) (1975), Word Order and Word Order Change, University of Texas Press, Austin and London.

_____ (1976), Subject and Topic, Academic Press, New York.

Liu, Shiru (1964), Xiandai Hanyu Yufa Jiangyi, Shangwu Yinshuguan, Beijing.

Lü, Shuxiang (1942—1944), Zhongguo Wenfa Yaolüe, Volumes I—III, Shangwu Yinshuguan, Chongqing.

_____ (1979), Hanyu Yufa Fenxi Wenti, Shangwu Yinshuguan, Beijing.

Lü, Shuxiang & Zhu, Dexi (1978), Yufa Xiuci Jianghua, Zhongguo Qingnian Chubanshe Bianjibu, Beijing.

Malinowski, B. (1923), The Problem of Meaning in Primitive Languages, Supplement I in C. K. Ogden & I. A. Richards, The Meaning of Meaning, Kegan Paul, London.

_____ (1935), Coral Gardens and Their Magic, George Allen & Unwin, London.

Muir, James (1972), A Modern Approach to English Grammar: An Introduction to Systemic Grammar, B. T. Batsford, London.

Pan, Jiajing (1979), Hanyu Xiuci Changshi, Tianjin Renmin Chubanshe, Tianjin.

Teng, Shouhsin (1975), A Semantic Study of Transitivity Relations in Chinese, University of California Press, Berkeley, Los Angeles, London.

Wang, Li (1944—1945), Zhongguo Yufa Lilun, Volumes I & II, Shangwu Yinshuguan, Chongqing.

Xinan Shifan Xueyuan Zhongwen Xi "Xiandai Hanyu Jichu Zhishi" Bianxie Xiaozu (1973), Xiandai Hanyu Jichu Zhishi, Xinan Shifan Xueyuan, Chongqing.

Young, David, J. (1980), The Structure of English Clauses, Hutchinson, London. [115]

"Yufa" Bianxie Zu (1978), Yufa, Shanghai Jiaoyu Chubanshe, Shanghai.

Zhongguo Yuwen Zazhishe (ed.) (1956), Hanyude Zhuyu Binyu Wenti, Zhonghua Shu Ju, Beijing.

Zhu, Dexi (1980), Xiandai Hanyu Yufa Yanjiu, Shangwu Yinshuguan, Beijing. [116]

(上述参考文献中涉及的中国学者的文献附译于下)
语法修辞.1973.北京:商务印书馆.
现代汉语语法知识.1979.北京:北京出版社.
陈望道.1978.文法简论.上海:上海教育出版社.
丁声树.1979.现代汉语语法讲话.北京:商务印书馆.
高名凯.1948.汉语语法论.上海:开明书店.
郭绍虞.1979.汉语语法修辞新探.北京:商务印书馆.
胡裕树.1979.现代汉语.上海:上海教育出版社.
现代汉语词汇知识.1973.武汉:湖北人民出版社.
刘士儒.1964.现代汉语语法讲义.北京:商务印书馆.
吕叔湘.1942—1944.中国文法要略.卷一至卷三.重庆:商务印书馆.
吕叔湘.1979.汉语语法分析问题.北京:商务印书馆.
吕叔湘,朱德熙.1978.语法修辞讲话.北京:中国青年出版社编辑部.
潘嘉静.1979.汉语修辞常识.天津:天津人民出版社.
王　力.1944—1945.中国语法理论,卷一,二.重庆:商务印书馆.
现代汉语基础知识.1973.重庆:西南师范学院.
语　法.1978.上海:上海教育出版社.
汉语的主语宾语问题.1956.北京:中华书局.
朱德熙.1980.现代汉语语法研究.北京:商务印书馆.

(柴同文整理)

第二部分

现代汉语及物性的进一步研究
（附：主语的重新定性解说）

彭宣维　著

第一章 小句的及物性(1)：
物质过程和处所关系过程

1. 引言

本章及随后两章讨论小句的语义范畴：前者叫做"及物性"。笔者拟按照周晓康的作格分析思路，讨论物质、关系和心理三个主要过程类别；必要时关注环境成分，并根据具体语言现象对周晓康模式给予补充和修正，从而使相关问题的讨论走向深入。下面是分析框架（彭宣维 2011；略有变动；注意"(及物性)过程"和"主语"所在位置；关于主语性质的理论阐述，见附录）。

	语	境（情景语境和文化语境）		
	语域：语义配置	语篇语义学：意义	语篇语法学：词汇语法/措辞	语篇语音学/语篇书写学
		所指→		能指
语境	语式→	语篇	主题→	主位→	调核化
			信息→	语序→	
	语场→	概念意义	过程→	主语→	语调化
			级差→		
			时间→	时制	
	语旨→	人际意义	互动→	语气→	声调化
			评价→	评判→	
			权势→	语体	
→	链接	代码化、结构组织化、实例化、体现		

本章的基本议题包括：
（一）与小句的语义概念"及物性"有关的问题（第 2 小节）；
（二）物质过程（第 3 小节）；
（三）处所关系过程（第 4 小节）。
但这里及随后两章只关心描写各种可能的语用现象，不讨论周晓康模式中涉及的计算机编码问题。

2. 与及物性有关的基本问题

先前(彭宣维 2011)在讨论动词词组时确立了两个有关范畴,即连带和范围;本小节拟说明这些成分在小句中究竟发挥什么作用,同时涉及其他相关现象;具体内容包括:(一)及物性的特征和定义;(二)及物性中一部分过程的环境成分可能同时做参与者;(三)参与者有直接和间接之分,直接和间接有一个程度问题;(四)部分参与者与过程之间、部分环境与过程之间存在纠葛。

首先是及物性的定义。小句的具体语义范畴是一个相对完整的语义结构"及物性"(Transitivity)。这里涉及两个方面。一是及物与不及物的关系。周晓康(1999;Zhou 1997:5—6;以下涉及 Zhou 1997 者仅标页码)根据韩礼德的观点总结道:传统语法将动词分为两类,即及物与不及物,依据是它们只带主语,或者同时带主语和宾语①。但问题是,有的动词既是及物的,又是不及物的,如"吃",我们既可以说"他吃了",也可以说"他吃了苹果了";因此,"及物"与否并非动词本身的特点,而是小句性质的(另见王力 1947:59)。再说,传统的划分方法是二分的:要么及物,要么不及物;事实上,在及物与不及物之间存在大量中间状态,无所谓主动或被动的中性小句就是证明,如"杯子破了"、"雨住了"、"水流走了"等;韩礼德(Halliday 1985:114;对比 Halliday 1994:125)认为英语的 BE 动词就没有什么特殊的被动形式(对比 Chao 1968:665 等)。而在本书的体系中,及物性是一个经由语法手段结构化了的语义概念。

二是及物性的定义。韩礼德(Halliday 1985/1994:106)对及物性的定义是:

(1) 我们关于经验最深刻的印象,是它包含的各种"事件"——发生(happening)、做(doing)、感知(sensing)、意指(meaning)、以及是(being)和变成(becoming)。所有这些事态都在小句语法中得到分类整理。因此,小句不仅是一种行为模式,一种给予和索取物品-服务与信息的模式,它也是一种反映模式,

---

① 我们不取"宾语"称谓,而将主语及动词述语以外的成分一律称为"补语"(见彭宣维 2011,第九章末)。

一种为不断的变化和事件流动赋予秩序的模式。实现这一目标的语法系统就是及物性。及物性系统把经验世界识解为一组可以操作的过程类别(process types)。

韩礼德的及物性模式分为"及物"与"作格"两个次类。及物分析(Transitive analysis)指外在和内外经验流程在小句语法介入的情况下加工确定的过程类别,功能上分为过程本身(Process)、参与者(Participant)以及环境(Circumstance)三个基本成分;在类别上包括物质(Material)、心理(Mental)、关系(Relational)三个主类,以及行为(Behavioural)、言语(Verbal)、存在(Existential)三个次类;外加一个气象(Meteorological)小类。

福赛特(Fawcett 1980;1987)按照他的理解对及物性做了系统探讨。(一)他将范围看作关联角色(Associated Role),与参与者并列。即是说,他对参与者取韩礼德的早期做法,即参与者角色(Participant Role);环境即环境角色(Circumstantial Role),该成分不属于及物性的范围。因此,其及物性=参与者角色+过程+关联角色。(二)在具体语用过程中,并非所有参与者都出现:出现的,叫做"显性参与者"(Overt);不出现的是"隐性参与者"(Covert)。(三)他的体系中只有物质,关系和心理三类,将韩礼德的关系、存在和一部分物质过程统归为关系过程,将行为、心理和言语归为心理过程。(四)福赛特用韩礼德早期使用的术语"施动者"(Agent)和"受动者"(Affected)[①],重新做了界定,并以此为依据考察关系过程和物质过程中的复合参与者。周晓康以福赛特的上述模式对汉语的及物性进行了系统描写。

下面首先按照笔者(彭宣维 2011)的体系讨论小句的环境和参与者。先看过程的环境。笔者(彭宣维 2011)在讨论动词词组中基本事件的跨级类连带范畴时指出,它们同时在小句中做相关过程的环境。

---

① 韩礼德后来在保留"施动者"、用"中介"(Medium)代替"受动者"的基础上,构拟了与上述六个过程(称为及物性之下的"及物分析"Transitive analysis)并行的"作格分析"系统(Ergative analysis),以解决及物性的使动意义问题。笔者赞同这种处理方案,并证明作格意义应该是在及物意义基础上的进一步抽象和概括;作为小句经验意义(及物性)的形式范畴主语结构,则又是在作格意义上的进一步抽象和概括。因此,及物意义的抽象和概括程度最低;作格意义居中,但已经带有相当程度的形式特点;主语结构抽象程度最高,形式特点最突出。具体论述见彭宣维(2007a,2007b;附录)。这个模式对下面的议题,尤其是主语的认识具有实质性意义(见后文)。

这些成分在汉语中一共有八个次类(见前一章):

（2）处所(I),跨度,伴随,起因,角色,方式,事情,角度

从语言级阶的角度说,正是这一类成分充分表明了动词词组到非典型小句、典型小句、甚至复句之间的连续性;但从语言单位的角度看,所有这些范畴成分均在小句的及物性关系结构中做环境。

但这里需要进一步说明和对比有关现象。先看以下实例。

（3）何平比娅高却比娅瘦弱得多(姜利敏:《且乐》)
（4）他的智力明显高于娅。(出处同上)
（5）保不定我们这辈子还不如娅过得好呢
（6）沟道仍然象山那面一样狭窄。(路遥:《平凡的世界》)

这是一种带比较对象的"对比方式",因为这样的实例同时符合方式和对比两个条件;所不同的是,(一)前面引述的现象主要涉及动词词组;这里主要针对的是形容词词组,与后面要讨论的关系过程有关;(二)动词词组直接做过程,而形容词词组在这里除了具备过程(动词)的特征外,还有参与者(名词)性质,即属性(见后文)。

周晓康(1999)在具体处理上遵从福赛特的处理方案:"小句的及物性结构主要取决于过程的参与者/相关者角色,环境角色既然不直接影响句子的及物性结构,则完全可以将其排除在及物性系统之外。这也是 Fawcett 体系与 Halliday 体系的一个重要区别之一"。对此,笔者发现这种处理方案对于环境做属性的环境关系过程来说就不合适。例如,she is near him in appearance(她在长相上跟他接近),如果不关心环境成分 in appearance(在长相上),"她跟他接近"指的是物理空间上的距离,与原意相去甚远。但在实际操作上,这样处理自然有其方便性,为下文所从。

从理论上讲,环境与过程和参与者之间的关系,可以用心理学的"图形-背景"理论做出解释。即是说,过程和参与者在整个小句的及物性关系结构中为图形,而环境好比背景。在具体编码中,背景成分也可能被选择来做参与者,此时相关背景成分便被认知性地推到了小句及物性的图形位置上。这实际上是选择的结果:相关成分在选择环境成分的同时,还被选择为参与者,如处所关系过程。这样,我们区分广义及物性和狭义及物性。前者指包括环境在内的整个过程,即小句的语义范畴结构;后者仅包括过程、参与

者和范围;除了关系过程,环境只作背景看,在汉语中不直接参与及物性建构。

(7)

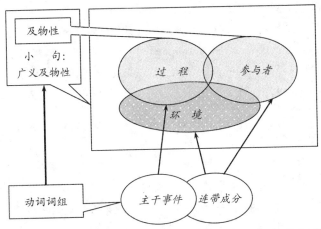

再看过程的参与者。这里涉及三组参与者:典型参与者和非典型参与者,直接参与者和间接参与者,以及基本参与者和准参与者。它们之间有重叠。

从典型性看,参与者可分为典型参与者和非典型参与者。例如,(3—6)中的"何平""他的智力""我们"和"沟道"均属于典型参与者,因为它们都是从世界的变化流程中,经过认知处理而分离出来的典型事物范畴,是参与过程运作的存在体。这一类应当包括事物性范围(彭宣维2011,第八章)。

(8)事物性范围范畴:处所(II),言语内容,认知内容,道具,配料,用具

这些成分均做基本参与者,因为事物性范围是过程发生或运作所涉及的对象性范围,包括幅度和延伸范围。这一类成分与先前谈到的非范围类典型参与者连成一体(Halliday 1985/1994:148—149)。

另一方面,上述实例中的"高""瘦弱得多""好"和"狭窄"等形容词组,则属于非典型参与者,因为按照先前的分析结果,这些成分同时带有一定的过程性质,即(一)可以带基本副词,(二)其中有些形容词具有动词的一系列特征,如后附"了""着""过""起来"等(可见李泉

1997a;另见 Chao 1968:88;张国宪 2000)①。这些成分在包孕关系过程中做归附属性参与者。

跨级类连带成分中的一些范畴成分,如处所、手段方式中的一部分工具和施动者、协作性伴随成分和起因等成分,均可在选择过程中被选择成为参与者:有的可做直接参与者(Immediate Participant),有的做间接参与者(Mediate Participant)。我们把这一类环境成分叫做"环境性参与者"(Participant of Circumstance 或 Circumstantial participant)。例如,

(9) 船头蹲着一个跟明子差不多大的女孩子(汪曾祺:《受戒》)
(10) 老辈子的时候,有这么一家子(阿城:《棋王》)
(11) 子弹中了姑娘的眼睛(引自谭馥,2001)
(12) 她是特地来和我谈心的。(姜利敏:《且乐》)
(13) 和他一起还来了个女的。
(14) 为这事儿还死了一个人
(15) (作为)代表来了一位女同志

其中加下划线的成分在句中都是参与者,但与前面提到的典型的参与者相比,它们同时是相关事件运作的环境,所以笔者把这些环境成分看作一类非典型参与者。其中,第一、二句是空间处所和时间处所成分在相应句子中做直接参与者;第三句是工具手段,也是直接参与者;(12)"我"是伴随性环境成分做间接参与者,当然也可能被配置为直接参与者,如(13);(14)是起因环境成分做直接参与者;(15)是起因类的利益成分,做直接参与者。可能还有其他类似情况。显然,直接与间接是认知处理的结果;从这个角度说,经验事理与经过认知加工处理的语义范畴结构之间就存在不一致的情况,从而表明经验知识和语义范畴的确应该分离开来处理(也见彭宣维 2011,第二章)。

除了具有过程特征的属性参与者与具有环境特征的环境性参与者外,还有一类非典型参与者,即事件性范围:

---

① 事实上,郭锐(2002)通过论证,支持朱德熙(1982/1999:63—65)区分"区别词"和"形容词"的观点:能做谓语的属性成分叫"形容词",修饰名词的特征成分叫做"区别词";如果这种划分合理的话,我们就可以依据笔者的体系,为这两类词分别确立一个功能称谓,即"属性词"和"特征词"。

(16) 事件性范围范畴——准构成成分：别称，事件，气象，度量，配备

我们已经指出，事件性范围成分在句中做准构成成分（Quasi-component），即准参与者，因为这一类成分要么是过程的别称（别称类），要么是对抽象过程的具体表述（事件类），要么过程的特征包括在范围成分之内（气象类），要么过程的有关特征在度量中得到具体化（度量类），要么范围是过程发生涉及的具体部位（配备类）。可见，与前一类范围成分相比，这些做参与者缺乏足够的语用事理；但从语义角色的角度看，它们又与典型参与者相当，尤其是当它们以受动者的身份出现时情况更是如此，如"这首歌她唱了几十年了"或者"她把这首歌唱了一遍又一遍"。

按照福赛特的模式，参与者中有一个比较特殊的类别，这就是第三施动者（Third party agent）；周晓康沿用了引动者（Causer）这一术语（Halliday 叫做 Initiator 启动者）。例如，

(17) 这消息使风起云涌的双水村更加激荡起来。（路遥：《平凡的世界》）

(18) 金富给他家送过来的礼物，他都让老婆客气地退回去了（出处同上）

这就是人们说使动句。不过，即便我们保留这一称谓，相关成分在不少情况下对后面的事件并不具有"使动"性质，而是引动性质的，如上例中"这消息"和"他"。试比较，

(19) 他曾经"揭发"过他，让他失了面子。（出处同上）

(20) 他要独立完成这件事，而不准备让哥哥出钱（出处同上）

(21) 父母提起让少安带着秀莲去县城扯衣服，使少安马上想到了县城教书的润叶。（出处同上）

第一个例子中的"让"是使动性的，但第二、三例中的"让"和"使"就并非相关事件"（哥哥）出钱"和"想到"的使动者，而是引发有关事件的促动因素。我们将会看到，正如这些实例所表明的，引动者会出现在所有的三种基本小句类别中。

下面是有关直接参与者与间接参与者以及基本参与者和准参与者的对应关系距阵。

(22)

身份 \ 地位	基本参与者	准参与者
直接参与者	张三打得重,张三死得惨 妈妈给我 钱,妈妈把钱给了我 由小李处理这事儿 船给人沉了,苹果(我)吃了 他每周六都去爬山,我明天去广州 风停了,杯子破了 这事儿叫我很为难 张三都告诉我这事儿了 从前有一个国王,屋后栽了好些树 母亲比不上他 张三有三间茅草屋 这间教室长20米,张三高 米饭一碗,馒头两个	老太太哭瞎了眼睛 (由)小李处理贷款的事儿 苹果(我)吃了,我明天去广州/爬山 李四干过革命,这事儿叫我很为难 太阳偏西了,他打破了杯子 刚才下过大雨了,下午会出太阳 张三会画山水画,他会唱民歌 张三都告诉我这事儿了 小姑娘流下了眼泪,张三打了一个喷嚏 她很痛苦,张三高,他是非洲国王 演唱会在周三,张三有三间茅草屋 从前有一个国王,张三今天在家 米饭(每人)一碗,馒头(每人)两个
间接参与者	张三要和李四结婚了;船被张三沉了;这段台词都给他说烂了	张三打得重,张三死得惨 张三跳得高,张三跑得快

这里将被动语态中的施动者、"得"字结构中的属性看作间接参与者,因为这些成分在大多数情况下可有可无,并不影响相关及物性结构。这些成分同时具备两种功能:(一)均可看作过程的环境成分,如上引两个"得"字句,分别为"打"和"死"的质量方式环境,这一点和被动态中由"被"等引导的施动者地位相当;(二)同时修饰前面的参与者"张三"和"张三(的智力)",尤其是在"张三跳得高"一类小句中,"跳"还可作手段方式环境看,而"高"为"张三"的属性。据此,这一类成分倒是和环境关系过程的环境属性相当。

这里有几点结论。(一)环境成分,尤其是短语性环境成分同时带有过程特征,自身可独立成句;(二)一部分环境成分可能以直接参与者的身份出现,如处所成分;(三)参与者分典型参与者和非典型参与者,后者包括关系过程中的归附属性、以手段方式环境的身份出现的施动者、伴随性环境成分、以及事件性范围成分。

至此,我们可以为小句确立一组特征。

(23) a. 典型小句是由基本名词词组和基本动词词组构成的语言级阶单位;

　　　b. 其基本语义功能是表达相对完整的及物性;

c. 基本语用功能是再现一个经验事件的过程；
d. 其语法功能是将相关及物性做抽象处理，从而表现为主谓语关系结构；
e. 可以体现为一个完整的语调单位"声调化"(Tonality)。

下面拟对上述特征中的前三点做进一步说明；第四点已在彭宣维(2011)中专门讨论过；最后一点暂不涉及。

第一，何为"基本名词词组"和"基本动词词组"？两者的基本内涵是指，构成名词词组和动词词组的成分，如果内部仅出现低于或者等于自身级阶的构成成分(动词除外)，该成分就可以看作是基本的；如果有高于自身级阶的成分出现，该成分就不再是基本的。例如，"那两个可爱的小女孩儿"中的每一个构成成分："那"、"两个"、"可爱"、"的"、"小"、"女"和"孩儿"，都是词项性的；而"他那不断挥动的臂膀"中就有动词词组"不断挥动"，这是一个动词词组经过级转移后来做名词词组的一个成分的单位，因此，整个名词词组就不是基本名词词组。又如，"(我)马上走"、"(他)在屋里"和"(她)会跳芭蕾"中的"马上"、"走"、"在"、"屋里"、"会"、"跳"和"芭蕾"都是词项性的，因此，三个动词词组都是基本的；但"(他)在沙发上睡了一晚"中的"在沙发上"是一个短语，因此整个动词词组就不再是基本动词词组。而由此构成的小句就不是典型小句。

第二，在(23c)的定义中，我们是把小句的基本语用功能看作"再现一个经验事件的过程"的。为什么要用"再现"一词？根据笔者(彭宣维 2011)的体系，经验事件与语言意义之间是有分别的，语言在处理"无尽的变化和事件的流程"的经验时，已经将语言自身的序列关系添加上去。因此，这一语言化了过程就是"再现"经验知识的过程。

第三，(23e)是说，一个完整小句会以一个完整的语调单位的方式出现，即有相对完整的"语调曲线"(Intonation contour)；这个音系单位的生成过程叫做"声调化"(Tonality)。达奈什(Daneš 1960)指出："就某一孤立的语句而言，语调能将其整合为一体；而就一个连成一体的话语而言，语调则确定每一个语句的界限，并将整个话语分成若干小段。"(转引自 Esser 1987)切夫(Chafe)指出："在实验中发现学术界人士谈话中有70%的语调地位是完整的小句，考虑到个体变异，其幅度在 60%—80%之间"(引自胡壮麟 1994：160)。但这是就英语的情况说的(见彭宣维 2002：26—27)。汉语的实际语用过程如何，还需要做具体调查；但估计汉语口语会有很大出入,出入在于一个语调曲线可能包含多个小句。

总之,严格地说,典型的小句是由过程和一个或一个以上的参与者或范围,外加一个或多个环境成分构成的。但在进入正题前,还需要说明的是句子中相关成分的语序、成分显隐与概念意义的关系。试比较,

(24) a. 主席团坐在台上。
　　 b. 主席团在台上坐着。
　　 c. 台上坐着主席团。

(25) a. 停电了。
　　 b. 这里/这时停电了。
　　 c. 电停了。
　　 d. 这里/这时电停了。

对比第一组和第二组内的句子。在第一组内,三个句子所描述的为同一经验现象,语序上的变化是出于各成分信息价值上的考虑,因此与各句的概念意义无关;在后一组例句中,有无处所信息(时间或空间)似乎没有太大的差别,除了语体上可能存在一定区别外,相关处所信息的显现或隐没并不能给彼此带来实质性的差异,差别在于句子的冗余度,这是信息价值的识解问题。也就是说,对于概念语义结构来说,句子成分的语序不是本质性的,而是信息性的。信息性是以概念意义为基础的另一种语义范畴,不在这里的讨论范围内(见彭宣维2000:79—118)。此外,参与者的显隐会影响到其它成分的语法地位。例如,"他在山上种了很多树"与"山上种了很多树",虽然两句的非标记语境会有一定差异,但施动者隐没,则意味着空间处所成分由环境提升为直接参与者。

下面拟系统分析现代汉语小句的语义和语法范畴,但重点是前者:及物性的过程类别及其相关问题。本章随后两个小节讨论"物质过程"以及以关系过程中的"处所"类;下一章讨论关系过程中的"包孕"和"属有"类;第三章分析及物性的心理过程。

3. 物质过程

这里首先说明物质过程涉及的范围和本书作者确立的描写框架,然后展开讨论。

3.1 物质过程的界定、分类及其相关理论描述

物质过程(Material process)是有关"做"的过程,即某个存在体"做"某事,可能涉及另一个存在体(Halliday,1985/1994:110;另见胡壮麟等 2005)。周晓康对物质过程的定义是(Zhou 1997:1):物质过程指关于物质世界里过程的经验,包括状态(如"李四坐着"),发生("李四摔倒了"),动作("李四打中了球"),事件("下雨了")等等。她的实际分析包括韩礼德说的行为过程的一部分和所有气象过程,如"李四打喷嚏","下雨了"。她还依据福赛特的观点,认为环境成分(相当于传统语法说的状语)不属于及物性范围。

对于物质过程,周晓康在福赛特(Fawcett 1980,1987)的基础上为汉语确立了两个参与者,一是"施动者"(Agent),二是"受动者"(Affected)(对比 Halliday 1985/1994:109—112),两者扮演的是"参与者角色";还有关联角色"范围"(Range;Halliday 1985/1994:146—149)。用我们的话说,就是事件性范围在句中的语法地位。这里不妨将她拟定的模式引译如下(Zhou 1997:60;周晓康 1999)[①]。

(26)

本文	传统语法	例句
单参与者:唯受动者过程	不及物	(1)小兔子死了。
单参与者:唯施动者过程	不及物	(2)兔子跑了。
单参与者:唯受动者带范围过程	及物(带同源宾语)	(3)李四打喷嚏。
单参与者:唯施动者带范围过程	及物(带同源宾语)	(4)小王在洗澡。
双参与者:受动者中心带隐性施动者过程	不及物	(5)船沉了。
双参与者:受动者中心过程	及物	(6)他们把船沉了。
双参与者:施动者中心带隐性受动者	不及物	(7)张三打得很重。
双参与者:施动者中心过程	及物	(8)张三打李四。

对于周晓康的汉语描写模式,笔者有几点不同处理方案。

首先是术语使用以及物质过程参与者的分类问题。看以下实例。

---

① 该表是从她 1999 年以论文形式发表的汉译文中引录的。其中倒数第三个类别在原文中是 Affected-centred,但译文中是"施动者中心过程"。这里根据她的两个版本的具体论述确定为"受动者中心过程"。

(27) 有水送过来,大家就掏出缸子要水。(阿城:《棋王》)
(28) 我的背被谁捅了一下(出处同上)
(29) 棋开始了。(出处同上)
(30) 下雨了。
(31) 打钟了。

韩礼德和福赛特在分析中采用了不同术语。据韩礼德,第一句中的"大家掏出缸子"是主动句(Active),第二句是被动句(Passive),第三句是中动句(Middle);前两例中的"大家"和"谁"叫做"动作者"(Actor:动作的发出者或施为者),意为"做(事)"的人或人格化事物;(27)"缸子"和(28)"我的背"叫做"目标"(Goal:动作的接受者或过程行为的承受者)。而(29)和(30)中的"棋"和"雨"一类成分,则可看做过程的延伸,即范围;在采用作格分析法时将参与者"大家"和"谁"看做agent,"棋"和"雨"则是Medium(中介)。

福赛特(Fawcett 1980:141)直接沿用韩礼德早先使用过的两个术语agent和affected(如1964,1967),而不是韩礼德后来统一使用的动作者和目标,周晓康(1999)分别翻译为"施动者"和"受动者";内涵均有所改变:agent指"过程的启动者",affected的"语义性质为过程的承受者或受影响者"。这样,福赛特实际上是将韩礼德说的中动语态的有关参与者一分为二:把(29)中的"棋"看作agent,"小兔子死了"一类句子中的参与者现象归入affected。

对此,笔者有几点自己的看法。第一,二分法不如三分法好:前者抹杀了动作发出者和动作接受者的中间状态,如(29)中的"棋"。第二,agent的"施动者"这一译文,很容易与韩礼德的动作者混为一谈,因为其中的语素"施"容易让人与主动"添加"某种行为(如这里的"动")发生联想。为此,笔者主张物质过程参与者三分原则,即针对主动句、被动句和中动句中参与者的性质,在保留韩礼德的术语Actor和Goal内涵的基础上,沿用"施动者"和"受动者"两个翻译术语;另用"中动者"(Middle)来指称中动语态中的参与者,这样,汉语的三个术语"施动者"、"受动者"和"中动者"可以分别表明三种参与者的内涵特征。笔者拟启用"介体"(Mediator)这一术语,作为含盖三类参与者的无标记术语。这样,在具体分析中就可以一并涉及范围成分在句中可能带上的介体性质,因为这一类成分所带的基本上是受动特征和中动特征(见后);当然,这样来处理并不排除它们同时具有范围特点。

事实上,如果接受福赛特和周晓康的处理方案,那么"树死了"中的"树"就是受动者,而"树活了"中的"树"就是施动者,这似乎还说得过去。但"风停了"中的"风"则难说是施动者还是受动者。因此就某一话段而言,如果语境不提供相关信息,如"门"是因为受风吹、还是自己无缘无故"开了"或"关了",在语义范畴的确认上就没有必要过多地寻求事理作依据,因为语言中大量的比喻现象,如"姑娘是一朵花",是无法通过直接寻求经验事理得到合理解释的;语义范畴虽然基于经验事理,但其自身具有相对的独立性。

此外,运用周晓康自己拟订的测试办法,也能说明采用二分法的不足之处。对于施动者,其测试手段是"X所为是";对于受动者,测试手段是"X所受是"。像"风停了"这样的小句,其中的"风"用两种测试方法都通不过。

第二个不同点是,周晓康和福赛特一样,采用语序("施动者中心","受动者中心",并结合"范围")来区别概念语义范畴,目的是为了能够在计算机上实现句子的生成;笔者对此有不同看法。直言之,从描写的角度看,以何者为"中心"容易引起误会,因为这样很容易和信息价值联系在一起,而从他们的实际操作看更是如此。此外,其模式中倒数第三个"受动者中心"的例子是"他们把船沉了",其中"船"为什么是"中心"?叫人不得而知;如果我们说"他们"是中心,似乎也很难说不可以,因为句首位置很重要。

第三,我们赞同区分参与者角色和关联角色(范围)的做法,但这里将根据关联角色在句中的作用,同时纳入参与者"介体"的分析范围内;而在后面的关系过程和心理过程中仍然保留"范围"的分析方法。

考虑到参与者的显、隐性问题,我们就得到(32)这个有关参与者介体及其特点的描述模式(方括号内者为补足的隐没成分)。

(32)

参与者		施动者	受动者	中动者
直接参与者	显现	他在打人 我吃了水果	他给打了 苹果给我吃了	杯子破了,他醒了 子弹中了姑娘的眼睛
	隐没	苹果[我]吃了	你[麦子]割得慢 [这首歌]她唱了三遍了	
间接参与者	显现	她就要和我结婚了 苹果被/给我吃完了	小林想跟她理论花瓶	她打了他一耳光 他打了一个喷嚏
	隐没	她就要[和我]结婚了 苹果被/给[我]吃完了	小林想[跟人]吵架	她打了他[一耳光] 他老哭[鼻子]
			基本参与者	
			准参与者	

还有几点说明。第一是隐没和省略的关系。隐没是有意无意回避有关参与者;而省略是信息问题:说话人有意省去那些语境中可以恢复的信息;当然,很多时候两者之间难于划清界限(具体讨论见 Zhou 1997:107—112)。不过,一个小句如果孤立地看不存在语法问题,就该看作是隐没,否则就是省略问题。如"我吃过了",其中隐没了"饭";但如果说"吃过饭了"就是省略问题("我")。第二,三类参与者都可能在一个小句中出现,如"她打了他一记耳光"中有基本施动者"她",有基本受动者"他",还有准中动者"一记耳光"(同时为范围)。第三,鉴于祈使句的基本功能不是概念性的,而是人际性的,所以这里不涉及。第四,也存在准参与者被选择为受动者的情况。例如,

(33) 咱得给他上个供。(刘震云:《一地鸡毛》)

(34) 这供如何上?(出处同上)

仅就前一例看,"供"似乎是中性的,无所谓施动或受动;但后一例"这供"就有明显的受动特征,是及物性结构的直接参与者。看来,准参与者只涉及受动和中动,与施动无关。这正是本书坚持将事件性范围成分同时做参与者分析的基本原因。

此外,准受动者和中动者之间有游移现象,例如,

(35) "听说他会做诗,会画画,会写字?"(汪曾祺:《受戒》)

按理,"诗",第二个"画"和"字"均属于相关事件的一部分,从而形成三个准参与者:它们是中性的,即准中动者。但它们又可能以相对独立的名词词组的身份出现,这样就很像准受动者。例如,

（36）"画一朵石榴花！""画一朵栀子花！"他把花指来，明海就照着画。到后来，凤仙花、石竹花、水蓼、淡竹叶、天竺果子、腊梅花，他都能画。（出处同上）

这一语段的前两个小句就是准参与者成分内部有数量修饰成分"一朵"；最后一个句子的同源宾语（朱德熙的"准宾语"）在主语之前。这些从事件中分离出来充任参与者成分，具有较为明显的受动性。

第三，我们将"言语"归入物质过程而不是心理过程：虽然这样的小句在事理上是心理与生理之间的过渡现象；从语义表述的方式看是物质的，也符合物质过程的定义和测试方式。

下面是有关准参与者在物质过程中有关特征的描写矩阵。

（37）

参与者类别		施动者	受动者	中动者
直接参与者	显现	我吃了水果了 她就要和我结婚了	他给人打了 小林想跟她理论花瓶	杯子破了 他醒了
	隐没	苹果[我]吃了 苹果被/给[我]吃完了	你[麦子]割得慢 小林想[跟人]吵架	—
准参与者	显现	—	这首歌她唱了三遍了 将革命进行到底	她打了他一耳光 她又流泪了
	隐没	—	老太太哭瞎了[眼睛] 小林又在跟人吵[架]	她打了他一耳光 外面又下上[雨]了

于是有三个大类、七个次类的配置方式。其中，带点的成分是施动者，加下划直线的为受动者，既带点又加下划线的也是施动者，但同时带受动特征；双下划线的为准受动者（无例；见后）；单波浪线者为中动者，双波浪线者为准中动者，方括号内的为隐没成分。

（38）

		配置方式	例句
1	a	施动者显现＋受动者显现	张三打李四
	b	施动者显现＋受动者隐没	他吃[苹果]了
	c	施动者隐没＋受动者显现	苹果（被/给[他]）吃了
2	d	唯施动者＋准中动者	他接二连三打起喷嚏来
	e	唯施动者	他走了
3	f	唯中动者：基本中动者	船沉了，风停了
	g	唯中动者：基本中动者＋准中动者	价格回落了三成

这些大类之下还可能有不同次类。下面的讨论将给出具体语用

实例。

这里还有一点需要说明：伴随性环境成分在物质过程中的功能地位问题。我们说一个小句中有两个施动者，是从过程本身的角度说的，即对于有些行为，需要两个施动者协作才能实施，如"结婚"、"合影"、"交往"、"做买卖"、"吵架"等等；但从两个施动者之间的关系看，两者的地位不一定总是完全平等的。例如，

（39）到五点左右，爷爷奶奶与徐姐研究当晚的饭。（王蒙：《坚硬的稀粥》）

这个句子里的"爷爷奶奶"和"徐姐"，无论是就过程"研究"而言，还是就两个参与者的地位关系看，在很大程度上都可以说是平等的。但下面这样的例子有些不同。

（40）为此小林老婆还和保姆吵过一架（刘震云：《一地鸡毛》）

尽管"吵架"是双方的事，但从相关语境看，是"小林老婆"主动发起进攻的，从这个意义上说，"保姆"则带有一定的受动性。其实，这种现象很普遍。例如，

（41）十来年里这家人就和孙家断绝了交往（路遥：《平凡的世界》）

（42）大哥，有件事我早想和你拉谈拉谈（出处同上）

（43）小林就又气鼓鼓地想跟她理论花瓶。（刘震云：《一地鸡毛》）

（44）她要和我换美元。（姜利敏：《且乐》）

（45）娅故意在电话里和那边热热火火地扯个没完没了。（出处同上）

这些例子中既带点又加下划线的成分，是过程的施动者，但就前面的第一个施动者而言，它们又具有受动性。于是，形成一个过渡级差关系。以(44)为例，"她"、"我"和"美元"之间的"施动—受动"特征可描述为："她＞我＞＞美元"。即是说，"＞"左边的成分支配右边的成分，最左边的成分是典型的施动者，最右边的成分是典型的受动者，两个"＞＞"表示施动者和受动者之间的分界线（下同）。我们将会看到，这一模式能够解释后面将要涉及的一系列现象。

3.2 "施动者+受动者"物质过程

这里又分好几种情况:(一)单施动者+单受动者,(二)双施动者(直接施动者+伴随性间接施动者)+单受动者,(三)单施动者+双受动者(直接受动者+间接受动者),(四)施动者显现+受动者隐没,(五)施动者隐没+受动者显现。

先看施动者显现+受动者显现。一是由一个施动者加一个受动者构成的物质小句。其测试方法是"谁对什么人或东西做了什么";其序列模式是"施动者>>受动者"。下面是实例;这里只提取直接相关的小句,必要时才一并抄录别的部分;如果不是独立小句,引文结束处没有标点符号。

(46) 等众人下山后,俊武就设法和俊文相跟在一起走。(路遥:《平凡的世界》)

(47) 这事就由你们来安排!(出处同上)

(48) 我来接你!(汪曾祺:《受戒》)

(49) 水香已推开了西厢房的门。(邵振国:《麦客》)

(50) 晚风轻轻地吹着那棵老槐树(出处同上)

(51) 我他妈要谁送?(阿城:《棋王》)

(52) (我)被老板开除了(于晴:《为你收藏片片真心》)

(53) 果然,谈笑之间,两人就把那个批件给处理了。(出处同上)

(54) 书名为编者所加(俞平伯:《人生不过如此》)

(55) 在这里你得听我管!(王愿坚:《党费》)

(56) 一切有我应付!(出处同上)

(57) 看他一副瘸样,年轻时竟还和大领导接触过?(刘震云:《一地鸡毛》)

因为概念语义分析基本上不关心语序,所以施动者和受动者的顺序比较自由。注意(53)中的"给"。按曹逢甫(2002)的观点,上述"把"字句中的"给"属于相关句式的动词前缀,是从前面的"被/把"之类的成分演化来的。

这里可能会涉及到准参与者(范围)带受动特征的情况,例如(其他实例可见吕叔湘,1948/1984:184—185),

(58) 老张是我的老同学,当年在大学,我们两个都爱搞田

径!(刘震云:《一地鸡毛》)

(59) 我要写一首诗。(张承志:《北方的河》)
(60) 这么乱,下什么棋?(阿城:《棋王》)
(61) 岑松了口气,便和娅开了句玩笑(姜利敏:《且乐》)

最后一例中的"娅"是伴随环境成分。这些实例中的范围成分,都带有受动特征,至少一般来说人们会这样看待。

这里引出了周晓康(Zhou 1997:73—99)论述的相关现象,即身体部位参与过程建构的范围成分,称为"身体性过程"(Bodily process),如"伸了一个懒腰","打了两个喷嚏","耸了耸肩膀"。在本书体系中,"一个懒腰""两个喷嚏"和"肩膀"同时做准参与者分析。此外,她将"吃饭""结婚""过节""跳舞""洗澡""抽烟"等看作"文化性过程"(Cultural process);于是,如果其中的"饭""婚""节""舞""澡"和"烟"以独立成分的身份出现,同样是准参与者。在这里,相关准参与者出现在过程后面;但在有严格语境限制的情况下,也可能出现在过程成分之前,如"这个懒腰他伸了十秒钟",或者"这个舞他跳了十年了",此时它们带有一定受动特征。其实,即便不出现在过程前,有关成分也可能带受动性。例如,

(62) 早上起床后,他常常得半天直不起腰。(路遥:《平凡的世界》)
(63) 早先,我们这里也不会纺线(孙犁:《山地回忆》)
(64) 她正在烧火(出处同上)
(65) 他点点头。(扎西达娃:《系在皮绳扣上的魂》)

不过,并非所有的事件性范围在句中都具有明显的受动特征。例如,

(66) 大家都是露天就餐。(路遥:《平凡的世界》)
(67) 我感激地看她一眼(刘震云:《塔铺》)
(68) 少平……狠狠地打了他一记耳光。(路遥:《平凡的世界》)
(69) 她……从来没有挨过谁一下打(赵树理:《登记》)
(70) 到目前为止,你连外单位幼儿园的园长见都没见一面(刘震云:《一地鸡毛》)

范围成分"餐""一眼""一记耳光""一下打"和"一面"既不带施动

特征,也没有受动性质,而是中性的。所以,物质过程中的三类成分在这里都出现了,只是这里的中动者是准参与者,而非基本中动者:施动者＞＞受动者＞＞准中动者。

也有施动者和受动者系同一所指的,如"他打了自己一耳光"。

下面看由两个施动者(直接施动者＋间接施动者)加一个受动者、或者一个施动者加两个受动者(基本受动者＋准受动者)构成的物质过程小句。先看前一种情况,这又分两个次类,即受动者分别是基本参与者和准参与者。例如,

(71) 不过孩子……还和印度女人的孩子拉着手,玩得很愉快。(刘震云:《一地鸡毛》)
(72) 好多次我想趁着他心情好的时候和他好好谈谈这个问题。(姜利敏:《且乐》)
(73) 她和岑商量出那些办法(出处同上)
(74) 金家户族的人……和外村的王姓展开了一场混战。(路遥:《平凡的世界》)
(75) 兰花却死心塌地跟他过日子(出处同上)

其中,前三例中的"手""这个问题"和"那些办法"都是范围性的基本受动者;后两例中的"一场混战"和"日子"分别是"展开"和"过"的过程性准受动者。这些都是两个施动者针对一个受动者的现象,其测试方法是"谁和/与谁对什么人或事做了什么";其序列是:直接施动者＞间接施动者＞＞基本受动者/准受动者。这里可能出现引动者。例如,

(76) 你先坐着,叫我给你弄饭去!(路遥:《平凡的世界》)

其中"叫"可以改成"让"或者"由"。这一格式里的"叫""让"或"由",按吕叔湘(1980:405—406,555)的解释,仍作介词看待,引入施动者。在这种情况下,我们也可以说"你让/叫我给你弄饭去"。

这里的第一个施动者可另拟名称"引动者",因为它不一定就是动作的发出者。又如,

(77) 这使他们再也不敢频繁地接触了。(路遥:《平凡的世界》)

下面是一个施动者针对两个受动者的情况。这又分两种情况:或者两个受动者都是基本参与者,或者其中一个是准参与者。

(78) 小林将这想法向小林老婆说了(刘震云:《一地鸡毛》)

(79) 润生……和他打了个照面就走了。(路遥:《平凡的世界》)

(80) 老张……照小林头上打了一巴掌(刘震云:《一地鸡毛》)

前一种情况如(78)中的"这想法"和"小林老婆";其序列是"言语内容>受话者"。后一种情况的基本序列是:"基本施动者>>基本受动者>准受动者",如随后两例。

吕叔湘(1980:184,186)还引用过下面这样的例子。其中加双下划直线的系同一类功能成分:它们和相应的基本受动者之间,存在部分和整体的关系。

(81) 把衣服脱了一件。

(82) 我把一个南京城走了大半个。

(83) 把妮子缚了两只手。

(84) 我将他活剥了血沥沥的皮,生敲了支刺刺的脑,细剔了疙蹅蹅的髓。

(85) 把一长青拴了双手。

其中带双下划直线的成分都是范围成分,在句中做准受动者。

这里有两点需要留意。第一,上述结构和兼语式不同,后者是两个小句压缩在一起构成的中间级阶状态。例如,

(86) 老板派娅和司机小张去接他。(姜利敏:《且乐》)

也不要和环境成分混淆了。例如,

(87) 索恩……更不想给自己找麻烦(出处同上)

(88) 敏儿为她打开车门(出处同上)

二例中的"自己"和"她"是环境成分,不是受动者(见彭宣维 2011 动词词组一章有关讨论)。所以,这样的例子应该归到单一施动者和单一受动者一类中去。

第二,还有以下复制情况:

(89) 这大王被司令官救过他一次(《沈从文散文选·一个大王》)

如果认可这个句子的话,那么生成语法的空语类理论就会受到严

重威胁(也见彭宣维 2011 有关主语分析中涉及的现象及其论述)。

其次是有施动者和受动者同时参加的物质过程中,其一隐没的现象。这又分两种情况:或者施动者隐没,或者受动者隐没。先看"施动者显现＋受动者隐没"的情况。例如,

(90)"什么时候,才能打败鬼子?"……"……我们总是要打下去,我们不会悲观的。"(孙犁:《山地回忆》)

倒数第二个小句中"打"后面隐没的成分应当是"日本鬼子",但这里不便补出;有上文作基础,这里也没有必要说出来。又如,

(91)张木匠打罢早走了,婆婆连看也不来看(赵树理:《登记》)

(92)让我念给你听!(出处同上)

在第一例中,受动者应该是"打"的对象,即前文说的"小飞蛾",这里没有出现;第二例中"念"后面隐没了报纸上刊载的有关"婚姻法"的文件。第三例隐没了基本参与者,最后一例隐没的则是准参与者。

(93)你别骂!(张弦:《被爱情遗忘的角落》)

(94)我能考上吗?(刘震云:《塔铺》)

(95)我再找找看。(徐星:无主题变奏)

(96)水香劝着。(出处同上)

(97)看你割得慢!(邵振国:《麦客》)

(98)他抽泣着,再也说不下去了。(出处同上)

(99)他会画!(汪曾祺:《受戒》)

(100)我在写呀!(徐星:无主题变奏)

(101)林震嗫嚅地说:"我吃过了。"(王蒙:组织部来了年轻人)

(102)田五,亮开嗓子唱!(路遥:《平凡的世界》)

这里前面六例中隐没的都是基本参与者,最后四例隐没的则是准参与者。

再看"施动者隐没＋受动者显现"。这里又分两种情况,一是只有一个受动参与者,二是有两个受动参与者。下面数例都是单一受动者小句。

(103)俺不烧了!(汪曾祺:《受戒》)

(104) 罗汉钱丢了！（赵树理：《登记》）
(105) 她的第二次考试已经录取了！（出处同上）
(106) 饭到底还是做了，做的还不错（刘震云：《一地鸡毛》）

第一例中的"烧"是指"烧戒疤"，但"戒疤"不是自己"烧"，而是由别人来"烧"，所以"俺"是受动者；但这里施动者隐没，也不便补出。(104)"罗汉钱"是说话人自己弄丢的，这里没有必要说出来。(105)的行为"录取"是由说话人实施的，但施动者在这里并没有出现。最后一例中的"饭"是准参与者。

注意下面的例子，它不再是典型的物质过程，而是与物质过程有关的关系过程。

(107) 前排的两个小弟兄终于病倒（刘震云：《塔铺》）

这里的"倒"是属性参与者，而"前排的两个小弟兄"是受动者载体（见下一章）。

下面是出现两个受动参与者的实例。

(108) 他和田福堂都在接受批判；他接受思想的批判，田福堂接受良心的批判。（路遥：《平凡的世界》）
(109) 实棒棰灌米汤，滴水不进（引自吕叔湘）
(110) 这早晚后门早已上了锁了。（出处同上）
(111) 清朝，近几年拍了很多电影。（实录语）

在各句的两个参与者中，要么两个都是基本参与者（带单下划线者），要么其中一个是基本受动者，一个是准参与者（带双下划线者）。

3.3 唯施动者和唯中动者物质过程

这里先讨论唯施动者物质过程，有四种情况：（一）单一施动者，（二）基本施动者＋准中动者，（三）双施动者（基本施动者＋伴随者）＋中动者，以及（四）双施动者。先看单一施动者物质过程。

(112) "妈，晌午了，你不歇着？""哦，我娃回来了……"（邵振国：《麦客》）
(113) 掌柜的走了，麦客们躺下了（出处同上）

引号内的"你不歇着"和"我娃回来了"都是典型实例。这里只有施动者"你"和"我娃"与过程"不歇着"和"回来了"。这就是传统语法说的不及物动词句。下面是其他实例。

(114) 我先回去了。(出处同上)
(115) 他哥,早些睡吧,明天早起咱早些走。(出处同上)
(116) 他抽泣着(出处同上)
(117) 五婶、张木匠、小飞蛾三个人都要动身了(赵树理:《登记》)
(118) 小织笑了。(张炜:《秋天的愤怒》)
(119) 小英子喊起来(汪曾祺:《受戒》)

再看下面的实例,这是有关双施动者的用例。

(120) 李向前终于如愿以偿地和润叶结了婚。(路遥:《平凡的世界》)

由于"结婚"是双方的事,因此,"李向前"和"润叶"都应当看作施动参与者;而"结婚"这一事件在这里被分开处理成了过程"结"和对象"婚"。其序列是:"基本施动者＞伴随者＞＞准中动者"。又如,

(121) 她和我小时候同过学(出处同上)
(122) 我……还和一个人吵了一架(路遥:《平凡的世界》)
(123) 女儿和一个泥腿把子谈恋爱(出处同上)
(124) 山里有人和他开个玩笑(出处同上)
(125) 从此以后,人们……再也不敢和这个老祖宗打交道了。(出处同上)

其中带双波纹线的成分,相对于(74—75)中的"(展开了)一场混战"和"(过)日子",不大一样:这里的成分基本上不带受动特征,也就是说,它们基本上是中性的。而从构词的角度说,汉语中已经形成了大量类似成分。比较(121—125)和下面三例。

(126) 索恩偶尔会来和弗兰克打打网球。(姜利敏:《且乐》)
(127) 登云和他从来没公开红过脸。(出处同上)
(128) 他……和一位山西姑娘一块过光景了。(出处同上)

其中的"网球""脸"和"光景"似乎带有一定的受动性,虽然严格地说,这些成分都应当看作中性成分。

以下例句中的"交火"就已经形成一个典型的词了。

（129）当然，眼下他还不敢和他正面交火。(出处同上)

其他类似成分如"打架"，"吵架"，"相约"，"约会"，"相好"，"相会"，"相处"，"争论"，"公事"等等。不过，这一类成分中的范围，如"婚"，也可能带上受动特征，例如，

（130）这婚你恐怕是和她结不成了。

在双施动参与者中，其中的伴随性施动者可能隐没。例如，

（131）人家就要结婚了！（路遥：《平凡的世界》）

也有准中动者隐没的。例如，

（132）明儿别到河里洗脸去了，到我们这里洗吧（孙犁：《山地回忆》）

（133）老人家还没睡么？（刘震云：《麦客》）

前一句后一个小句的基本过程成分"洗"后面没有出现"脸"，这显然不是省略问题。后一句是"觉"隐没。

注意下面的用例（出自电视连续剧《失乐园》2003年5月1日晚9:12江西一套）。

（134）妈，你让舅舅让爸爸进来吧！

这里有三个参与者，其中"爸爸"是施动者，"你"和"舅舅"都是引动者，但"舅舅"和"爸爸"都带有一定的受动特征。

最后来看唯中动者小句。例如，

（135）天已经完全黑了。（张弦：《被爱情遗忘的角落》）

也就是说，任何一个小句，其与参与者有关的认知兴趣点，只要不涉及施动和受动特征，这样的小句基本上就是中动物质过程。其他实例如下。

（136）高考结束了。（刘震云：《塔铺》）
（137）一旦世事变了（出处同上）
（138）雨不知什么时候已经停了（出处同上）
（139）那座黑黝黝的秃塔……似要马上塌下。（刘震云：《塔铺》）
（140）风停了。（出处同上）
（141）早饭的时辰过了（邵振国：《麦客》）

(142) 太阳已经偏过了(出处同上)

(143) (哪怕我一个人割不倒,)麦就黄过头了!(出处同上)

(144) 山崩了(扎西达娃:《系在皮绳扣上的魂》)

(145) 棋开始了。(阿城:《棋王》)

(146) 太阳终于落下去(出处同上)

(147) 天已黑了(出处同上)

(148) 下一场考试的钟声响了。(刘震云:《塔铺》)

(149) 两天过去了。(出处同上)

(150) 事情过去了(出处同上)

(151) 不久,这条线正式营运(铁凝:《哦,香雪》)

(152) 天气……终于放晴了(《沈从文散文选·辰河小船上的水手》)

此外,唯中动者小句可能带范围性准中动者。例如,

(153) 河水半月来已落下六尺(出处《同上·一个多情水手与一个多情妇人》)

其中的度量范围成分"六尺"可作准中动者看待。

注意,(140)和(147)等与韩礼德所说的"气象过程"(Meteological processes)不同。试比较。

(154) 天照样刮风下雨(路遥:《平凡的世界》)

在这里"天"似乎是"刮风"和"下雨"的施动者;其实,这只是表象,因为"风"和"雨"不是"天""刮"和"下"起来的,"天"只是处所环境,就像"外面下大雨了"、"山上起雾了"、"地上打霜了"等等一样。它们和"天晴了"不一样,因为后一例所说的,是"天"本身怎样变化,而不是"天下雨了"那样,"天"仅仅是一个环境身份。又如,"下起雨来了"和"雨下起来了"之间,从概念意义的角度说,两者是一样的。但它和"雨住了"不同:后者的兴趣点在于"雨"本身所发生的变化。类似小句如果没有句首的处所环境成分,句子照样成立。下面是另外几个实例。

(155) 今天下着小雨(刘震云:《一地鸡毛》)

(156) 窗外下起雨来(陆文夫:《小巷深处》)

(157) 起风了(刘震云:《塔铺》)

前一例中"小雨"是过程性范围成分,故为准参与者;"今天"是处

所成分,是非典型参与者。中间一例中"雨"与前一相同,只是处所环境是空间范畴;最后一例的处所环境隐没,"风"仍然是准参与者。

其实,如果将这些小句和下面这样的现象进行比较,其间的差别并不大;差别只在于参与者地位而已。

(158) 天边涌起一轮满月(茹志鹃:《百合花》)

总之,气象小句没有典型参与者,只有两个准参与者,且处所环境往往隐没。也许正是基于上述原因,韩礼德没有把气象小句当作一个基本过程类别处理。只是在这里,相对于其他类型的处所关系句而言,这一类小句是准参与者小句。

3.4 余论与小结

前面从参与者的角度考察了相关物质过程的类别;最后,我们从过程本身来看看物质过程。物质过程涉及到两种过程类别,一是"单物质过程小句",即基本过程成分只涉及一种物质过程;二是"双过程物质过程":其一为基本行为,其二为相关行为的结果。前面涉及的现象都是单过程的;这里看看双过程(动作+结果)现象。例如,

(159) 现如今这案子又倒折腾回来了!?(郭宝昌:《大宅门》)

(160) 如果我考取了,他会不会……(徐星:无主题变奏)

这些例子属于朱德熙(1982/1999:143—159)说的"述补结构",只是这里的"补语"都是动词。在第一个例子中,"这案子"是"折腾"的受动者,施动者隐没;它又是"回来"的施动者。(159)与(160)相当:"考"是"我"所发出的行为动作,但对于"取"来说,"我"又是受动者。由此看来,这样的句子是由两种物质过程套叠在一起构成的一种复合过程小句。我们把这种句子称为"动作—结果双物质过程句"。这样的动作结果句不限于物质过程,在归附包孕关系句中尤其多见(见下一章)。

当然,对于下面的过程成分"接装",应该当作一个临时词看待,而不是系统成分,因为这里是将"接"和"装"组合在一起试图涵盖相关事件的整个过程。

(161) 工人正在接装电话(出处同上)

可见,临时构成的词与固定成型的词,在功能上是相当的。这一

点对于双物质过程、对于跨类过程小句来说,具有普遍意义。如在"他哭瞎了双眼"中,"哭"和"瞎"属于两个不同的范畴:前者是物质过程性的,后者是一个包孕关系成分,但可将两个成分看成一体(见下一章有关实例及其讨论)。

还有一种现象,跟语序有关。例如,

(162) 回避啦您呐(郭宝昌:《大宅门》)

(163) 掏钱吧您!(出处同上)

(164) 跑得了我们俩,跑得了白家老号吗?(出处同上)

第一句是单施动者句;第二句是单施动者加单受动者;第三句是双施动者句。但所有的过程都在参与者之前。

至此,我们将前面讨论的有关物质过程的主要类别及其次类用系统模式的方式做如下总结性描写(对比 Zhou 1997:53;周晓康 1999)。

(165)

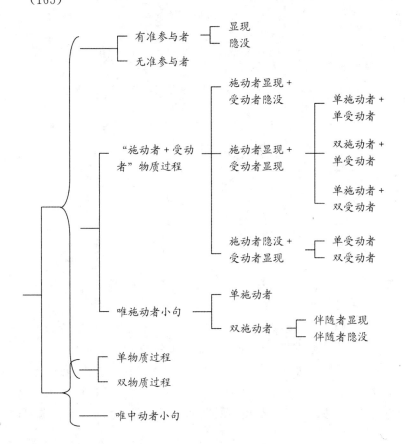

我们将这里的系统选择模式,用下表的方式加以总结。
(166).

		配置方式		例句
1	a	施动者＋受动者	单施＋单受(基本)	张三打了李四,苹果我吃了
			单施＋单受(准)	他已经唱过歌了
			单施＋单受(基本,隐)	他吃了
			单施＋单受(准,隐)	他已经唱过了
			单施(隐)＋单受	苹果吃了
			单施(隐)＋单受	李四挨/被/给打了
			单施＋单受＋准中	张三打了李四一巴掌
			双施(全显)＋单受(基)	张三还在和李四争论这事儿
			双施(一隐)＋单受(基)	张三还在争论这事儿呐
			双施(全显)＋单受(准)	张三又和我做了几笔买卖
			双施(一隐)＋单受(准)	张三又做了几笔买卖
			单施＋双受(双基)	张三把这想法向李四说了
			单施＋双受(一基+一准)	他把后门上了锁,他被人绑了手脚
			单施＋双受(一隐)	张三向李四说了
			单施＋双受(一隐)	张三说过这想法
			单施＋双受(全隐)	张三说过了
			单施(隐)＋双受(全显)	后门早已上了锁了
2	b	唯施动者	单施	张三走了,她老叹气
			单施＋准中	张三接二连三打起喷嚏来
			双施(全显)	张三和李四打起来了
			双施(全显)＋准中	张三和李四早结了婚了
			双施(全显＋准中隐)	张三和李四早结了
			双施(一隐)＋准中	张三都结过五次婚了
			双施(一隐＋准中隐)	他早结了
3	c	唯中动者	基本中动者	船沉了,风停了
			基本中动者＋准中动者	太阳偏西了

从上面的分析我们看到以下几点。第一,环境和参与者连成一体,如果选择需要,部分环境成分就可能被同时选作参与者,此时的环境性参与者都是直接参与者。第二,准参与者没有以施动者身份出现的;准参与者可能带受动特征,还可能在受动和中动特征之间游移:有的准参与者受动特征相对突出,有的中动特征明显,还有的介于两者之间。第三,从计算机识别和生成看,我们肯定福赛特和周晓康模式的优势,即从总体来说显得简洁些,便于操作;但人为因素太大;而

本章的模式有利于做到深入详尽,尤其是将关联范畴成分纳入及物性关系中时,这一点就体现得比较明显。(四)同时有施动者和受动者参与的小句,其配置类别最多;但从整体上看,各种配置方式之间并非总是对称和均衡的;这就为表达提供了更多的灵活性,也为语言发展和变化提供了可能性。(五)各类参与者之间存在地位的级差序列:基本施动者/基本受动者/基本中动者＞准受动者＞过渡性成分＞准中动者。(六)从过程的角度看,既有单物质过程,也有双物质过程,从而在物质过程中出现复合过程的现象。

对物质过程的系统描写,有利于以此为基础,考察关系和心理过程中的复合参与者。

4. 处所关系过程

前面指出,处所关系过程是关系过程的次类。在汉语中无所谓存在过程,这里一律划到处所过程中;此外,在英语中对相关现象的称谓是环境关系过程,即环境成分同时做属性参与者,但汉语主要以处所的方式出现,故周晓康用处所这个术语,而这恰好与福赛特的术语一致,尽管内涵上有差别。

为了讨论上的方便,我们需要对整个关系过程有一个总体把握。先看以下三组例句。

(167) a. 门外是一条河
　　　b. 李四在(张三)前面
　　　c. 客人进了屋
　　　d. 地里种着庄稼
　　　e. 山上起雾了

(168) a. 张三很勇敢
　　　b. 老太太哭肿了眼睛
　　　c. 不过洋人总和咱们不一样
　　　d. 他当选为主席
　　　e. 她看起来很忧郁

(169) a. 他有一台笔记本电脑
　　　b. 我丢了一本新书

c. 他在银行里存了一大笔钱
d. 我们一人才不到十块
e. 他赔了一大笔银子

以上各组分别代表一类关系类别。第一组系处所关系过程;第二组系包孕关系过程;第三组系属有关系过程。本小节的基本议题就是探讨现代汉语中的处所关系过程;包孕关系过程和属有关系过程将在下一章讨论。进入正题前有几点交代。

一是理论框架。我们讨论关系过程的基本框架仍然是周晓康(Zhou 1997)在福赛特(Fawcett 1987)的基础上改进来的汉语模式(对比 Halliday 1985/1994:119—138)。笔者的工作主要体现在两个方面,第一,根据汉语现象对周晓康的模式进行必要的修正和补充。例如,周晓康留下了(168c)这样的语言现象无法解释,也没有涉及(168e);其整体描写系统中,有的也需要做一定的修正,例如,按照本书的体系,事件性范围成分,仍然作准参与者看待;这一点将在讨论各大类关系句时逐一做出具体说明。第二,周晓康在分析中所采用的例句仍然都是她凭语感自拟的,这是客观需要,目的是建立系统描写的基本框架,这样做也有经济原则上的考虑;留给我们的工作,就要求我们必须转向实际语言现象,因为具体语用过程中会出现许多"变异"性标记现象,这就需要做出进一步的具体分析;所以,我们只在十分必要时才自拟例句。

二是关系过程的基本构成。首先,既然叫关系过程,就必然涉及两个存在体(entities);而物质过程小句中可能只出现一个存在体,也可能是两个甚至三个,但关系过程中必须有两个基本的存在体;这些存在体包括事物、品质、处所等。其次是这些存在体的功能关系,即是说,所有的关系过程都有一个基本的参与者,叫做"载体"(Carrier),另一个基本的参与者是属性(Attribute)。第三,根据这些不同的基本参与者的性质,关系过程进一步划分为处所、包孕和属有三个次类:处所关系过程由"载体+处所"构成,包孕关系过程由"载体+属性"构成,属有关系过程由"载体+属有者/被属有者"构成;同时,根据相关过程成分的性质,这些次类的载体进一步分为"单纯载体"(Simple Carrier)和"复合载体"(Compound Carrier),单纯载体句就是相关小句的典型存在方式,复合载体句除了具有典型载体句的一些基本特点外,还与别的基本过程,或者连成一体,或者套叠在一起:连成一体者系不宜截然划定界线的现象,这主要表现在不同基本过程类别、以及同一过程内部不同次类之间;套叠在一起者指两种基本过程重叠在一起、同时发挥两种及物性功能的语用现象。因此,结合前一小节所涉及的现象、以及随后两章的具体分析我们仍然会看到,语言级阶是如何由典型词组向小句和复句过渡、从而形成连续体的。

处所关系和典型的物质过程的区别在于,在处所关系中,时间或/和空间处所成分是直接参与小句的及物性结构建构的,而物质过程中出现相关处所成分,仅仅是为过程和参与者提供补充信息的环境,不是参与者。例如,

(170) 景琦不是要<u>在海淀</u>盖个花园子吗?(郭宝昌:《大宅门》)

(171) <u>从十六岁</u>提亲的人都跑破了门坎子。(出处同上)

此二例均系物质过程,虽然都有处所成分,但不是相关过程的直接参与者,而是环境性的。事实上,在处所关系过程中,相关成分隐没(注意是隐没而不是省略),就是为了体现相关处所成分与另一个参与者之间的关系。例如,"窗台上摆了一盆风信子花",这里隐没施动者,目的就是为了体现"窗台"这一处所与"风信子花"之间有处所关系。即便两者位置互换,说成"一盆风信子花摆在窗台上",彼此的关系仍然没有改变。又如,

(172) 在那儿我几乎每个周末都在当地人家里度过。(姜利敏:《且乐》)

在这个例子中,"几乎每个周末"和"当地人家里"与"度过"也有关系,但"我"与"度过"的关系比"当地人家里"、"在那儿"和"几乎每个周末"与"度过"更紧密。也就是说,在这样的小句中,"当地人家里"处于比"我"低一些的地位上。打一个比方。一个人在甲单位是副处长,他上面还有正处长,因此,其作用就不够突出;另一个人在乙单位也是副处长,但这里没有正处长,他行使着正处长的权力。两人都是副处长(对应于处所),但各自的作用不同,由此形成的权力关系也就有差别。所以,(172)这个句子是纯粹的物质句而不是关系句。

4.1 对周晓康系统模式的修正

周晓康将处所关系过程(Locational Clause)分为两类,即"单纯载

体—处所"(Simple Carrier_Location)和"复合载体—处所"(Compound Carrier_Location)。在两大类之下又分"存在型"(Existential)和"非存在型"(Non-existential)。她举的例子有:

(173) a. 前面是一条河
 b. 从前有一座山
 c. 李四住在北京
 d. 故宫坐落在市中心
 e. 床上坐着一个男孩
 f. 对面来了一个年轻人
 g. 客人坐在床上
 h. 会议开了三小时
 i. 天下雨了

周晓康把前四类句子叫做单纯载体—处所句,后四类叫做复合载体—处所句;其中,a,b,e和f是存在型,余者为非存在型。她在区分存在型与非存在型时提供了五点理由。现概括性地转述如下。

(174) a. 动词的类不同:存在型用"有"和"是",非存在型的动词更具体,如:住,坐落,位于,存在,活;
 b. 两者没有同系对应关系,即非存在型的动词不能换成存在型动词;
 c. 非存在句中"在"是必需的,但存在句则可有可无;
 d. 存在句中载体大都是不定的;
 e. 存在句中的载体不能省略,非存在句中则可以省略,因为存在句中的载体是新信息,非存在句中的载体是已知信息。

对此,笔者有自己的看法。从语义范畴的角度看,没有必要划分存在型和非存在型。现就周晓康提出的五条理由逐一做出答复。

先看最后一点。我们的看法是,存在句和非存在句之间的语义差别是信息价值方面的:就存在句而言,句首的时空等成分是作为已知信息看待的,它们出现的目的是为了引入新信息;对于非存在句而言,句首的名词词组是已知信息。根据信息表达原则,在不影响语义关系的情况下,已知信息可以作为冗余度省略或隐没。因此,处所关系句中载体能否省略与语序有直接关系,也就是说,与它们的信息价值有直接关系。由此可见,周晓康的第五点实际上与概念意义关系不大,或者说关系不直接。

再看第四点。其意思是说存在句中的载体也可能是有定的。但一个存在体是否有定与其在信息单位中的信息价值无直接关系。换言之,存在句中的有定载体在交际功能上均与前面的时空已知信息相对,是作为新价值看待的。例如,在"在另一节车厢里睡着他的父亲"中,"他的父亲"是有定的,但这里处于信息单位的焦点位置,是新信息。与此相应,非存在句的载体同样可能是不定的,如"一个男孩坐在床上"中的"男孩"。因此,从载体的有定和不定的角度来说明存在句和非存在句的语义性质,值得商榷。

现在看第三点。非存在句中"在"是必需的,因为该成分具有标明载体与处所之间的关系的作用,按照我们的看法,这是一个具有逻辑语义关系的成分,目的是连接载体和处所两个经验存在体。而对于存在句而言,处所出现在句首,此时处所和载体之间有过程成分,"在"在相当程度上失去了直接发挥逻辑纽带的作用,故常省略。因此,周的第三点同样既不充分也无必要。

下面来看第二点。即便我们接受周晓康的见解,即她所说的那些单纯载体的非存在型动词的确合理,那么虽然它们和存在型动词"是"和"有"没有直接的同系对应关系(agnate),但彼此之间的转换是有规律的,并且转换前后的概念功能相当。例如,"前面有/是一条河"→"一条河在前面","李四住在北京"→"(在)北京住着李四"/"李四在北京住着","故宫坐落在市中心"→"(在)市中心坐落着故宫","床上坐着一个男孩"→"一个男孩坐在床上","对面来了一个年轻人"→"一个年轻人从对面来了","客人坐在床上"→"床上坐着客人"/"客人在床上坐着"。也就是说,如果不考虑转换前后信息价值上的差别,就空间处所而言,转换前后要么衔接成分有系统变化,要么基本过程成分存在系统对应关系:"有/是"←→"在","着"←→"在"。有对应转换关系的,两者的概念功能都一样:"有/是","在"和"着"都是静态的标志(见 Zhou 1997:277—282;刘一之 2001)。直言之,相应小句转换前后的功能没有根本改变。因此,第二点也缺乏足够的说服力。

最后我们来看最关键的第一条,即动词类别不同。这一点表面上看来似乎很有说服力,其实不然。事实上,两类动词没有对立关系。即是说,非存在型实际上就是她说的单纯载体—处所句,应当划归复合载体类;或者不能看作纯粹的单纯载体句,因为这样的小句中都有

"在"(或"于"),而"住","坐落","位于","存在","活"等与周晓康在复合载体句部分论述的、与"动态"过程相对的"静态"过程类别,可以说没有什么本质差别;对比(173c)和(173e)。她举的与"静态"有关的其他例句有:"沙滩上站着一个人","沙滩上立着两只仙鹤","中间立着烟几","脚上穿着一双皮鞋","头上戴着一顶帽子","书架上搁着一本字典","桌子上放着一块桌布","瓶子里装着葡萄酒"。既然难于辨别,不如取消单纯载体的非存在类。即便我们接受周晓康的见解,即她所说的那些单纯载体的非存在型动词的确合理,根据我们对周晓康第四点的看法,也不存在"存在型"和"非存在型"的绝对对立:对立在相当程度上是出于信息分布上的考虑,而不是及物性概念意义上的差别。

余下的问题是时间处所句,如前面引述的"从前有一座山"和"会议开了三个小时"。就前一类小句而言,这是一种固定说法,即"时间处所+'有'+载体"。所谓固定说法,一是没有相应的所谓非存在句"*一座山在从前",二是不能将"有"说成"是";而"李白活在封建时代"这样的话我们一般也不说;要说,过程成分也是"生活",这就应该做复合载体类看待。因此,就单纯载体小句而言,取消存在和非存在两个语义范畴就有了可能性。

就复合载体—时间处所看,则只有周晓康说的非存在型(如"她昨晚只睡了两小时"),没有所谓的存在型(这一点在英语中常见,only two hours did she sleep last night)。所以,就这一点看,也没有从语义范畴上区分存在型和非存在型的必要。

总之,就周晓康划分的"存在型"和"非存在型"两个大类看,其实是语序上的变化,这在相当程度上是信息分布上的需要,而不是概念意义因素;我们所说的没有语序变化的时间处所句、或者有变化且意义也有所不同的标记句和非标记句之间,与语用对比等其他因素有关。例如,"故宫坐落在市中心"与"市中心坐落着故宫"两句,前一类是一个相对的非标记句,是常规信息传递方式;如果是后一句,就可能有对比语境,例如"北京市的布局有些奇怪:市中心坐落着故宫,(市)西北郊是颐和园和圆明园,这好理解。但为什么(市)东北郊却没有任何类似建筑?西北是开门,东北是生门,东北郊也应该有类似建筑才合理!"没有对应的语序变化,在很大程度上也是出于信息分布上的考虑,"从前有一座山"是这样,因为在这种语境下没有可资利用的已知成分,只好借用时间这个与叙事者直接相关的认知因素来做铺垫,从而引入新信息。就"会议开了三个小时"而言,这里显然只能是"会议"作为已知信息出现在句首,而不是"开"延续的时间,后者正好是信息尾重所在。

基于以上认识,周晓康的系统模式的总体框架可以修正为(175)(对比 Zhou 1997:267)。

(175)

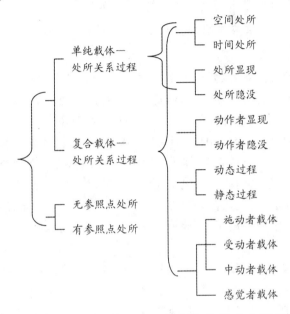

这里有几点补充说明。第一,上述系统总模式中涉及到了"感觉者载体"。例如,"我们彼此认识好多年了";按理,"认识"是下一章要讨论的典型心理成分,属于其中的认知类,但该句所关涉的主要是相识的时间跨度,因此,"我们"是一个感觉者载体。第二,这里仍然坚持前面确立的标准,即处所关系中的处所,在地位上是一个非典型参与者。第三,各具体范畴之下的次范畴和次次范畴仍然赞同周晓康的处理方案。因此,在下面的分析中,我们只从总的方面讨论相关基本范畴,具体的分类描写见周晓康有关章节(Zhou 1997)。

4.2 处所类别

根据周晓康的模式,处所分两类,一类有参照点,另一类则没有。例如,(173)中的小句的处所都没有参照点。下面是没有参照点的实例。

(176) 一九五六年年底,陈景润再次从南方海滨来到了首都北京。(徐迟:《歌德巴赫猜想》)

(177) 我同这几个水手在这只小船上已经过了十二个日子。(《沈从文散文选·辰河小船上的水手》)

前一例的"首都北京"是空间处所,后一例中的"十二个日子"是时间处所。但都没有参照点。现在对比(176)和下面一例。

(178) 两边铁似的河岸后面,又是漫无边际的黄土山。(出处同上)

前者的载体是"陈景润",处所是"首都北京",该处所成分不含参照因素。后者是一个存在句,参照点是"两边铁似的河岸",即"后面"是相对于"河岸"而言的。其中,(176)的"首都北京"是一个名词词组,指向一个地点。(177)中的"后面"这样的成分叫做"处所标"(localiser;沿自 Chao 1968:397);根据我们对名词词组的讨论,参照点"两边铁似的河岸"系名词词组的限定成分,在(178)这样的实例中它是处所参与者的一部分。从这里我们看到了名词词组中出现前置修饰成分对分析小句中相关语用功能的作用。下面拟从周晓康的系统逐一给出实例,并加以说明。

处所标可分为"绝对"(Absolute)和"相对"(Relative)两大类。前者又分"基本类"(cardinal)和"非基本类"(non-cardinal)。基本类包括"东""南""西""北""东北""东南""西北"和"西北"等空间方位。例如,

(179) 另一面的窗子朝南(阿城:《棋王》)

该例中的方位成分"南"就是一个说明处所的处所标;但与(176)不同,这里的参照点是隐没的,实际上说的是"车厢/火车"的南面。

非基本处所标涉及"上"和"下"两个范畴。例如,

(180) <u>土圪崂</u>上面就是高高的神仙山。(路遥:《平凡的世界》)

(181) 乔伯年不言不语立在<u>人行道的一棵中国槐</u>下。(出处同上)

这里两例的处所成分前都冠有参照点,分别是"土圪崂"和"一棵中国槐"。

但需注意下面的用例。

(182) 在那上面可以结出同样美丽的、红脸蛋似的苹果来（出处同上）

　　(183) 在相距很远的两棵杨树之间,配着一根尼龙绳,上面晾晒着医院白色的床单和工作服。（出处同上）

　　(184) 金家湾过去有钱人家多,打碎的瓷器往往又细又好看,上面还釉着许多美妙的花纹。（出处同上）

　　(185) 一头黑发散乱地披在肩头,上面沾着碎银屑似的水珠。（出处同上）

这些例子中的"上面"没有(180)和(181)的"上面"和"下（面）"那样的绝对空间位置意义。其实,它们应该归入无参照点的一类处所关系句,其中的"上面"与(176)中的"首都北京"一样。

周晓康对这一范畴划分了三个次类:"线性"（linear）,"中心"（centric）和"内外"（areal）。

　　(186) 冯世宽主任走在前面;后面是副主任张有智和马国雄;再后面是几个常委和老资格中层领导。（出处同上）

　　(187) 洞中央坐着一个特大的石佛像;左右站着两个。洞两边有两道走廊,走廊上又分别立十八个大石佛像。（出处同上）

　　(188) 对面的崖畔上,开满了五彩斑斓的野花。（出处同上）

　　(189) 他恍惚地立在汽车站外面（出处同上）

　　(190) 车里面看来没坐几个人（出处同上）

　　(191) 他……只好灰心地又回到自己的铺盖卷旁边（出处同上）

这些实例中的处所都是从特定角度说的。其中(186)的三个小句都是有关线性处所关系的:"主任"在"前面","副主任"在"中间","几个常委和……"在"后面"。该例中"前"、"中"、"后"都有了。(187)中的前三个小句和(188)是有关中心和非中心处所关系的:"（洞）中央""左右""（洞）两边"和"对面的崖畔上"。最后三例分别是有关"外面"、"里面"和"旁边"的"内外"关系。

笔者发现,还有度量性空间做参照的处所成分。例如,

　　(192) 二十几步远近就是她家的米店（马凌:《八重樱下》）

以上都是与空间位置有关的实例;下面是与时间处所有关的实例。

(193) 两个星期以后就传来了玛丽莲·梦露自杀的消息。(周增祥:《八个故事》)

(194) 六年前一个冬日的午间,天空中还陆续飘着零星小雪。(瞿沙蔓:《长大的一刻》)

(195) 此时此刻,居然来了个保罗!(姜利敏:《且乐》)

(196) 元朝末年,也曾出了一个嵌口磊落的人。(吴敬梓:《儒林外史》)

(197) 这时传来一个消息(刘震云:《塔铺》)

(198) 她死在三星期后。(张爱玲:《花凋》)

(199) 我曾在非洲呆过两年。(姜利敏:《且乐》)

这里"以后""后"和"一个冬日的中午"是处所标;"两个星期""三星期"和"六年前"分别是参照点。

就整个处所范畴看,有时间、空间处所同时出现的。如前面的(186);又如:

(200) 河中长年有大木筏停泊(《沈从文散文选·一九三四年一月十八》)

(201) 这时外面大厅来了一个瘦小的老年妇人(周增祥:《八个故事》)

(202) 文林街一年四季,从早到晚,有各种吆喝叫卖的声音。(汪曾祺作品自选集·职业)

(203) 有一个寒冷的冬天,东北大兴安岭的森林里落了一场大雪。(周大新:《边塞传说》)

这里倒数第二例中的"有"系"泛指,跟'某'的作用相近"(《现代汉语词典》修订本,1995年第1528页),因此,与前面诸例中的"有"不同。

下面是时间和方式同时出现的:

(204) 这时慌慌张张跑来了一些人(出处同上)

从这里分析的实例看,处所的类别既涉及单纯载体句,也与复合载体句有关。

4.3 载体类别

从观察载体类别入手考察处所句,就意味着得同时考察相关过程成分。我们先看单纯载体类,典型的是"有"和"是"做过程。例如,

(205) 独门独户,岛上只有这一家。岛上有六棵大桑树(汪曾:《受戒》)

(206) 门外是一片很大的打谷场。三面都是高大的柳树。山门里是一个穿堂。(同上)

周晓康认为,两者的差别是语体上的,"是"是"有"的语体变异;"是"只出现在空间处所句中,如她认为"从前有一座山"中的"有"不能换成"是"(第288—289页)。此前,曹逢甫(Tsao 1990:76—77)认为,"是"存在句所表达的是穷尽性或全部,"有"除了表达相关部分外,还有其他部分或事物。

笔者取曹的看法,并做如下说明:第一,"是"字句是"囊括性过程"(covering),"有"涉及视点的移动问题:一次选择一个对象,可称为"挑选性过程"(selective)。比如,我们可以说"门前有一座山,有一条河,有一块好几丈高的大石头,还有……",其中的"有"不能换成"是"。"是"的囊括性是指,叙述行为排除了还将涉及其他存在体的可能性;但"有"没有这种限制。第二点是信息意义方面的:"是"引入新价值是说话人假定听话人可能已经知道或容易推知的,但"有"引入的新信息则缺乏这一点。例如,周晓康说的"从前有一座山",实际上就是故事刚开始,叙事者要讲一个故事,而这个故事从叙事者的角度说就是假定此前听话人所不知道的。我们杜撰一个话段:"她们正在兴头上。这时突然有人敲门。小红说:'都这么晚了,(门外)可能是谁呢?'"此话语中的"有"和"是"不能互置。可见,除了信息价值因素外,"是"仍然带有一定的识别性经验意义(见下一章第一节)。

下面是时间处所存在句。

(207) 以前有一位印第安酋长(霈清:《比赛》)

(208) 那一天,没有月亮,也没有星星。(邹德学:《得意的萤火虫》《读者文摘》2003年第6期17页)

(209) 许多年以前,有个年轻的美国律师(周增祥:《八个故事》)

(210) 老辈子的时候,有这么一家子(阿城:《棋王》)

(211) 那天晚上微雨(张爱玲:《色、戒》)

最后一例就是周晓康说的无动词处所关系句;由于无法确定隐没的动词可能是"下",还是"是/有",所以直接归入单纯载体—处所句之内。

而对于下面的实例,我们仍然认为是时间作处所的关系过程。

(212)冬天是一件旧外套(鲁迅:《藤野先生》)

理由很简单,我们的依据是就小句本身而言的,这也是本书的基本思想之一。

至于周晓康说的"非存在型"单纯载体—处所句,笔者有自己的看法。如果按照周的处理意见,在复合载体—处所句中划分"静态"和"动态"过程,即便"是"和"有"不归入其中的任何一类(至少学界认为"是"是这样),那么其他相关过程成分却很难说。前面对此已有初步说明。又如,

(213)胡雪岩是在第一条船上。(高扬:《红顶商人胡雪岩》)
(214)那小子就在窑里面(路遥:《平凡的世界》)
(215)火车站位于城市中心。(出处同上)
(216)索恩的房子坐落在距市中心数公里的郊区的一块高地上。(姜利敏:《且乐》)
(217)那时,中苏关系正处于蜜月时期(出处同上)
(218)人生旅程时刻处于"零公里"处。(出处同上)

对于其中的"在","位于","处于",我们没有任何理由说它们不属于静态事件。因此,笔者假设,从典型的静态特征到典型的动态特征,是一个级差过渡连续体。例如,这里举的例子中,相关动词所体现的可以说都是典型的静态事件;而"躺","坐","站"等,当后面带"着"时,则以静态为主,但这些事件本身涉及人的动作行为,所以具有一定的动态性;而"来","去","跑","跳","追"等则是典型的动态事件。不过,同一个动词后面跟不同的时态成分,其动态与静态特征将随之出现。例如,"站着"在相当程度上是静态的,但"站了起来"中的"站"就是典型的动态事件了。这个问题比较复杂,需要整个的论文甚至专著来处理,这里暂时搁放一边。因此,截然划分有些武断。至于"静态"和"动态"的划分及其进一步分类描述,下面的讨论只涉及一些典型实例,不作为重点讨论(具体讨论见 Zhou 1997:315—345)。

与此同时,本书将(213—218)这样的例子看作典型的静态关系句。在这些实例中,"在"是一个同时具有动词和介词特征的复合功能成分,这一点与周晓康明确阐述的"在"不是动词完全不同(第 277—282 页)。我们的理由很简单:如果承认"处于"或"位于"是两个融动

词和介词一体的成分,那么就得承认"在"与它们的功能相当,尤其是(213)和"他今天在家里"这样一类小句中的"在",抛开它是从基本动词发展而来的事实不谈,这里的动词特征仍然明显。

如果上述假设成立,那么(213—218)中的载体"那小子""胡雪岩""火车站""中苏关系""人生旅程"同时是"中动者",因为相关小句中的过程成分,相对于这些参与者来说,既非动作的发出者,也非接受者,而是介于两者之间的事件的相关主体。所以,笔者把这一类载体叫做"中动者载体"。其他过程成分包括周晓康说的"坐落(于)""存在(于)""生活(于)"等。但我们可以清楚地看到,这些小句的关系特征突出,因为略去处所成分后,整个句子要么意思改变,如(213)变成"那小子在"(与"不在"相对),要么不成话,但由于仍然可以说"那小子在呢",这就是典型的物质句了。

其他实例如下(对比周晓康的有关论述)。

(219) 时间过了半个世纪(《沈从文散文选·附记》)

(220) 日子过去了三年(出处同上·老伴)

(221) 四月中起了战事(出处同上·女难)

(222) 这中间一定发生了一些什么事情。(张爱玲:《十八春》)

(223) 一月,下大雪。(《汪曾祺作品自选集·葡萄月令》)

(224) 在四月落了点小雨(《沈从文散文选·我读一本小书同时又读一本大书》)

(225) 从家里到医院门诊部要一个小时的时间(笑冬:《生命属于你只有一次》)

(226) 有的地方出劁猪的,有的地方出织席子的,有的地方出箍桶的,有的地方出弹棉花的,有的地方出画匠,有的地方出婊子,他的家乡出和尚。(汪曾祺:《受戒》)

(227) 你的身影悄无声息地消失在那道白砂的河岸后面。(张承志:《北方的河》)

(228) 这里的一切都常常出现在他们的睡梦中(路遥:《平凡的世界》)

(229) 高先生已经死了几年了。(《汪曾祺作品自选集·故里杂记》)

其中有的载体是基本中动者,如(219)中的"时间";有的载体是准中动者,如(223)"大雪"。我们把上述这些实例一律看作单纯载体—处所句。下面是有关复合载体—处所句的实例。其中的载体是那些同时具有施动特征的成分。

  (230)后面盘膝坐着一个穿大红满金绣袈裟的和尚(出处同上)

  (231)船头蹲着一个跟明子差不多大的女孩子……(出处同上)

  (232)门开处进来了一个年事极轻的妇人(《沈从文散文选·一个多情水手与一个多情妇人》)

  (233)靠墙的床上,躺着一个干瘦如柴的中年人……床前围着几个流鼻涕水的孩子;床头站着一个盘着歪歪扭扭发的中年妇女。(刘震云:《塔铺》)

  (234)黄昏里,街上各处飞着小小的蝙蝠。(《沈从文散文选·街》)

  (235)他两口住北房,艾艾住西房(赵树理:《登记》)

  (236)我哭了七天(《沈从文散文选·一个大王》)

  (237)在龙潭我住了将近半年。(出处同上)

  (238)我家就住在那个坡子上(孙犁:《山地回忆》)

  (239)他们早年间住过俊海家的窑洞(路遥:《平凡的世界》)

  (240)她坐在他旁边(出处同上)

  (241)一个马趴栽倒在了地上(出处同上)

  (242)我们睡在一间大房子里。(姜利敏:《且乐》)

  (243)河面长年来往着湘黔边境各种形体美丽的船只。(《沈从文散文选·五个军官与一个煤矿工人》)

  其中,(230—234)是存在句,余者为非存在句,都是施动者载体。宋玉柱(1988/1995:95—100)将这一类存在句称作"假存在句"。

  在下面这个小句中,时间空间成分同时出现,还带有方式连带范畴。

  (244)就这样,在一处呆子可以连杀上一天。(阿城:《棋王》)

  其中"呆子"是施动者载体,"一天"是时间处所,"在一处"是空间处所,"就这样"是方式连带范畴。下面的例子也算。

(245) 一时呆子的大名"王一生"贴得满街都是(出处同上)

注意下面这样带比较范畴的用例:

(246) 索恩比平时晚来了半小时。

这里"平时"是比较对象,比较者是与过程成分"来"直接相关的连带范畴,但这里隐没了,大致是"今天"之类的成分。

下面是有关受动者载体的实例。

(247) 金家族里受伤的人,分别被抬回了自己家里。(路遥:《平凡的世界》)

(248) 有的村庄实在没办法,就被挤在了干山上(出处同上)

(249) 这种无偿劳动往往进行到很晚。(张弦:《被爱情遗忘的角落》)

(250) 你不该生在这个家!(郭宝昌:《大宅门》)

(251) 餐厅里立刻掀起一阵欢愉的喧哗和骚乱。(路遥:《平凡的世界》)

(252) 房檐下一边种着一棵石榴树,一边种着一棵栀子花(汪曾祺:《受戒》)

(253) 佛像前的大供桌上供着鲜花、绒花(出处同上)

(254) 天井……铺着青石,种着苍劲翠柏。(出处同上)

(255) 正面法庭上摆着两个锡胆瓶,里面插着红绒花(出处同上)

(256) 头上一边插着一朵栀子花,一边插着一朵石榴花。(出处同上)

(257) 庙里走廊两头的砖额上,都刻着他写的大字。(出处同上)

(258) 这个《自传》,写在一九三一年夏秋间(出处同上)

(259) 事情闹腾到半夜。(张弦:《被爱情遗忘的角落》)

(260) 解剖实习了大概一星期(鲁迅:《藤野先生》)

(261) 那次公开考试是在那间古色古香的大厅里举行的。(何为:《第二次考试》)

(262) 荒荒抓走已经三天了。(张炜:《秋天的愤怒》)

(263) 房子才修了三年(汪曾祺:《受戒》)

(264) 我关在庙里。(出处同上)

(265)荸荠庵收来的租稻也晒在场上。(出处同上)

其中(251—257)是存在句,余者为非存在句。这里的存在句,宋玉柱(1982/1995a:62—67)称为"动态存在句"。下面是受动者载体句中同时出现施动者的实例。

(266)就这样,孙少平被田晓霞引到了另外一个天地。(出处同上)

(267)他迅速将脑袋扭向了窗外(阿城:《棋王》)

此外,这些例子中的处所都是显性的,也有隐没的用例。如,

(268)出什么事了?(路遥:《平凡的世界》)

这里既隐没了时间处所,也隐没了空间处所。正如周晓康指出,处所隐没的情况只出现在存在句中;非存在句则不能隐没或省略。

这里注意两点。第一是有结果出现的过程成分参与的复合载体—处所关系句。例如,

(269)院里。站满了人(郭宝昌:《大宅门》)

其中,"站"是自主动词,因此"人"是施动者载体;同时,"满"是描述"人"与所在地"院里"的关系的。所以,这个复合载体—处所句带有包孕句的特点,其中"满"为属性,"人"为载体。

还有一个问题,即学界说的"他死了三天了","他们吃了三个小时了,早饿了"和"他们吃了三个小时了,还在吃"前两句属于一类,即事件"死"和"吃"完结以后的时间,后一句是动作行为本身"吃"所持续的时间。两句中的时间跨度都是参与者。

4.4 小结

从上面的实例分析我们可以看出,这里的讨论所依据的框架已与韩礼德的模式相去甚远;而我们的实际操作也与福赛特和周晓康有所不同,主要表现在(一)这里和周处理"单纯载体"和"复合载体"的方案有差别:笔者以为,周在分析单纯载体句时同样涉及到了静态动词;为此,笔者提出"动态"和"静态"的相对性和级差连续性,从而在单纯载体和复合载体之间形成一个连续体,单纯处所句和复合处所句连在一起;如果将含"是/有"的小句看作典型的单纯载体处所句,那么"位于","处于","坐落于"等就带有一定的一般静态动词的特征,相关处

所关系中的载体也就带有一定的动作者特征;而"走","冲","跃","吃"等如果后面不跟"着"一类静态标志,相关小句就是典型的动态处所句。(二)笔者认为周晓康的分类"存在"和"非存在"的应当看作语法形式的范畴,两类句型之间,如果存在对应的转换关系而意思不改变,彼此的概念意义就是相当的。

下面一章探讨包孕和属有关系过程。

第二章 小句的及物性(2)：
包孕关系过程和属有关系过程

1. 引言

前一章讨论了与及物性有关的问题、基本物质小句以及处所关系过程；本章讨论关系过程的另外两个次范畴：包孕和属有；它们也分单纯载体和复合载体两类。周晓康据福赛特称为属性小句；但这样的叙述容易和"载体—属性"结构关系中的"属性"混淆；再者，其他两类关系过程的有关参与者（环境和被属有者）也是属性，即所有三个次类的小句均可称为属性小句，所以我们还是主张使用韩礼德的术语；而这样变动也不会造成混乱。我们将会看到，还有物质过程小句和关系过程合二为一的现象。其中将涉及到的"引动者"，既可能是施动者或受动者，还可能是中动者甚至别的动作者。我们还将看到：句子是如何从典型小句经由复合参与者跟双过程小句重合的现象向复句过渡的。具体议题包括：

（一）关系过程：包孕类（第 2 小节）；

（二）关系过程：属有类（第 3 小节）。

下面将先以周晓康的模式为基础进行实例分析，然后根据具体语料做出必要的补充和修正，最后总结出修正模式。

2. 包孕关系过程

周晓康将包孕关系过程分成两个大类："单纯载体—属性"类（Simple-Carrier_attribute）和"复合载体—属性"类（Compound-Carrier_attribute）。例如，

(1) a. 你这同学倨傲不逊（阿城：《棋王》）

   b. 这个人是对的。（出处同上）

(2) a. 倪斌是个好人。（出处同上）

b. 陆武丽很乖的模样。(池莉:《你以为你是谁》)
(3) 她今年五九岁(王蒙:《坚硬的稀粥》)

这些都是"单纯载体—属性"小句,其中第一个成分(主语;见彭宣维 2011 第九章末)是"载体",加下划线的成分就是"属性";属性被归附到载体上;这些是单纯包孕句,因为除了"载体"这一单一功能外,再没有别的作用;其相应的属性不涉及任何行动。根据属性的性质,该类又分为三个次类:"质量属性"(Attribute_as_quality),如(1);"事物属性"(Attribute_as_thing),如(2);以及"数量属性"(Attribute_as_quantity),如(3)。再看下面的例子。

(4) a. 金俊武在三兄弟中排行第二。(路遥:《平凡的世界》)
　　b. 他吃胖了(引自周晓康)
　　c. 他演汉姆雷特(引自周晓康)

其中的"排行""吃"和"演"系物质过程的过程成分。可见,这一类小句同时包含物质过程的特点:其中的载体同时带有施动者的特点。周晓康把这样的特点划分为两类:"起始"(Inchoative)和"行动"(Actional),均以属性和过程特点为依据。对此,笔者原则上是赞同的;但这里将对复合载体重新做出分类,包括介体载体和感觉者载体两个大类,即载体成分同时发挥物质小句和心理小句中有关参与者的双重作用。

2.1　单纯载体—包孕关系过程

2.1.1　质量包孕关系过程

质量类又分"归附"(ascribing)和"特性"(characterizing)两种。周晓康举的例句分别有"李四很勇敢","李四是一个好人";两个"李四"都是"载体";前一句中的"(很)勇敢"是归附(属性)参与者,后一句中的"一个好人"是特性(属性)参与者。下面先看有关归附类的实例(本小节所引例句,未注明出处者,均出自阿城的短篇小说《棋王》;引文结束处没有标点符号的,表明原文句子未完;被省略的地方系原文与这里讨论的现象无关;下面三例中带点者为载体,带下划线者为属性)。

(5) 你恐怕还是有些呆
(6) 王一生简直大名鼎鼎。
(7) 第二天你的伙食水平不低

这显然就是学界说的"形容词谓语句"。其中,载体由名词词组体现,属性是形容词词组。因此,这一类小句是将属性作为一种性质特点归附到载体上的。下面是其他实例。

(8) 我可不是这样。

(9) 你两天的热量还是可以的。

(10) 他日子不多了。

(11) 其实杰克·伦敦那个故事挺好。

(12) 晚上黑灯瞎火。

(13) 呆子的吃相可能更恶了。

(14) 你还挺麻利的。

(15) 王一生……当然更了不起。

(16) 队里的活儿稀松

(17) 这里乱糟糟的

对于属性来说,除了直接用形容词词组,还有用代词的,如(8)。此外,这些小句往往带一些别的成分:要么用"是……的",如(1b)和(9);要么带程度副词,如(6)中的"简直",(11)和(14)中的"挺",(15)中的"更";或者程度副词加"的",如(14);或者只有的"的",如最后一例。

这里,周晓康区分了强调/确认和非强调/确认两类。她(第184—191页)指出,这一类小句如果有"是"出现,它就是一个人际性的强调或确认标记。下面是两个实例,前一例的"是"表达人际性的强调语气,后一例的"是"为确认功能。

(18) 钱是不少,粮也多,没错儿,可没油哇。

(19) 老头儿说我的毛病是太盛。

我们不主张做这种区分,因为这种差别不是概念意义方面的,而是人际功能性的评价意义(拟另议)。

按照周晓康的看法,这一类小句还可能带范围。她引用的例子之一是"象鼻子长",其中"象"是载体,"鼻子"是配备范围,"长"是属性。因此,其语序是"载体＞配备范围＞属性"。

学界早就发现了部分和整体分裂、并将部分放到属性之后的语用现象,这一类结构的目的是体现有关语用意图(有关系统综述及"部分—整体"分开的例句,可见徐杰,1999;笔者2011讨论句子主语时有引

用)。例如,

(20) 棋呆子红了脸

按照笔者的理解,"配备范围"当为准参与者(见第一章)。于是,两个基本参与者和准参与者的语序是:"载体＞属性＞准参与者"。其实,(20)与"棋呆子的脸红了"的关系意义是一样的。出现"部分—整体"分裂,是信息表达上的需要。

还有其他情况。例如,李泉(1997b)举的例子中有"错了三个字"和"差了一道题",其中的"三个字"和"一道题"是度量性范围,做准参与者(见前一章有关讨论)。

我们做三点说明和补充。一是属性成分可能像基本事件成分(动词)一样,会带上状态成分"起来"、"下来"等。例如,

(21) 敏儿的脸红了起来。(于晴:《为你收藏片片真心》)

(22) 围观者愈发多了起来。(池莉:《你以为你是谁》)

(23) 忽然人群乱起来

(24) 王一生的身子软下来

(25) 车厢开始平静下来。

(26) [他很惊愕地看着我,忽然像明白了,]身子软下去[,不再说话。]

(27) 她[肤色晦暗干涩,]嘴唇瘪了下去(池莉:《你以为你是谁》)

还有带"着","了","过"等的。这些语境中的相关成分,除了具备典型形容词所具有的品质特征外,还带有一定程度的事件性。例如,(21)中的"红",通常表状态;但这里与"了"和"起来"共现,根据戴耀晶(1997:35—41;94—108)的观点,"了","起来"和"下去"均具有"动态性"(也见李泉 1997b,2001 等);也就是说,它们与"红"结合在一起,表明主体的"脸"处于一种变化状态中,即逐渐变"红"。这里引用的其他实例也有类似特点。它们显然和(21)的情况大致相当。因此,我们不排除这些属性同时具有品质和事件特征。如果这一观点成立,那么这里的相关载体就带有一定的中动参与者的性质(见前一章)。也就是说,这一类载体同时具有中动性质。

二是典型的"单纯载体—属性"小句中,除了周晓康注意到的整体和部位的关系外,还可能出现连带范畴。例如,

（28）他对吃是虔诚的,而且很精细。

这里的"吃"是一个角度性的连带成分,即从"吃"这一方面或这一角度看,"他是虔诚的"和"精细"的;这就排除了在别的方面具有类似属性的可能性。又如,

（29）一般来说,武汉男人普遍比较瘦小(池莉:《你以为你是谁》)

（30）作为餐厅的店名无疑它很文化很别具一格。(出处同上)

（31）对工作索恩是从不马虎的。(姜利敏:《且乐》)

从形式上看,这里后两例中带下划线的成分均可看作不完整小句;但结合属性看,它们与(29)中"普遍"一样,都是提供环境信息的。因此,如果完全排除环境成分,及物性的语义关系就会受到影响。

这一类环境成分主要是针对属性的。在这一点上,相关属性成分与物质小句中的过程成分相似(见前一章;另见 Chao 1968:88;张国宪 2000);所以,可将属性成分看作带有一定过程特征的参与者。而韩礼德(Halliday 1985/1994:214)是把英语的形容词直接看作名词词组之下的一个小类的。

三是有些属性带比较性质(对比朱德熙 1982/1999:118—119)。如(5)"有些呆"是和听话人此前言语中表现出来的"呆劲儿"相比;(9)"还是可以的"指与叙事者自己的情况相比较;(10)"(日子)不多了"的比较意义很明显;(12)"黑灯瞎火"是与"白天"相比;(13)和(15)"更可恶"、"更了不起"很显然;(14)"挺麻利"与叙事者事前的设想相对;(16)"稀松"是就言语事件发生时说的,之前有一段时间不是这样;(17)"乱糟糟的"是和别的地方比。但所有这些情形的比较意义都是隐含性的,比较对象不出现。我们要留意的是下面的情况。

（32）他目前和以前没有什么不同(路遥:《平凡的世界》)

（33）棋道与生道难道有什么不同么?(阿城:《棋王》)

第一例是同一载体的不同时期比较,第二例则是两个不同存在体之间的比较。在这种情况下,"不同"仍然是属性;但这里的两个例句中都出现了环境性的比较对象:前一例是两个时间环境之间的比较;后一例中的比较对象与被比较者功能相似。可见,比较对象具有一定的参与者特征,跟伴随者有相似之处。

上面所谈的是归附类关系过程；下面看特性类关系过程。

(34) 吃饭倒是不重要的事。

(35) 象棋是很高级的文化。

(36) 他很可怜的样子

(37) 你真是呆子。

这一小类与前一小类的相同之处在于，都是后一个属性成分将评价特征指派到前面的载体上。周晓康从形式上还做出了三点总结，其中有一点很重要，即载体和属性的位置不能交换（第 179—180 页）。与归附属性的不同之处有两点。（一）从语义的角度说，两者指派属性的角度不同：前一类是从品质上说明载体的属性，后者则从类别特性上加以描述。例如，如果说"倪斌好"，说话人就将品质"好"归附到"倪斌"身上；而"倪斌是个好人"中的"好人"则是说明他属于"人"中的一类，从而出现分类上的评价意义。（二）从语法形式上说，归附属性成分是单纯的形容词词组；而特点属性成分是带评价形容词的名词词组。即便"呆子"中没有修饰性的评价形容词，但该成分本身是评价性的。(37) 中出现了一个人际性成分"真"，表强调。这一点拟另做讨论。

下面的用例，亦属特性类归附小句。

(38) 我们老李<u>人</u>不错（出处同上）

(39) 老头子<u>腿瘸</u>（刘震云：《一地鸡毛》）

(40) 小林与小林老婆<u>脸上都一赤一白的</u>（出处同上）

(41) 这孩子<u>脑子反应很快</u>（路遥：《平凡的世界》）

这四例都是传统上说的双主语结构；其中带下划线的名词词组都是配备性范围，它们属于相关属性的一部分（对比前一章讨论的配备范围成分）。

2.1.2 事物包孕关系过程

周晓康将事物属性也分成两类：识别（identifying）和详述（elaborating）。先看前一类。它又分为两个小类："是/识别"（being）和"命名"（naming），后者包括"全名"（full name）和"姓"（surname）。例如，

(42) 我们祖上是元朝的倪云林。

(43) 我姓王，叫王一生。

前一例是识别性的，"我们祖上"和"元朝的倪云林"可以易位：

"元朝的倪云林是我们祖上",即属性和载体在性质上等同,只是看说话人是将何者作为识别另一者的属性,何者为被识别的载体。(43)有两个小句,前一句的属性是"王",后一句的属性是"王一生",区别在于识别性过程成分本身:"姓"和"叫"。

就识别类而言,笔者基本赞同周晓康的观点,认为比喻性"是"字句也属于这一类。她举的例子是"太阳就是毛主席"。我们也可以仿举一个实例:

(44)我是一匹来自北方的狼(齐秦歌词)

我们说基本赞同,因为还有进一步的考虑,即这里毕竟还存在象征意义,即可以同时看作象征类。这个问题还将在后面提到。

注意下面这一类实例。

(45)今天我们就绅士一次(池莉:《你以为你是谁》)

这里的"绅士"具有双重作用:同时具有过程和参与者的功能,相当于"当一次绅士"。我们把这一类句子也归到事物属性中,但这里的"绅士"还有归附属性的特点。

对于下面的小句,韩礼德(Halliday 1985/1994:119,130—132)是将它们看作环境关系过程的(Circumstantial);但在本书的体系中,它们和(44)一样,也是识别性的;或者更准确地说,它们还带有特点包孕句的特征,因为其中两个存在体的位置不能互换。

(46)第二天是一个星期日(张爱玲:《十八春》)

如果没有表示识别的动词出现,相关句就成了学界说的"名词谓语句"。例如,

(47)骆驼,你沙漠的船(郭沫若:《骆驼》)

其他如"鲁迅绍兴人","我四川人"等也属于这一类。

就命名类而言,还有其他过程成分。例如,

(48)其中有一条余数定理……名为孙子定理。(徐迟:《歌德巴赫猜想》)

但要注意下面的现象。第一,(49)中的"原名"是一个范围成分,"黑老"是载体。当然,如果在两者之间插入"的",就需另做解释。

(49)黑老原名叫黑耀其(路遥:《平凡的世界》)

(50) 王一生外号棋呆子

第二,下面的实例同时具有识别关系过程和物质过程两种功能。

(51) 数千万光年中的七尺之躯,与无穷的浩劫中的数十年,叫做"人生"。(丰子恺:《静观人生·阿难》)

过程成分"叫做"是前人早已"叫"顺了的称谓,可以在前面加上"人们"之类的成分。这样,"人们"之类的隐没成分就是施动者,"叫做"之后的整个成分是受动者;与此同时,(51)中的前一个成分"数千万光年中的七尺之躯,与无穷的浩劫中的数十年"(相当于"数千万光年中的七尺之躯在无穷的浩劫中的数十年中")与"人生"之间的确存在关系意义:后者对前者做识别性的说明,"叫做"相当于"就是"。"读作""念作""写作"等做过程成分,也属于这一类。因此,这是一个同时具有识别关系过程与物质过程的复合功能小句,或者说是典型的识别过程与物质过程相重叠(或糅合)的现象。不过,这与那些过渡现象有所不同,因为过渡现象与两种相关的典型现象相比,都不显著。

下面我们看详述类。按照周晓康的定义,详述关系指两个存在体之间存在相同、相似或相关关系,并进一步分为三个次类:"相似"(resembling),"象征"(signifying)和"关涉"(concerning)。她举的例子分别有"弟弟像姐姐","红灯表示危险","这个工程关系到国家利益"等。根据她在系统中对"相似"范畴中两个次范畴的描述,即"相同"("being_alike")和"相似"("being_similar")。

先看第一个小类。在周晓康的模式中,除了她实际说明的"相象"一个次类外,还有"相同"类。但这里采用二分法不如采用级差观合理,因为语言现象中不仅存在"相同"和"相似"关系,还有处于中间状态的"相当"以及处于对立面的"相反",从而形成"相同"和"相反"连续体,中间包括周晓康说的"相关"关系。当然,这也包括"相同","相似"和"相反/相对"的否定形式。

先看相同类。前面(32—33)是相同关系。其中的"(不)同"是属性,尤其是当比较对象出现在它前面的时候,"(不)同"的品质属性就很明显。对比下面的实例。

(52) 这种心理决然不同于他和郝红梅的那种状态。(路遥:《平凡的世界》)

如果这个句子在"不同"之前就终止了,显然是一个完整的归附类关系过程;但实际上比较成分出现在后面。笔者征求过好些人的意见,看(52)和(32—33)在意义上有什么不同,他们都认为是一样的。这些被询人都不了解系统功能语法;因此,他们认为比较对象出现在"(不)同"之前和之后是相同的,这是就概念意义说的,排除了由语序带来的信息意义上的差异。对此,笔者试图做如下说明。一方面,既然两种语序下的关系意义相当,那么"(不)同"的属性意义仍然存在。另一方面,这里的比较对象仍然符合环境的定义,只是带有一定的参与者特征。比较对象出现在句尾是出于信息配置上的需要。简言之,鉴于句子的"尾焦"原则(End-focus),即句子结尾部位设置新信息很重要,故将焦点信息"(不)同"放到了最后。

还有过程成分是"相等"或"等"的。例如,

(53)(1+2)有什么了不起?1+2不等于3吗?(徐迟:《歌德巴赫猜想》)

在这种情况下,过程成分是否仍然具有一定的归附特征值得考虑,因为它可能以属性的身份出现。例如,

(54)铜城矿务局是"国中之国",和市政当局没有隶属关系,级别也与其相等。(路遥:《平凡的世界》)

这与(32—33)的情况相当。其中最后一个小句中"级别"系"铜城矿务局"的"级别",与"市政当局"的"级别""相等"。这里被识别的属性(由"其"指代)由一个介词提到过程成分之前,也是出于信息价值分布上的考虑。此外,如果补足(54)的相关项,则有"铜城矿务局的级别等于市政当局的级别"。鉴于界定关系过程的出发点是两个存在体之间的语义关系,因此我们主张将这一类关系句看作双包孕句,即"品质属性+事物属性"。

此外,上述"等于"应与下面的情况区别对待。

(55)平常看棋的时候,棋盘不等于是横着的?

该例是说明"棋盘"的状态的,因此"横着"具有属性特征,"等于"为过程。再看下面的例子。

(56)结婚虽然已经几个月,但他还是等于一个光棍(路遥:《平凡的世界》)

这里的"等于",其意义与"相当于"相当,"一个光棍"为属性。

又如,

(57) 一百五十斤高粱可不是一个小数字,几乎快等于一个人一年的口粮了。(出处同上)

(58) 社员欠集体储备粮一千三百多万斤、相当于全县近一年的征购任务(出处同上)

再往后就是周晓康讨论的"相似"类。她举的例子有"弟弟像姐姐"和"毛主席像太阳"(第 197 页)。笔者以为,只有前一类例子才属于"相似"类;后一类例子属于下面要讨论的象征类(关于两者的差别,可见陆俭明、沈阳 2003:72—77)。

(59) 他没想到,他的朋友的思想竟然和他如此相似!(出处同上)

(60) 四世同堂一起吃饭,太象红楼梦时侯的事了。(王蒙:《坚硬的稀粥》)

这里主要是两个存在体在某一方面相像,限制条件是相对比的两个存在体必须是同类事物;如果出现非同类事物的比较,就应当看作"象征"类,如"他像一头狮子"或"(那姑娘)真像一根杨柳"(张承志:《北方的河》),就不是这里说的"相似"范畴。

下面是一致关系的实例:

(61) 岑说深点的肤色最合西方人时下的审美观。(姜利敏:《且乐》)

(62) 这都符合政策(路遥:《平凡的世界》)

下面是"相反"和"相对"的例子。

(63) 晓霞和她哥的性格截然相反。(出处同上)

(64) 两座建筑隔路相对,形成奇异鲜明的对比。(《沈从文传》)

(65) 它与文物研究中历来承袭的以文献为主的传统方法相对立。(出处同上)

从这些实例我们看到:(一)汉语中被比较对象出现在品质属性之前的语序很常见,这仍然是信息组织上的需要带给结构上的影响;(二)如果比较对象出现在属性之前,又没有明确的动词,相关形容词则同时带动词特征;如果比较对象出现在之后,属性的动词特征就相对明显,甚至变成静态动词,如"等于",此时,两个比较对象之间就构成典型的包孕关系。

下面看象征类,即通过"意味(着)","表示","象征","代表","体现","反映","标志","表明","显示(出)","展示(出)"等基本过程表达的两个存在体之间的关系。例如,

(66)这古老的罐子应当象征古老的生活。(张承志:《北方的河》)

(67)锁子随时都为他留心各方面的事情,象一条忠实的牧羊犬。(路遥:《平凡的世界》)

(68)晓霞头稍稍歪着,烂漫的笑容象春天的鲜花和夏日里明媚的太阳。(出处同上)

就第一例而言,"古老的生活"从"象征"的角度对"这古老的罐子"做详述,因而,"这古老的罐子"就成了被赋予"古老的生活"这么一种属性的载体。后二例相当。在下面这个话段中连续出现了多个类似关系句,过程成分分别是"暗示(着)","意味着","(决不)意味着"和"反映(了)"。

(69)淋滴不断的水滴、同事们、莫名其妙的住处、睡法,都暗示着你现状的窘迫;众人纷纷搬迁房间意味着对这一现状的一种公众态度,而你独自拒搬决不意味着你反对这一唯一明智之举,只不过反映了你在前途依然无卜的情态下对现状的厌憎又留恋、无奈又无为的逃避心理(姜利敏:《且乐》)

下面是表达"关涉"意义的实例。

(70)坚决维护上海的稳定,关系到全市人民的切身利益。(高新、何频:《朱熔基传》)

一个存在体关系到另一个存在体,从而显示出两个存在体之间的本质关系;"坚决维护上海的稳定"这件事与"全市人民的切身利益"相关联,彼此之间出现了被阐述和阐述的相互关系。又如,

(71)这个劫关乎"东南半壁"的存亡(高扬:《红顶商人胡雪岩》)

(72)这世界现在一切都和他毫不相干!(路遥:《平凡的世界》)

(73) 他不仅关系到他的名誉(《曹禺传记》)
(74) 棋品连着人品(阿城:《棋王》)
(75) 它们与我以前对生活的认识太不合辙(出处同上)
(76) 他们实际上没有涉及所谓的爱情(出处同上)

下面这个例子也应当属于这一类。

(77) 她的结局将和我的结局连在一起。(巴金:《怀念肖珊》)

常见的类似过程成分还有"关联","关乎","涉及","干","无关","无干","不相干","了不相涉","漠不相关"等等。

周晓康提出了三类无法解决的问题,如相似类"他们俩很像",象征类"红灯是危险"和"红灯是表示危险",关涉类"这本书是关于越南战争"。对于"他们俩很像",根据我们前面提出的分析方案,"很像"当作品质属性看待;这里的比较对象和被比较对象通过代词化的方式变成了一个词,于是整个小句就是典型的品质包孕小句。对于象征类,过程成分为"是"。这个问题我们在前面涉及识别关系过程时,已经提到了,即将这一类小句看作"识别+象征"的混合类,这一点尤其能从后一类小句"红灯是表示危险"得到进一步说明。至于"关于"类的"这本书是关于越南战争",似乎也不存在多大问题:这是一个"识别+关于"的混合类。

这里小结一下。详述关系过程所表达的是一个存在体对另外一个存在体做"相像","象征"和"关涉"等方面的述说;在三类事物包孕小句中,"相像"是一个总体概念,涉及到从"相同"到"相似","相反"和"相对"的一个级差模式;"相像"和"相关"有三个相似之处:(一)它们都有对比对象,带有参与者特征,(二)比较对象可能出现在动词/形容词之前,(三)如果出现在之后,发挥比较功能的形容词则可能和相关介词一起,变成一个典型的过程成分。因此,是否有必要将"相像"和"关涉"两个次类合并成一个类,值得考虑;如果这一处理方案在一定程度上可以接受的话,那么前面提出的级差模式中就要包括"相关"在内。与周晓康不同,属性又分两类:一是基本属性,即由名词词组表达的事物性范畴,故有事物属性之称;二是有些过程成分本身同时具有品质属性的特点,这与动词连成一体。此外,各小类属性范畴之间,根据原型理论,存在诸多过渡或混合现象。这一点也将体现在下面的数量属性中。

2.1.3 数量包孕关系过程

下面笔者拟先以周晓康的模式提供实例,然后提出自己的看法。数量属性即对载体加以说明的属性是数量成分。例如,

(78) 白灰五千斤(路遥:《平凡的世界》)

(79) 她的工分在妇女中数第三。(张弦:《被爱情遗忘的角落》)

(80) 对手共是十人

(81) 生意人三个一伙,五个一群(路遥:《平凡的世界》)

第一例是对"白灰"做"度量"(measure)说明的;这里没有出现过程成分,但根据可能的变异表达方式,载体和属性之间可能出现"是",也可能是"重"。(79)是描述"她的工分"的,即它在相关"妇女"中这个序列上的名次;因此,"第三"是用来说明"她的工分"的,这是从"数量"(number)方面做出的描述:这个数量成分是属性,"她的工分"是载体,过程成分在此例中是显性的"数"。与(79)相似,(80)也是从数量方面对载体"对手"加以说明的,但是基数。(81)有所不同:相关成分是数量词组,而非纯粹的数量词。

就度量属性而言,它可能是多方面的。龙日金(Long 1981)举过的相关例子有"张永身高一米七","猪重六十公斤","这辆汽车值一万元","这块地长二十米,宽十五米"(前文第35页)。龙将这些成分一律看作度量范围;在周晓康的模式中没有提到这一点。但它们被处理为参与者,具体归纳为"重量""高度""长度""宽度""深度"等类别;并被定义为度量存在体的大小:以特定标准或度量单位为依据确定载体的大小(第204页)。当然,我们还可以据此增加别的范畴,诸如"厚度""幅度""进度""刻度""亮度""浓度""坡度""热度""速度""纬度""经度""温度""响度""偏心度"等等。下面是其他实例。

(82) 男劳一天三元,女劳一天一元五角。(出处同上)

(83) 她自豪地宣称,她在街上走过时,男人们的"回头率"达到了百分之九十以上!(出处同上)

(84) 根据中央和省委的指示,地区一级新的领导班子年龄在五十岁以下的要占三分之一,大专文化程度的要占三分之一。(出处同上)

(85) 按当时河口摩崖刻字记载的水位换算,实际水位近二百六十米,流量接近三万四千秒立方米。(出处同上)

(86) 少安的砖确实也好,压力系数都在一百号以上(七十五号以上就是国家标准)。(出处同上)

(87) "就我所知,我们国家全员工效平均只出 0.9 吨煤左右,而苏联、英国是 2 吨多,西德和波兰是 3 吨多,美国 8 吨多,澳大利亚是 10 吨多。同样是开采露天矿,我国全员效率也不到 2 吨,而国外高达 50 吨,甚至 100 吨。(出处同上)

(88) 一斤豆腐才值几个钱?(刘震云:《一地鸡毛》)

(89) 摊主有两个人(出处同上)

(90) 那些人只有一米二三高(路遥:《平凡的世界》)

(91) 他昨晚上在百货店看中的帽子,实实在在是二元五一顶(高晓声:《陈奂生上城》)

周晓康指出,这一类小句还有另一种形式,即以"是"为过程成分,如"三公斤是这个西瓜的重量",其中的"是"不能省略。她认为两种形式的区别是人际性的正式程度方面的(第 210 页)。笔者赞同这一见解,我们将对此另做系统讨论。

就数量属性而言,它又分两个次类:"基数"(cardinal)和"序数"(ordinal)。(79)是序数,(80)是基数。基数性成分做属性的关系过程是指一个存在体的数量特征的。其中后一个名词包含至少一个数字,一个度量单位,和一个可有可无的中心词;载体和属性的位置不能互换(第 212 页)。下面是实例。

(92) 这本诗集印一两千册,其中征订数不足二百(路遥:《平凡的世界》)

(93) 今年的粮食产量有希望突破历史最高纪录,达到十三亿市斤左右(出处同上)

(94) 马国丈贩来的六七个四川农村姑娘中,25 岁的一名,24 岁的两名,23 岁的三名(刘绍棠:《蛾眉》)

对此,周晓康明确指出,第一,这一类小句中的前一个名词词组是有定的,后一个是不定的,两者位置不能交换;第二,如果出现"是",它是基本动词,即过程成分,不是肯定或对比性的标记(第 212—213 页)。

笔者发现,下面这样的实例含有被隐没了的比较对象,这个比较对象就是"我"眼下的高度。

(95) 如果我个头再高它个五公分,那就疯掉啦。(姜利敏:《且乐》)

其中有一个"它"。这个成分在很大程度上词义已经虚化,省掉并不影响整个句子的意思,所以,这是一个已经语法化的成分(拟另议)。这一现象与陆俭明(2002)讨论的"吃他三大碗"中的"他"("三大碗"的属有者)虽然有渊源联系,但从共时的角度看,毕竟已经不同了。

此外,数量描述并非总是直观数目,也可能是模糊数量词。例如,

(96) 粮食一囤一囤的

这里通过"一囤一囤的"来描述"粮食"的量大,但不关心具体数量。这一类小句也可以换说成"粮食很多",或"粮食多的是/得很",改造后的小句就是典型的品质包孕小句。因此,(96)拟看作品质和数量之间的过渡现象。

下面是有关序数成分作属性的用例。

(97) 他年年都在班上考第一名(路遥:《平凡的世界》)
(98) 他在全公社的考生中,名列第一。(出处同上)
(99) (他)一十三省数第一!(汪曾祺:《受戒》)

周晓康指出(第 213—215 页),序数关系过程是指载体在一个序列上的位置;如果载体和属性之间没有"是"出现,如"我第一",两者位置不能互换;如果出现"是",则没有强调意义,属性和载体可以易位。例"我是第一(名)"("第一(名)是我")。语序上的不同是语境中信息价值的分布原则造成的,没有概念意义上的本质差别。

这里,笔者需要对周晓康的模式做些说明和补充。第一,从上面提供的实例我们看到,度量和基数属性之间难以截然划分出界限。例如,前文引的例(3)是从年龄方面说明"她"的,下面的(100)是从"直径"方面说明"圆盘"大小的,这既像度量,也像数量属性。

(100) 圆盘直径有十米左右(路遥:《平凡的世界》)

当然,如果一定要坚持"载体+'重'一类的成分+数量"这样的格式为度量范畴,除此之外则是基数属性,似乎不好处理。例如,如果将(3)说成是"她年龄五十九",把(100)说成"圆盘直径长十米左右"就该是度量属性类;而现在这样很像基数属性类。因此,这里有两种处理方案。一是将度量属性和基数属性看作连续过渡现象:"他高 1.75

米"是典型的度量属性,"他们是三人"为典型的基数属性类;二是将两者合二为一,即将现有模式中的两个范畴任意取消一个,只保留其中之一。笔者倾向于后者,理由是,度量和数量之间的界限很模糊,同时为了和前面讨论的度量范围相区别。

第二,笔者接受周晓康对"这个西瓜重三公斤"作度量包孕句的处理方案:其中的过程成分"重"与前面说的归附属性不同。周虽然没有提供足够的理由,但这一点很容易说明:这里所说的不是载体"西瓜""沉"("重"),而是它的具体重量"三公斤";从周自己提供的、将"重"放到句尾"这个西瓜三公斤重"也成立的例句(比较例句32—33),也能看出"重"只是说明"三公斤"是"这个西瓜"的度量的一个方面,因为还可以说明"这个西瓜长20公分"等。但是,对于下面的用例,我们该如何处理呢?

(101) 王一生比倪斌矮下去两个头

这一句主要是说"王一生矮",而"两个头"是说明"矮"的度量范围的。因此,该句拟做归附类包孕句看待,只是另带比较环境成分(有参与者性质)和范围成分。

至此,我们讨论了三类基本包孕关系句。还有带标记语序的情况。例如,

(102)(你?半吊钱都不值!)二百五吧你!(郭宝昌:《大宅门》)

这都是载体在后、属性在前的实例,也就是传统说的倒装。这一语序跟英语不同(见 Halliday 1985/1994:121)。

作为本部分的结束语,我们想顺便看一个与包孕关系句有关的环境成分。

(103)命运对人太不公平了(路遥:《平凡的世界》)

除了大致相当的载体和品质属性外,还有一个成分"人",该成分是通过介词"对"引入的。这应当归属于受惠者。但下面的情况须区别对待。

(104)而她对待他却不甚公平。(出处同上)

此例中"她"是"他"的施动者,"对待"是物质过程;"不甚公平"又是"她"的品质属性,"她"是载体。因此,该句既有物质过程、也有关系

过程、且物质过程的施动者和关系过程的载体由同一个成分体现，"她"是复合载体。这就是我们下面要讨论的问题。

2.2 复合载体—包孕关系过程

周晓康将这一个大类分成两个次类："发端"类（Inchoative）和"行动"类（Actional）。发端类又分"结果"（resultative）和施为（performative）；"结果"之下又分"物质"（material）和"行为"（behavioural）。对此，笔者有自己的看法。首先，根据前一章有关物质过程的定义，我们将韩礼德的行为类归入物质过程中，或者说是典型的物质过程和心理过程的过渡现象。所以这里不采用"行为"说。其次，既然周已经将经典模式中的"行为"过程分别归入物质过程（实际操作所涉及的一部分现象）和心理过程（理论描述和一部分实际操作对象），而在笔者看来应当归入物质过程，顶多看作物质过程和心理过程之间的过渡现象，那么，笔者以为没有必要单列行为类；有关现象，尤其是她所说的"范围＋载体"类，笔者在赞同其基本观点的同时，仍然坚持前一章讨论的将范围纳入介体的范围（即"准参与者"），从而有"准受动者载体"。这又引出第三个与周的不同之处：根据前面的标准，笔者确立三大类、五小类的复合载体。三大类是："施动者载体"，"受动者载体"，"中动者载体"；五小类是："基本施动者载体"，"基本受动者载体"，"准受动者载体"，"中动者载体"和"环境载体"。这些复合载体句可从功能上进一步区分为"变成"，"结果"和"施为"三个意义小类；它们与各类物质参与者之间是合取关系，即上述五类参与者从参与关系过程建构的角度看，有"变成"，"结果"和"施为"三个复合关系过程类别。第四，我们发现，语言现象中还有同一个成分充当"载体"和"感觉者"的情况，如"他感觉挺好的"中的"感觉"是一个心理动词，"他"既是感觉者又是载体。这样，周晓康的系统模式可以改造为(105)。

(105)

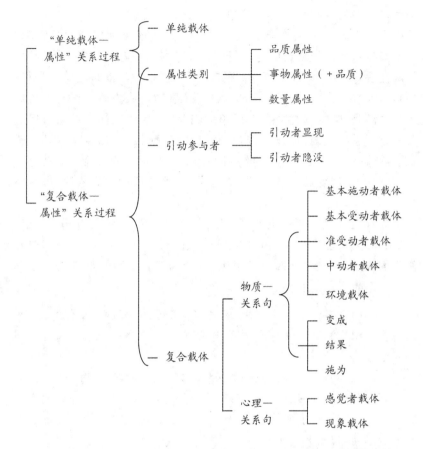

在上述修正后的模式中,"引动参与者","属性"和"复合载体"是合取关系。我们在后面的实例分析中还将看到,有载体成分同时带施动者和感觉者特征的情况。先看一组例句。

(106) 这时呆子倒成了棋主
(107) 我走累了(路遥:《平凡的世界》)
(108) 油绳全卖光了(高晓声:《陈奂生上城》)
(109) 一队的社员就一致推选他当了队长。(路遥:《平凡的世界》)
(110) 眼睛哭瞎了(琼瑶:《青青河边草》)
(111) 小林前几年爱足球,看得脸红心跳,觉得过瘾(刘震云:《一地鸡毛》)

从施动者的类别看,(106)中的"呆子"和(107)中的"我"是基本施动者,(108)的"油绳"和(109)的"他"是基本受动者,(110)的"眼睛"是准受动者。从相关物质过程看,(106)是变成类("成了"),(108),(109)和(110)是结果类("走","卖","哭"),(109)是施为类("推选")。从属性看,(107),(108)和(109)的"累","光"和"瞎"都是品质(归附性的),(106)的"棋主"和(109)的"队长"是事物。从心理过程看,(111)的"小林"是"觉得"的感觉者,现象应当是"看足球这件事过瘾";但从关系过程看,"过瘾"可以看作"小林"的品质属性。因此,"小林"是感觉者载体。最后,从引动者的角度看,(109)的"一队的社员"是施动者。下面拟以"变成","结果"和"施为"三类过程意义为依据,做具体分析。

先看变成类。根据周晓康(第 218—226 页),该类又分为"成"(becoming),"变"(changing)和"长"(growing)(对比 Long, 1981)。她举的例子分别有"李四成了医生","李四变富了"和"妹妹长高了"。下面是笔者提供的实例。

(112) 现在生米都做成了熟饭(路遥:《平凡的世界》)

(113) 他父亲后来成了前后村庄有名的二流子。(出处同上)

(114) 从此,在扬州的山前水畔,世纬等三大两小的"五人行",就增加了石榴一个,变成"六人行"了。(琼瑶:《水云间》)

(115) 院子里,四个警察加上谷玉农,和子默、梅若鸿等人分成了两组(出处同上)

(116) 这份合约书有问题,报价单上您少写一个零字,十万块的生意变成一万块了!(出处同上)

第一例的载体"生米"同时是基本受动者,属性是"熟饭"(事物);第二例通过"有名的二流子"使整个小句成为特性关系句;第三例是识别性的;第四、五两例都是数量性的。

但如果"成"前面没有别的物质过程成分出现,它自身则肩负物质和关系过程双重身份。只是通常前面会出现各种物质过程动词,上面例句中出现的有:"做"(112),"分"(115);其他如:"演化/变成","读成","写成","笑成","打成","换成"等等;(114)和(116)中是"变成",这是和"变"合在一起的用例,并且已经基本上固定成词了。当然,也有在"成"后面出现"为"等情况的,并且"成为"也已经变成了词。

就"变"而言，如果后面有"成"，就是上面说的情况：要么是事物属性，如(109)，要么是数量，如(116)；如果后面没有别的动词，或者所跟的是"得"，都只有品质属性（归附）一个小类。如上面引用的"李四变高了"，后面就没有跟别的动词；下面一例，是"变"后面跟"得"。这也属于前一章说的动作结果句，只是在这里，结果不再是物质性的，而是归附属性——一个同时具有过程特征的参与者。

(117) 至于你爹娶姨太太的事，不就变得很渺小了吗？（出处同上）

如果是事物，如"变鬼变魂"（出处同上），或者只有过程成分，如"我变了"（出处同上），此时相关小句仍然是单一的物质过程小句，与关系过程无关。

与此相仿，"长"要么和"成"搭配，后面出现事物属性成分，要么和"得"搭配，体现品质属性。例如，

(118) 你长大了！（出处同上）
(119) 她知道自己长得美（琼瑶：《水灵》）
(120) 妹妹已经长成了大姑娘（路遥：《平凡的世界》）

当然，在"长"后面出现形容词，后面还可能有数量准参与者（范围）出现，如"他近两个月长高了三公分"中的"三公分"。

周晓康在讨论上述现象时指出，对于"孙悟空变成了一座庙"中的"孙悟空"，如果是巫师使他变的，那么"孙悟空"就是受动者载体；如果按《西游记》书中描述的那样，"孙悟空"就是施动者载体。

根据以上分析，我们可以总结出三个相关标记成分，一是由动词"成"直接充当的，后面的属性是事物；二是"得"，后面的属性是品质；三是零标记，如"长高了"。第三和第一不同：对于第三例，"成"可以附着在"长"等后面；而(118)中的"长"前就不能加。

再看结果类。严格地讲，上面谈到的"变成"类也应该属于"结果"类；只是为了描述上的方便才沿承了周晓康的处理办法。前面提到，就笔者说的结果类看，周晓康是分成"物质"和"行为"两个次类的。前一个次类她举的例句有"爷爷喝醉了（酒）"和"这堵墙造歪了"；后一个次类她举的例子有"那个老太太哭瞎了眼睛"。但正如前面指出的，仅从动词"喝"和"哭"看，似乎很难分出明确的界限，所以我们不做这种区分；而相关现象也能在我们的模式中得到解释。看一组实例。

(121) 他竟然真的喝醉了(路遥:《平凡的世界》)

(122) 他昨晚上喝醉了酒(出处同上)

(123) 金家湾的金光亮掼烂鞋子[跑遍了东拉河两岸的家户]。(出处同上)

(124) 孙若西的影子放大了(冯德英:《迎春花》)

(125) 她的外衣都淋湿了(新鲜人:《反正我说了你也不信》)

(126) 向前的腿被压坏了(路遥:《平凡的世界》)

(127) 这块碾盘终于在他手里用坏了。(出处同上)

(128) 你的眼睛睁这么大(出处同上)

(129) 春玲兴奋得墨黑的大眼睛也笑细了(冯德英:《迎春花》)

(130) 太阳升高了(出处同上)

(131) 我这个头长不高了吧(新鲜人:《反正我说了你也不信》)

(132) 贝师爷已听得目瞪口呆(郭宝昌:《大宅门》)

这些都是结果性的。(121)"他"是施动者载体,物质过程成分是"喝",属性是"醉",系归附类关系句。(122)相仿,但准参与者"酒"显现。(123)"金家湾的金光亮"是施动者载体,"掼"是物质过程成分,"烂"是品质属性,"鞋子"是配备性的准参与者。(124)"孙若西的影子"仍然是施动者载体,物质过程成分是"放",关系过程属性是"大"。以上都是与施动者载体有关的关系过程。(125—127)中"她的外衣","向前的腿"和"这块碾盘"都是受动者载体。(128)和(129)中的"你的眼睛"和"黑黑的大眼睛"都是配备性准受动者。随后两例"太阳"和"我这个个头"是基本中动者载体。(132)的"听"是相关主体"贝师爷"主动发出的动作,故"贝师爷"为施动者,但"他"同时是"目瞪口呆"的载体,因此,该例与(121)相当。

在这里,如果按照周晓康的思路,(121)和(122)中的"喝"都是物质过程成分,而(128)和(129)中的"睁"与"笑"则是行为过程(属于她说的心理过程);后面的属性成分"醉","大"和"细"都是品质。但根据笔者的理解,三个过程成分在正常情况下都可能涉及意识状态(心理活动),也都是生理行为,因此,划分"物质"和"行为"缺乏依据。倒不如将相关动词一律看作物质过程成分,这样既便于识别,也易于描写。

下面是一个有关度量属性的实例(圆括号内的成分是笔者根据原

语境补上的;方括号系笔者所加,以便突出基本分析对象)。

(133)[(一家三口)数着米粒下锅,]只吃七成饱(刘绍棠:《蛾眉》)

这句话也可说成"只吃饱了七成",这样度量范围特征就突出了。"一家三口"既是"吃"的施动者,也是"饱"的载体。

下面我们来看看典型的物质过程和典型的包孕关系过程有机地重叠在一起的现象。周晓康举的例句中有"他们喊哑了嗓子","我笑疼了肚子","姐姐哭湿了手绢","宝宝尿湿了裤子"。其中,前两例属于她说的身体部位做范围的行为类;后两例是"配备"(accoutrement)做范围的行为类。周晓康的分析在这里采用了两种分析方法:她一方面认为各句的第一个成分都是复合载体,但另一方面后面的配备性范围成分又是范围性载体。

这一类句子也可以看作物质小句和关系过程套叠在一起的现象,这一点尤其体现在"宝宝尿湿了裤子"中的"裤子"变成"我的裤子"等情况以后,此时"我的裤子"不再是"宝宝"的配备性范围。为此,笔者建议只采用重叠法进行具体处理,即周晓康的后一种分析方案。

(134)

(a)	他们	喊	哑了	嗓子
周(1)	参与者:载体	过程:物质	属性	范围
周(2)	参与者:施动者	过程:物质(行为)	参与者:属性	范围:准受动者载体

(b)	宝宝	尿	湿了	妈妈的裤子
	参与者:施动者	过程:物质	参与者:属性	参与者:受动者载体

下面是实例。

(135)春天的细雨,从轿子的布蓬里飘进,吹湿了她的衣衫。(柔石:《为奴隶的母亲》)

基本动词"吹"不可能是"细雨"自己"吹",只能是被风"吹",施动者在这里隐没。因此,这里是两个类别的过程重叠在一起的:"春天的细雨被吹"和"她的衣衫湿了",前者是施动者隐没的物质过程,后者是归附关系过程,"她的衣衫"是受动者。

这里得借助第三个范畴,即福赛特(Fawcett 1987)说的third party agent(第三方施动者),周晓康称作"引动者"(Causer)(第 244—254 页)。根据以上分析,该范畴从物质过程的角度看既可能是施动者(她哭瞎了双眼),也可能是这里说的受动者。例如,

(136)

春天的细雨	(被风)吹	湿了	她的衣衫
参与者：受动者/引动者	过程：物质	参与者：属性	参与者：载体

而在下面的实例中,"眼泪"则可看作"沾"的带中动性质的引动者,因为它在这里是有关过程"沾"的主体。

(137) 禁不住的眼泪又沾湿了枕巾(姜利敏:《且乐》)

就引动者而言,还可能有无法归入物质小句参与者中的任何一类的情况。周晓康举的例子有"那场战争使李四变富了/变成了富翁",其中的"那场战争"既不是施动者,也不是受动者,更谈不上中动者。我们姑且称为"促动者"(Provoker)。引动者还可能是范围性的,例如(以下前二例引自陆俭明、沈阳 2003:226):"这种书把我看腻味了","这首歌把她唱红了"和"这首歌唱红了她",其中的"这种书"和"这首歌"就是。因此,我们得到五类引动者,即施动引动者,受动引动者,中动引动者,促动引动者和范围引动者。

最后是施为载体关系句。(109)的"推选"就是一个施为性的事件成分,从而使"他"与"队长"这一角色发生联系。又如,

(138) 他被选成了"劳动干事"(路遥:《平凡的世界》)

(139) 他已经被命名为铜城矿务局的"青年突击手"(出处同上)

(140) 那里农村的贫困已经可以宣布为紧急状态。(出处同上)

(141) 王满银自告奋勇要演他自己(出处同上)

(142) 哼,让他也坐上几天官位!(路遥:《平凡的世界》)

(143) 我这时正代理一个管三四个人的小组长(阿城:《棋王》)

是这些例子中的施为事件"选","命名","宣布"以及"演",使各相关小句的载体同时成了施为者,如(141)中的"王满银";或者被施为者,如(138)和(139)中的"他",(140)中的"农村的贫困(状态)"。周晓康举的例子中还有"当"(如"王太太当/坐庄家")。这几例中的施动者

均处于隐没状态。

在上面的初步分析中,有些例子中的引动者是显性的,如(109)和(141),其余的都是隐性的。同时,引动者不只出现在施为载体关系句中,也可能出现在任何别的复合载体关系句中,只是有时被隐没了,不易让人觉察出来。此外,引动者可能以多种方式出现,最直接的是用"使"或"让"。例如,

(144) 这使他们的脸如同火一样烫热。(路遥:《平凡的世界》)

(145) 这顿饭使两个买卖人成了朋友。(出处同上)

正如学界已有的定论,这里的"使"不是一个基本动词;周晓康本人也持这一观点。

也有用"把"将复合载体引出来的。例如,

(146) 你那副嘴巴把娃娃都亲疼了(出处同上)

(147) 孙少安这阵势几乎把他父亲也弄成了石圪节集市上的"明星"。(出处同上)

(148)(我)早晨一着急,把镜片给摔碎了(新鲜人:《反正我说了你也不信》)

其中,"娃娃","他父亲"和"镜片"都是受动者载体。但需注意以下不同情况,通过被动语态的方式,将施动者引出,如以下一例中的"不幸的女儿"。

(149) 眼下两个娃娃总算被不幸的女儿拉扯大了。(路遥:《平凡的世界》)

在这里,"两个娃娃"是受动者载体,"大了"品质属性,"拉扯"是物质过程成分。

(150) 你妹妹刚才把你找苦了(阿城:《棋王》)

此处"你妹妹"是施动者载体,后面的"你"是"找"的受动者,与关系过程无关;"苦"是描述"你妹妹"的,故为"你妹妹"的品质属性(其他实例可见吕叔湘1948/1984:190—194关于结果补语的例子中,绝大多数都属于这一类)。这样的句子显然不再是单纯的小句了。

最后来看一看几种在周晓康的模式中没有论及、或者我们另有解释的现象。

第一是她说的容量关系句(Capacity)。她举的例子是:"这个瓶子装两公升水","这个大厅容纳/坐三千人","这张床睡三个人"。笔者认为这样的句子是单纯的倒装小句。又如,

(151) 一盆水养三条金鱼
(152) 一亩地打八百斤稻子
(153) 四张纸糊一个窗子
(154) 一张纸包两本书
(155) 五斤草铺一个炕(以上五例引自李临定、范芳莲 1960/1994:1—2)
(156) 一间屋子住五个学生。
(157) 一小时讲两个人。
(158) 一锅饭吃三十个人。
(159) 一条板凳坐两个人。
(160) 一匹马骑两个孩子。(以上五例引自宋玉柱 1982/1995b:200)

其实这些都是典型的小句。我们选择一部分作分析。
(161)

(a)	一盆水	养	三条金鱼
	一亩地	打	八百斤稻子
	一张纸	包	两本书
	环境:手段方式	过程:物质	参与者:受动者
(b)	一锅饭	吃	三十个人
	一条板凳	坐	两个人
	一小时	讲	两个人
	非典型参与者:准受动者	过程:物质	参与者:施动者

第二是心理过程和关系过程重叠在一起的情况。也就是说,有关载体既有心理过程的感觉者或现象、也有物质过程的施动者或受动者等意义特征,这可能是最复杂的一种过渡现象,是周晓康的识别类无法解释的。

(162) 我虽孤身一人,却算不得独子
(163) 她实质上是在将索恩当作一块可能助她到彼岸的跳板(姜利敏:《且乐》)

一方面,"独子"是描述"我"的属性成分,因为它对载体"我"从类别上加以阐述,鉴于属性和载体的位置不能易位,这应该是一个特性类关系过程。但另一方面,基本事件成分"算"是一个表心理过程的成分:《现代汉语词典》对"算"相关义项的解释是:"认做,当作"。这显然是一种认知事件;这样"我"就是"算"的"现象"(Phenomenon),因为这里说的是:按照有关政策规定"我"不够"独子"的标准,所以"我"就不能被看作是"独子";"感觉者"(Senser)在这里隐没了。因此,这应该是一个"现象性载体＞特性属性"关系过程。(163)属于同一现象,只是"她"是施动感觉者(见下一章),"索恩"是受动者,但同时是"一块……跳板"这一事物属性的受动者载体。这一议题后面还要讨论。又如,

(164)唐春早兴奋得满脸通红(刘绍棠:《峨眉》)

(165)按说小林老婆在这方面还算开通(刘震云:《一地鸡毛》)

(166)这算是一次现场办公会。(路遥:《平凡的世界》)

(167)他肯定已将自己视为他的一个最好的朋友(姜利敏:《且乐》)

这里第一例是"唐春早兴奋"和"唐春早满脸通红"。第一小句是心理过程(情感类),第一小句是品质包孕关系句("开通")。因此这是一个典型的心理过程和典型的包孕关系过程重叠在一起的复合过程句。(165)中的"算"相当于"认做","当作",因此是一个心理事件成分做过程;但"开通"描述的是"小林老婆",所以,这是"现象载体"关系过程。(166)中的过程成分也是"算",但后面的属性成分是事物。这样的动词不少,其他如"当作/做","作为","认作/做","看成","看作/做","当","作","算作","算得(上)","不失为"。(167)与(163)相同:施动者和载体分离:"他"是施动者,"自己"为受动者载体。其他实例如,

(168)我还得装能。(新鲜人:《反正说了你也不信》)

(169)我还故作豪迈。(出处同上)

(170)他里里外外忙得一塌糊涂,一天跑下来,腿都疼得瘸了。(路遥:《平凡的世界》)

(171)我觉出有点儿冷(池莉:《你以为你是谁》)

(172)小林猜错了(刘震云:《一地鸡毛》)

就第一例看,《现代汉语词典》(1995:609)对"装"的解释是:"故意做出某种动作或姿态来掩饰真相"。这说明这个动词既是心理的(认知类),也是生理行为的(我们归入物质类)。是心理认知的,因为这涉及到主体的心理处理过程(有意回避自己知道或明白某事:"掩饰");是生理物质的,因为该事件必须涉及主体的外在表现"做出某种动作或姿态"。另一方面,"能"是描述"我"的品质属性,因此,这虽然也可以看作一种关系过程,但载体同时包括基本施动者(物质)和感觉者(心理)的现象,比前面提到的复合载体更为复杂。(170)中的"疼"也属于这一类,其意义是"疾病创伤等引起的难受的感觉"(同上,第1236页和第1268页),这种"难受的感觉"既是心理的也是生理的;因此,这里的"腿"是一个带有"准中动者＋感觉者"意义的载体。最后二例中的"觉出"和"猜"分别为感知和认知心理动词,因此"我"和"小林"都是感觉者载体。

最后是复合载体与单纯载体之间的过渡现象:"表现"类。例如,

(173) 在这方面,他表现得心灵手巧(路遥:《平凡的世界》)

(174) 紧闭的眼球显得比睁着时更大(姜利敏:《且乐》)

这里的"表现"和"显得"指事物的某些内在属性通过外观表现出来。我们仍将这一现象看作物质过程与关系过程的融合。其他类似功能成分有:"显示","看起来","来得","展示","预示","预告"等。这样的小句既有外观特征(物质),也有品质或事物属性(关系)。这应该看作单一载体和复合载体之间的过渡现象。

总之,以上分析表明,在典型的单纯载体功能出现的关系过程之外,还有许多过渡或重叠现象。一是单纯载体—属性小句内部各小类之间的过渡与重叠现象;二是事物属性小句中还有品质属性成分;三是包孕关系过程与物质过程小句之间的过渡与重叠现象;四是包孕关系过程与心理过程之间的过渡与重叠;五是存在同时与心理过程和物质过程有关的载体。

3. 属有关系过程

属有关系(Possessive relationship)涉及两个存在体(entities),其一是"属有者"(Possessor),另一个是"被属有者"(Possessed) 属有关系有两种表达方式:一是通过名词词组的方式,如"我的自行车",

"她的行李箱",其中的"我"和"她"是属有者,"自行车"和"行李箱"分别是各自的被属有者;二是通过小句来体现,如"他有一对烧制的貔貅",其中"他"是属有者,"一对烧制的貔貅"是被属有者。前一类现象笔者已经在名词词组部分涉及到了(彭宣维 2011 第六章);这里拟根据周晓康确立的框架对小句内的属有关系做具体分析;不同看法将随文指出。

根据周晓康的系统模式,与处所关系句和包孕关系句一样,属有关系过程也包括单纯载体—属有(Simple_carrier possessive)和复合载体—属有(Compound_carrier_possessive)两个大类。单纯载体—属有句由"有"(having)和"缺"(lacking)组成,如"他有一辆自行车"和"他们缺计算机":它们分别涉及"具体化"(specification)和"非具体化"两个次类。复合载体—属有句涵盖"施动者载体属有"(agent_carrier possessive)和"受动者载体属有"(affected_carrier possessive),如"他借到/丢失了一辆自行车"和"他获得了 500 万元人民币(的奖励)"。施动者载体属有关系句又涉及"临时属有"(temporary)和"非临时属有"(non-temporary);受动者载体属有关系过程又分"获得属有"(obtaining)和"终止属有"(cessation of possession)。复合载体类关系过程还可能出现第三个动作者,如"我把一辆自行车卖给了他"中的"他",是领受者(Client)(按照前面确立的标准,该参与者应当叫做"受益者";见彭宣维 2011 动词词组一章)。

此外,在周晓康的具体讨论中涉及像"李四被重感冒所折磨"这样的现象;在笔者看来这同时与心理过程有关,因为"受折磨"不仅是生理的,也是心理的。也就是说,属有关系过程不仅与物质过程连接或套叠在一起,也在一定程度上与心理过程连在一起。因此,这样的载体不仅是动作者载体,还是感觉者载体。而载体本身,不仅有"属有者"性质的,也有"被属有者"性质的。

3.1 单纯载体—属有关系句

根据周晓康的分类方式,单纯载体—属有关系过程包括"有"和"缺"两个次类,两者之下又分具体化和非具体化属有关系。但在随后的分析中我们将会看到,这里有两点与周晓康不同:(一)"缺"类属有句虽然也可以做出"具体化"与"非具体化"的划分,但周晓康涉及的相关过程成分中,只有"需要"等很少几个动词可以看作发挥了这一功能,"需要"的另一些用法、以及由其他一些相关动词体现的关系过程,应作为感觉者载体—属有关系过程处理;(二)单纯载体—属有小句中也可能出现第三个参与者"拥有者"(Owner);此时,拥有者和属有者错位。下面是关于"有"类属有句的实例。

(175) 这家子有一囤一囤的粮食。(阿城:《棋王》)
(176) 他可能有妻有儿,拥有幸福美满的家庭。(于晴:《为你收藏片片真心》)
(177) 毕竟,小小终究是他的,不是吗?(出处同上)
(178) 机遇毕竟不可能属于那些毫无准备的人。(《梁晓声小说集·京华见闻录》)

前四例系"有"类:(175)和(176)中的"这家子"和"他"是属有者载体,过程成分是三个"有"和一个"拥有",被属有者包括"一囤一囤的粮食"、"妻"、"儿"和"幸福美满的家庭";(177)和(178)中的"小小"和"机遇"为被属有者,过程成分为"是"和"属于",两者功能相当,"他"和"那些毫无准备的人"为属有者。在这四个实例中,(178)的归一度是否定的,其余的都是肯定的。

汉语中也存在不出现"有"一类过程成分的实例。例如,

(179) 这孩子这条嗓子(汪曾祺:《受戒》)

对于"有"类而言,周晓康认为,非具体化的过程成分总是由单音节动词"有"体现的,"从法定关系看,属有者和拥有者并非就很清楚",如她举例子说,"我有自行车"并不表示一定就是"我拥有自行车",而可能是"买/借/租/造"的;拥有者只是整个这一类属有者中的一个次类(对比 Halliday 1985/1994:132)。对此,笔者表示赞同,且看实例。

(180) 咱们终于在北京也有个房子了(刘震云:《一地鸡毛》)
(181) 李科长有一同学(出处同上)
(182) 我还有朋友(阿城:《棋王》)

就(180)而言,叙事者说他们"在北京""有房子",其实那房子是单位分的公房,而不是他们自己买的,他们只有使用权。(181)仅表明"李科长"和别的人("同学")之间的关系,并不是说这就是"拥有"关系。最后一例同理。所有这些例子均表明两个存在体之间的关系:不是属性,不是处所,而是某种属有关系:(180)按原文只是使用关系,后二例是社会人际关系。

上面所说的,是"有"类属有关系中,存在拥有者不具体的情况。

下面看拥有者具体化了的现象。对于具体化拥有者而言,过程成分分为"是"和"不是";前者如(177),后面是属有者加"的"构成的"的"字属有关系;后者如"李四拥有那栋别墅","他占有大量房地产"和"那栋别墅属于李四";在我们举的实例中是(176)的后一小句和(180)。按周晓康,这一类又分两个次类:载体导向类(carrier oriented)和属有导向类(possession oriented)。下面是有关载体导向的实例。此处带下划线的为被属有者。

(183) 他拥有<u>两家工厂和一家在镇上装修得最豪华的饭店</u>。(《余华小说选·命中注定》)

(184) 莫高窟确实有着<u>层次丰富的景深</u>(depth of field)(余秋雨:《莫高窟》)

(185) 山西在全国经济结构中曾经占据过<u>这样一个显赫的地位</u>!(余秋雨:《抱愧山西》)

(186) 你立即就具有了<u>与我一样的魔力</u>。(姜利敏:《且乐》)

(187) 这件事带有<u>一定的象征性</u>(余秋雨:《一个王朝的背影》)

(188) 我的导师在学术界享有<u>难以动摇的地位</u>(《张炜小说选·散文与文论》)

(189) 这片土地,竟然会蕴藏着<u>这么多的甘甜么</u>?(余秋雨:《流放者的土地》)

(190) 卢叔……对"野花"再也不存<u>半点浪漫</u>。(梁晓声:《一个红卫兵的自白》)

这些实例均系载体导向类,即后面的存在体为前面的存在体所属有,其中的属有者载体分别是"他"、"莫高窟"、"山西"、"你"、"这件事"、"我的导师"、"这片土地"和"浪漫"。由这些过程确定的载体都是单纯的,不带介体或感觉者特征。

下面看属有导向类。周晓康分为两类,即"是"类和"属于"类。实例如下,其中带下划线者为被属有者载体。

(191) <u>窑洞</u>……自然还属王彩娥。(路遥:《平凡的世界》)

(192) <u>你</u>显然应当属于我们地理学。(张承志:《北方的河》)

(193) 有的人历经政治运动越挨斗越胆大,有的人却看别人挨整也觉得害怕,<u>他</u>就属于后一种人(张贤亮:《浪漫的黑炮》)

(194) 然后,我把烂网套往墙根一撂:<u>这个地方</u>是我的了!

（出处同上）

(195) 全归你，连车都是你的了。(魏润身:《顶戴钩沉》)

(196) 只有这一刻他才踏踏实实地属于我，属于我独有。(姜利敏:《且乐》)

(197) 这不是我的发明!(路遥:《平凡的世界》)

最后一例容易和包孕关系句中的识别类发生混淆，这里，我们将此句加以改造，就可以清楚地看出(197)系属有类而不是识别类:"这发明不是我的"。倒数第二例还可以说成"为我独有";而常见的结构是"为……所有"。

如果"归"作"属于"用，它也属于这一类。对比下面两例。

(198) 你忘了我们的合同吗？你的一切归我们所有(王小波:《未来世界》)

(199) 家里五亩田归了人民公社(余华:《活着》)

前一例是有合同在先，因此，第二个小句所描述的就只是一种状态，相当于"你的一切属于我们";但后一例不同，因为它涉及到一个拥有权转移的过程(见后文)。

在实际语料中，也有"是"和"属于"同时出现的情况。例如，

(200) 它们也不明白山，不明白它们赖以生存的山是属于谁的。(张炜:《秋天的愤怒》)

(201) 这才想起父亲也是属于这个陌生的、不可理解的世界的。(张贤亮:《灵与肉》)

(202) 现在，连空气都是属于我的!(张贤亮:《绿化树》)

如果"是"和"属于"共现，则带有人际特征，即确认或强调。

单纯载体—属有关系过程的第二个范畴是"缺"类。周晓康举的例子是"我们需要两台计算机"和"我弟弟想要录像机"(第382—383页);而这里的"需要"和"想要"主要是心理性的，因此，上述两例应当看作复合载体句，即"心理过程"与"属有过程"的过渡现象。这个问题拟留到后文去讨论。但这并不排除"缺"类有"具体化"这一次类。下面是有关"缺"类关系句的实例。

(203) 剧本我已经写好了，就缺一个强有力的制片主任。(方方:《白雾》)

(204) 社会少了个寡廉鲜耻、假仁假义、自命不凡、趾高气

扬、放浪形骸、脑满肠肥、鼠目寸光的败类(于晴:《为你收藏片片真心》)

(205)我可不想欠他那种人任何一毛钱!(出处同上)

(206)他扯开大步,去找小福子。心中已看见了那个杂院,那间小屋,与他心爱的人;只差着一对翅膀把他一下送到那里。(老舍:《骆驼祥子》)

过程成分是"缺","少","欠"和"差";载体都是属有者,分别是"我","社会","我"和"他";被属有者分别是"……主任","……败类","一毛钱"和"一对翅膀"。

下面是其他有关实例。

(207)卢家的大人孩子不亏一副胃肠。(梁晓声:《一个红卫兵的自白》)

(208)社员欠集体储备粮一千三百多万斤(路遥:《平凡的世界》)

(209)日常在山里劳动,<u>大家</u>也都愿意和田万有在一块,听他唱几声,说几句逗人笑的话,<u>就少了许多的熬累</u>。(出处同上)

(210)她不具备这种泼辣性格!(出处同上)

(211)她也没有这种水平和智慧(出处同上)

(212)我现在摆的个小摊,短点本。(陆文夫:《小巷深处》)

(213)你还缺少像那些河流一样的、饱经沧桑的生活(张承志:《北方的河》)

(214)"九·一八"事变后,东北药材禁运,老号"百草厅"断了货源(郭宝昌:《大宅门》封四"内容简介")

其中,(210)和(211)是"有"类的否定形式,从而带上了"缺"的意义。但周晓康指出,"没有"并不意味着"需要";鉴于笔者将"需要"等事件看作有关小句的心理过程,我们没有必要在"有"和"缺"两个次类之间划分一条不可逾越的界限:两者应当看作是有对应关系的一对范畴,肯定与否定之间有类别上的对反关系。下面且看一例。

(215)英国说尚无伊使用大规模杀伤性武器的证据(香港凤凰卫视中文台 2003 年 3 月 27 日晨 10:44 滚动字幕)

这里说"无"即是"没有",亦即"缺(乏)"。由此可见"有"和"缺"之间存在对转关系:"没有"="缺"。

至于有关"缺"的具体化现象,可以从下面的例子得到证实。

(216) 你看需要不需要钱?(路遥:《平凡的世界》)

(217) 他正需要一只箱子——这些人显然知道他缺什么。(出处同上)

(218) 可是重开砖场需要资金。贷款是不可能了。(出处同上)

(219) 他问他们:"农民现在最需要什么?"老乡说:"最需要化肥!还需要自行车和缝纫机,不过,想要好的哩!"(出处同上)

(220) 黄原,需要现代文明的大冲击(出处同上)

(221) 象索恩这种人,只身来到中国,肯定十分需要一个理想的异性伙伴。(姜利敏:《且乐》)

但又要和下面这种情况区分开来:

(222) 在人民大会堂开会需要中共中央办公厅批准。(路遥:《平凡的世界》)

(223) 今天他……吃了一老碗肥肉片子,倒需要喝些茶水帮助消化。(出处同上)

前一例"需要"不能解释为"缺",而是一个能愿动词,"批准"为基本过程成分,因此(222)不是关系句,而是物质小句,"中共中央办公厅"为施动者;后一例的"需要"是一个能愿范畴,因为后面直接跟了动词"喝"。

此外,(205)中出现了第三个参与者"他那种人"。又如,

(224) 我欠了人一点钱(于晴:《为你收藏片片真心》)

(225) 去年国家贷款金额近一千万元,<u>人均欠款五十多元。社员欠集体储备粮一千三百多万斤</u>(路遥:《平凡的世界》)

在(224)中,"人"(即"别人")是拥有者,"我"是属有者,"一点钱"是被属有者。该例揭示了"拥有者"和"属有者"之间的错位情况:此处的属有者是"负"属有。在(225)中,第二、三小句都与"缺"有关,但最后一个小句中出现了显性拥有者"集体",载体是"社员";其实第二小句隐没了拥有者"国家"。

总之,单纯载体—属有关系过程是整个属有关系过程系统的基本类;我们与周晓康有两个基本不同点:一是在"缺"类属有句中虽然做"具体化"与"非具体化"的划分,但周晓康说的"需要具体化"中的某些

现象;在我们看来,应当归入后面将要补充的感觉者载体—属有句。二是拥有者不仅出现在复合载体—属有关系句中(见后文),在单纯载体—属有小句中也可能出现;此时,拥有者同样存在显性和隐性之别。以此为基础而出现的复合载体—属有关系句则是与其他过程(包括物质和心理)相交叉的重叠类或过渡类。

3.2 复合载体—属有关系句

按照周晓康的模式,复合载体—属有关系句分两个类:施动者载体和受动者载体;按照笔者的处理方案,汉语中有五个类,即除了上述两个外,还有中动者载体,受益者载体和感觉者载体。

施动者载体——属有关系句又分为临时属有和非临时属有。先看前一类。

(226)小林专门借了办公室副处长老何家的三轮车。(刘震云:《一地鸡毛》)

(227)镇上谁肯租房间给我们(三毛:《哭泣的骆驼·搭车客》)

(228)他从旧书店里买了两本哲学和政治经济学的小册子(张承志:《北方的河》)

(229)孙少安花了二毛五分钱(路遥:《平凡的世界》)

(230)我们储存着地球上所有人的资料。(出处同上)

五个小句涉及四种情况:(226)是临时属有中的临时获得,因为"借"来的东西终究要还,即只有使用权,没有处置权;(227)是临时属有中的临时终止属有,因为"租"出去以后"谁"还具有所有权;(228)和(229)都是非临时属有中的改变类,但前者是获得性的("买"就意味着永久拥有),后者是终止属有性的("花"掉以后就不再归自己处置);(230)是非临时属有中的非改变类,因此与前两例情况相对。

下面是有关临时获得性关系句的实例。

(231)河南师傅的家属可以借用他的一孔窑住宿(出处同上)

(232)吴仲平已经租好了船(出处同上)

(233)他放开胆量在公社信用社贷了七千元款,并且雇好一个可以操作制砖机的河南师傅。(出处同上)

(234)你干脆在公社信用社贷点款,个人再转借上一点钱

（出处同上）

(235) 少安知道请不动金俊文,于是就到山背后的王家庄请了一名高手;然后又在村中雇了几个关系要好的庄稼人,便开始大张旗鼓地为自己建造新屋。（出处同上）

(236) 他……又借出一本新的（出处同上）

(237) 我在南郊别墅租了栋房子（姜利敏:《且乐》）

(238) 还是小林和小林老婆好哄歹哄,才把人家留下（刘震云:《一地鸡毛》）

(239) 多少年来,兴隆场的田粮,以至于屠宰税码头捐之类都是由吴顺广家包去了的（路翎:《燃烧的荒地》）

临时获得性属有关系指以任何方式临时获得事物的使用权,典型的过程动词还有"租借""租赁""赁""佃""承佃""典当""当""抵押""典借""挪用""借用"等等,其中的载体同时是施动者,即动作行为的发出者。

与此相反的是临时终止属有关系,典型事件动词有"借(出/给)""放贷""放款""放帐""贷(出/给)""借支""出租""租借""出赁""招租""转租""包租""佃(出/给)""租(给)"等等。例如,

(240) 现在他们第一次给别人借钱了（路遥:《平凡的世界》）

(241) 我每人借给你们几十块钱（出处同上）

(242) 一是农场退出一部分地给农民;二是农场出租土地给农民。（出处同上）

(243) 三年前,她借给了这个多少有点亲戚瓜葛的船户五百块钱。（路翎:《财主底儿女们》）

与前一类比较,有些成分,如"借""租""贷",其内部的语义特征中同时包含临时属有和临时终止属有的语义特征。例如,

(244) 我们租下了一个小客栈的房间（三毛:《哭泣的骆驼·逍遥七岛游》）

(245) 我们在这一带每天借送无数东西给沙哈拉威邻居（三毛:《哭泣的骆驼·哑奴》）

(246) 信用社能给我贷一千块钱吗?（路遥:《平凡的世界》）

对比(244)和(242),后者是"租出去"的意思,而(244)是"租进来",矢量刚好相反;(245)中的"借"是"借出去"给"沙哈拉威邻居",但

(234)是从别人那里"借"来自己使用;(246)是"贷出去",但(233—234)中的"贷"是"贷进"。因此,这得依赖语境确定究竟相关过程所涉及的是临时终止还是临时获得属有关系,但相关事件同时具有对反的语义特征的事实是存在的,选择过程将剔除对立特征。

再看非临时复合载体—属有关系。它包括"改变"和"被改变"两类。前者又进一步分为获得性与终止性属有关系,如(228—229)。下面是有关获得性属有关系的例句。

(247)我把菱花送到接生站,抽空到信用社去存上了钱(张弦:《被爱情遗忘的角落》)

(248)朋友买了套西装(《百合小说集:长相守》)

(249)他牢牢地攫住了这夜晚的黄金时间(张承志:《北方的河》)

(250)美国一位专门研究超自然现象的专家自赖特·史德加博士,就写过一本《奇异的失踪》的书,收集了不少集体失踪事件(路遥:《平凡的世界》)

(251)有的人还跑到原西和黄原搞了营业执照(出处同上)

这些例子都是有关非临时属有中的获得类,相关过程成分是"存""买""攫住""收集"和"搞"。也就是说,一旦这些行为得以实施,在不考虑别的因素的情况下,相关获得者将具有占有和处置相关事物的权利:"钱","西装","这夜晚的黄金时间","不少集体失踪事件"和"营业执照"。下面是其他实例。

(252)莫非你正打算取得对她的监护权?(姜利敏:《且乐》)

(253)我是乐意娶一位中国妻子的(出处同上)

(254)我可不想在未来的三十年为自己招惹不必要的麻烦(于晴:《为你收藏片片真心》)

(255)除过买化肥和其他零七碎八,他现在还积攒了一千元。(出处同上)

(256)听说(张木匠)在外面找了好几个相好的(赵树理:《登记》)

(257)不知不觉之中儿子积累了这么多学问(王蒙:《坚硬的稀粥》)

(258)最好你金俊山一家人办个猪场,把队里的任务都包了!(路遥:《平凡的世界》)

(259) 咱大队自己炼出钢来啦！有了钢,咱就可以造拖拉机了。(茹志鹃:《剪辑错了的故事》)

(260) 儿子在外边搞上对象(浩然:《新媳妇》)

(261) 第五天,我穿上了新袜子。(孙犁:《山地回忆》)

(262) 你们跑了快半月,赚了多少钱？(出处同上)

(263) 少安……已经把烧砖的整个过程和基本技术都学会了。(路遥:《平凡的世界》)

(264) 那你们从哪里弄的土特产？(出处同上)

(265) 孙少平用劳动"掠夺"了这些人的财富。(出处同上)

(266) 我割了一斤肉,买了几斤白菜,还在中学大灶上买了几个白面馍。(出处同上)

(267) 这闺女！几时把我的罗汉钱偷到手？(出处同上)

(268) 我家大雁也会拣麦穗了。(张洁:《拣麦穗》)

(269) 小林……又用粮票换了二斤鸡蛋(出处同上)

(270) 她在厂里领了工资(理由:《中年诵》)

(271) 她一定是贪污了伙食费(王蒙:《坚硬的稀粥》)

(272) 王喜光黑了那么多钱(郭宝昌:《大宅门》)

(273) 提出这个绝妙办法的孙玉亭,几乎年年能"抓"到一头猪(路遥:《平凡的世界》)

(274) 叔本华曾说过:所有的男人都倾向于占有更多的女人(姜利敏:《且乐》)

(275) 几经折腾,现在不也终于混上了一个一居室的单元？(刘震云:《一地鸡毛》)

(276) 好好儿学,将来能拿大冠军呢！(阿城:《棋王》)

(277) 景琦赶忙编个理由支应着(郭宝昌:《大宅门》)

(278) (景琦)置办了一座更讲究的新宅子(出处同上)

(279) (我)不是想多讹他们一笔银子嘛！(出处同上)

其中,(273)中有一个"抓"字,是指通过"抓阄"的方式承担集体的养猪任务,谁抓上了"纸蛋"就是谁的事,所以,这也属于同一类。

总之,只要载体同时是施动者,过程成分与变更性获得义有关,被获得者是事物性的,就可以归为同一类。而"王一生赢了我"(阿城:《棋王》)应当作为典型的物质过程看待。这里的"赢"是"战胜"之意。当然,如果"赢"后面跟的是钱的数量或物品,如"赢了三千块",那仍然是非临时性改变类属有句。

下面是终止属有关系的实例。

(280) 有人走漏了消息(王愿坚:《党费》)

(281) 你去卖鸭子吧(刘振云:《一地鸡毛》)

(282) 就好象他在这地方丢失了什么贵重的东西(路遥:《平凡的世界》)

(283) 他不该把那床破被褥送了别人。(出处同上)

(284) 她很快把那张票向旁边"钓鱼"的人处理掉(出处同上)

(285) 狗贩子一口要价十五元。少平没讨价,付了钱抱起狗娃就走。(出处同上)

(286) 他把这半截纸烟扔掉(出处同上)

(287) 现在这些人用很便宜的价钱出售他需要的东西(出处同上)

(288) 交猪的人除多贴赔了几斤粮食,还得多耽误半天功夫(出处同上)

(289) 他们实在没办法,又开始千方百计贿赂收购猪的人(出处同上)

(290) 我不想掏这些财礼。(出处同上)

(291) 他发现他年纪的确大了,已经丧失尽了魄力。(出处同上)

(292) 我才不过二十一岁,这么快就掉入婚姻陷阱里,一点都不值得,起码过去五年所学的专长全浪费了。(于晴:《为你收藏片片真心》)

(293) 高手你入他很难,这就要损。损他一个子儿,损自己一个子儿(阿城:《棋王》)

(294) 人家打死我我也不舍你(赵树理:《登记》)

(295) (我们)快把她出脱了吧(出处同上)

(296) 礼品一周前他已经快件寄出了(姜利敏:《且乐》)

(297) 一年中,她花光了仅有的积蓄,还卖掉了两辆自行车。(理由:《中年颂》)

(298) 今天不容易,王一生来了,我再贡献一些。(阿城:《棋王》)

(299) 他把银子赌光了(郭宝昌:《大宅门》)
(300) 听说你还要辞了他?(出处同上)

下面的现象也属于这一类。这里的"白菜"不便作受动者理解,因为这是一个配备性范围成分,做载体。

(301) 白菜已经脱了好几层皮(刘震云:《一地鸡毛》)

但需留意不要和处所关系句混淆了。试比较下面的实例。

(302) 她就忙着为他泡了一杯茶(路遥:《平凡的世界》)
(303) 水盆里泡了一条雪白的毛巾。(出处同上)
(304) 一到中午,原西河里就泡着数不清的光屁股小孩。(出处同上)

第一例可以看作非临时性变更属有句,但后面两例是处所性的,因为涉及到处所成分"水盆里"和"原西河里"。

以上讨论的是变更性非临时属有关系句,包括获得性与终止性两个次类;下面看非变更性非临时属有关系句。例如,

(305) 整个社会依然保持着一种热热闹闹的局面。(路遥:《平凡的世界》)
(306) 他父亲下面的那座新坟,埋着去年去世的俊斌。阴间和阳界一样,俊斌旁边给俊文和他留出了一块地方(出处同上)
(307) 老人手里就留下一孔窑洞(出处同上)
(308) 她终于保全了名誉(出处同上)
(309) (我们)没办法为你老人家保存住这院子了(出处同上)
(310) 他揣着一摞硬铮铮的票子(出处同上)
(311) 他捧着一束花朵(出处同上)

所有这些过程成分"保持"、"留(出)"、"留(下)"、"保全"、"保存"、"揣"和"捧",都意味着各自的施动者载体"整个社会"、"金俊武"(按原文)、"老人"、"她"、"我们"、"他"和"他"在叙事的当时分别直接或间接拥有"局面"、"一块地方"、"一孔窑洞"、"名誉"、"这院子"、"一摞铮铮的票子"和"一束花朵"。这些属有关系不关心相关属有者是何时拥有这些东西的,也不关心以后是否会终止属有,所以与前一类"变更性非临时属有"关系句不同。

不过,有一些过程成分并非总是行使一种单一的功能。例如(311)中的"捧",表示那"花朵"此时归"他",不管这"花"是别人的,或者是暂时替人拿着。但(312)中的"捧"就没有属有的意思。

(312) 他捧起妻子泪迹斑斑的脸,吻了又吻。(出处同上)

但下面的实例又该如何看待呢?

(313) 人们的身上和头上都冒着热气(出处同上)
(314) 他头上冒着汗气(出处同上)

前一例好处理,因为"人们的身上和头上"可以作为处所对待,这样(313)就是一个处所关系过程;可是(314)呢?我们可以直接将这句话说成"他冒着汗气呢",即处所隐没。所以,笔者以为(314)这种情况当看作"属有"和"处所"双重关系句。

但问题是,即便"他"是载体,但该成分既无法归为施动者,也不是受动者,而"他"与"汗气"之间的确存在属有关系,即后者系前者属有。按照前面的标准和"冒"的特点,"他"从物质过程看应当是一个中动者。这样,(314)是一个兼跨"物质"、"处所"和"属有"两个大类(物质与关系)、三个次类的用例:"他"=中动者+载体。又如,

(315) 他身上装着赚来的六十元工钱(出处同上)
(316) 安锁子手里还提着一把电筒。(出处同上)

我们也可以将(315)说成"他(的)衣兜里装着……"或者"他在上衣口袋里装着/了……",可见其中"他"同样具有"中动者"和"载体"特征。

其实,仅就关系过程本身看,这种兼跨两个次类的语用现象不只和非临时获得有关。

(317) 反正我这里还缺几个服务生(于晴:《为你收藏片片真心》)

我们既可以说"这里还缺一个服务生",也可以说"我还缺一个服务生",因此,可将该句也看作属有一处所双重关系句。当然,这与纯粹的处所关系句不同。对比(315)和下面的例子。

(318) 老婆娃娃吃穿不缺,家里的木箱里面,还常压着千二八百的积蓄。(路遥:《平凡的世界》)
(319) 在小学大操场上,用白灰划出了许多道道和圈圈。

（出处同上）

这里"家里的木箱里面"是处所，施动者可能是指"老公"，这里隐没，后面的"千二八百的积蓄"是载体；过程成分"压"表明该句也含有一定的属有特征。但(319)不同，其过程成分"划(出)"主要指动作行为，而后面的"道道圈圈"则是结果。

最后是与前面讨论的"施动者载体—属有"和"中动者载体—属有"并列的第三个复合载体类，即"受动者载体—属有关系句"。按照周晓康的系统模式，该类属有关系又分为"获得"(obtaining)和"终止属有"(cessation)两个次类。下面是有关获得类的实例。

(320) 谁得了这种病？（出处同上）
(321) 她成熟了许多，但也不可避免地沾染上某些属于市民的意识（出处同上）
(322) 在上学期全校乒乓球比赛中，他竟然夺得了冠军，学校给他奖了一套"毛选"和一张奖状（出处同上）
(323) "冒尖户"除在春节后"四干"会上披红挂花"游街"以外，每户还要给奖励"飞人牌"缝纫机一架。（出处同上）
(324) 他得了一个全局男子单打第二名（出处同上）
(325) 这金俊山终究腿上挨了国民党的一颗枪子（出处同上）
(326) 孙玉厚一家人受到许多金姓人家的普遍尊重（出处同上）
(327) 他受到了教育局的奖励（王蒙：组织部来了个年轻人）
(328) 我相信很多普通电脑使用者曾经或多或少受到过"千万不要随意更改 BIOS 及注册表数据"的忠告！（友静：《揭开"BIOS"与"注册表"的神秘面纱》，中华读书报，2003 年 2 月 19 日）
(329) 这个名额可以让给你们（刘震云：《一地鸡毛》）
(330) 一个黄花大闺男，全给她们看光了。（于晴：《为你收藏片片真心》）

按照周晓康的系统模式，下面这些例子也应当属于受动者载体—获得性关系句的范围（见 Zhou 1997：372）。

(331) 如果他们获得我们的技术，就会……（路遥：《平凡的

世界》)

(332) 老祖母接过这块蛋糕(出处同上)

(333) 别人能得到的东西,你最终也能得到(刘震云:《一地鸡毛》)

这里的相关载体都相当于是"接"别人"给"的东西,因此相关载体是受动者;从这个角度看,周晓康是有道理的。只是相关成分的受动特征相对弱一些,而(332)中的"接过"同时具有一定的施动性。可见,这"施动"和"受动"只是一个相对概念;而且这里涉及到角度问题:从"给"东西的角度看,"接"东西的人带受动特征,但从被属有者的角度看,"接"东西的人又带施动特征。

不过,并非所有语境中的"接受"一类的成分都能构成属有小句。例如,

(334) 目前这些人正在接受调查(中央电视台一台2003年5月19日晚7:28新闻)

我们不能说这里的"调查"属于"这些人"所有,事实上,这个"调查"是一个过程性的准参与者,"这些人"是受动者。所以,这是一个带过程性范围的物质小句。

同样,我们也很难说下面这个句子和属有关系有关。

(335) 田福平接到地委办公室打来的电话(路遥:《平凡的世界》)

我们不能说"田福平"在"接到""电话"以后就有了"电话"。事实上,这仍然是一个带准参与者的物质小句。

另一个次范畴,就是与获得性属有关系相对立的终止属有关系。例如,

(336) 她给保安卸了一个戒指……保安把口里衔的罗汉钱送了她。(赵树理:《登记》)

在这里,"她"终止了自己对"戒指"的属有权,而"保安"把"罗汉钱""送"给"她",则是从"保安"的角度终止对"罗汉钱"的属有权。下面是其他类似实例。

(337) (王冕)七岁时死了父亲(吴敬梓:《儒林外史》)

(338) 那年我死了一个二姐(《沈从文散文选·预备兵的技

术班》)

  (339) 妻子失去了丈夫(路遥:《平凡的世界》)
  (340) 那座城市死了几千人,损失了几亿人民币(出处同上)
  (341) 一人罚款拾元!(出处同上)
  (342) 一双麻鞋磨掉了后跟(邵振国:《麦客》)

其中,(342)属于郭继懋(1990)说的"领主属宾句"。即主体与其中的一个部分在小句中被分离开来作为两个相对独立的成分出现。

(343)

王冕	死了	父亲
	过程:物质	中动者
载体:属有者	过程:属有	参与者:被属有者

在周晓康的模式中没有感觉者载体—属有关系句;笔者发现,虽然这一类现象不多,但毕竟还是存在的。例如,

  (344) 我存着侥幸的心理(张抗抗:《白罂粟》)

显然,这里的过程成分"存"与前面提到的情况有所不同,因为它所描述的是一种心理状态。因此,"我"同时是感觉者和载体,"侥幸的心理"是被属有者。又如,

  (345) 他需要大人的保护和温情(出处同上)
  (346) 我非要这个孩子不行!我早就想要个女儿了。(出处同上)

其他动词,如"指望""想""盼望"等,只要表明两个存在体之间一个对另一个具有属有关系,就属于这一类。

最后,我们来集中看一看那些同时具有三个参与者的实例,以及它们之间的关系(对比 Zhou 1997:406—413)。在笔者看来,它们与物质过程靠得很近。

  (347) 爸爸,你给老师买炭火了吗?(刘震云:《一地鸡毛》)

这里"买者"并非"炭火"的非临时性拥有者,"老师"才是。但施动者毕竟是"你(爸爸)","老师"虽然是最终的获得者,但毕竟不是过程"买"的施动者,因此,"你(爸爸)"具有占有和处置"炭火"的权利。该例中出现了第三个参与者"老师",是受益者,因此它在这里受益者载

体,"炭火"是被属有者,而前面的"你(爸爸)"是施动者。

(348) 春早,爹给你搞了个对象!(刘绍棠:《蛾眉》)
(349) 爸爸连个媳妇也给你娶不回来(路遥:《平凡的世界》)

此二例与(347)相比,虽然"老师"和"你"都是受益者,但前面的施动者"你(爸爸)"和"爹"的功能有所不同:对于前者来说,如果"你(爸爸)"不把"炭火"送给"老师",那东西还是购买人的;但我们不能说"爹"不把"对象"给"你",那"对象"就是"爹"的。差别出自被属有者"炭火"与"对象"上:后者有针对性(可见及物性是句性质的,不是词组性质的)。但无论如何,(347)和(348)属于同样的施动者载体—属有句,其序列是:施动引动者>受益者载体:属有者>被属有者。(349)也属于同一现象,只是被属有者被"连"字提到了过程成分之前,这是受主题化(Topicalization)的影响造成的(Tsao 1990:256—278)。

下面的情况该如何处理呢?

(350) 我让过去一个开车的朋友捎着买了一套钉鞋工具。(路遥:《平凡的世界》)

这里具体实施"买"这一行为的是"一个开车的朋友"而不是"我",但根据叙事者的口吻,是他自己"买了一套钉鞋工具","一个开车的朋友"只发挥了"捎"的作用。其中,"我"是属有者载体,"工具"是被属有者,"朋友"是施动者。其他实例如下。

(351) 我给你三天时间(方方:《桃花灿烂》)
(352) 糍……递给他一支烟。(出处同上)
(353) 七爷,咱们赔他二十块钱得了(张恨水:《金粉世家》)
(354) 他就把它留给了儿孙们。(张炜:《秋天的愤怒》)
(355) 这位小偷慷慨解囊,给王满银借了一百块钱。(路遥:《平凡的世界》)
(356) 他表兄前不久已把这活包给了别人(出处同上)
(357) 再说,他也不能悄无声息地给少安娶媳妇。(出处同上)
(358) 谁知新来的大学生……给他划了一个"迟到"。(刘震云:《一地鸡毛》)
(359) 我到农场来,我父亲给他带过信,请他照顾。(阿城:

《棋王》)

（360）我扔给她20元人民币（姜利敏：《且乐》)

这些实例涉及多种参与者关系。对于(351)，"我"是施动者，但不是拥有者；"你"是具有自由处置被拥有者"三天时间"的权利的主体；此例中"你"是属有者载体。(352—355)四例中的"牺"，"咱们"，"他"和"这位小偷"既是施动者，也是拥有者和属有者，三合一；"他"，"他"，"儿孙们"和"王满银"为受益性属有者（载体）。(356)中的"他表兄"可能是拥有者，也可能根本就不是，"别人"是受益性属有者。(357)中，"他"是施动者，"少安"是受益者载体，施动者和属有者错位。(358)与(357)同。(359)的情况稍复杂一点："我父亲"是写信的人，那么他就是"信"的拥有者，如果是替别人捎的信，"我父亲"就只是"带"的施动者，"他"是受益者载体，同时是"信"的属有者。(360)中"我"是施动者，"她"是受益性属有者，"20元人民币"是"她"的被属有者。

这里，我们来总结一下有关属有关系过程中参与者之间的两种关系。一是主要参与者之间的几种配置情况：（一）施动者＝拥有者＝属有者，如(352—355)；（二）施动者≠属有者＝拥有者，如(357)；（三）施动者≠属有者≠拥有者，如(356)；（四）施动者＝属有者≠拥有者，如(359)；（五）属有者＝受益者，如(357)。另一种关系是"属有"关系的角度问题以及属有者的类型。首先看(352—355)，在相关事件（"递"，"赔"，"留"和"借"）发生之前和之中，相关存在体，或"被属有者"（"一支烟"，"二十块钱"，"它"和"一百块钱"），为"牺"，"咱们"，"他"和"这位小偷"所有和属有；但当相关事件发生后，受益者"他"，"他"，"儿孙们"和"王满银"就成了属有者；因此，我们把这样的参与者叫做"受益属有者"，而"牺"，"咱们"，"他"和"这位小偷"则为"拥有属有者"。因此，我们得到几类属有者：施动属有者(350—358)，拥有属有者(352—355)，受益属有者(357)，中动属有者(313—316)和感觉属有者(343—346)。其间可能重叠，也可能错位。

因此，从系统上讲，周晓康的模式需要做如下修正（对于有三个参与者的关系句，这里只考虑拥有者和属有者之间的匹配问题，没有标出有关其他范畴的进一步分类）。

(361)

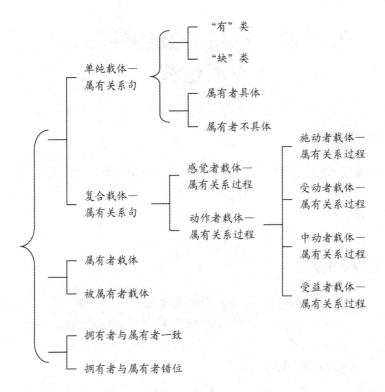

本章讨论关系过程,基本特点是描述两个存在体之间的关系,包括包孕和属有关系。基本框架是周晓康在福赛特基础上发展来的关系过程系统模式,具体涉及单纯载体句和复合载体句,但在具体分析过程中,笔者则根据现代汉语的实际现象,给予了相应修正与补充。

第三章 小句的及物性(3)：
心理过程

1. 引言

前面两章讨论了物质过程和关系过程；本章讨论心理过程。鉴于关于心理过程的描写是初步的，因此，我们将首先提出有关模式，然后提供论证。

2. 心理过程

心理过程，从典型性看，是物质和关系以外的第三类及物性语义关系。在论述小句的语义范畴结构"及物性"时，周晓康系统地分析了现代汉语的物质过程和关系过程；遗憾的是，由于篇幅所限，她没来得及涉及心理过程，只是附带提了一笔。

心理过程是有关人或高等动物的心理体验的。它有两个参与者。一是"感知者"(Senser)，即涉及心理体验的人或人格化的事物；另一个是被感知到的对象，即"现象"(Phenomenon)。所以，心理过程的功能结构是：感知者＋过程＋现象。这里有几点说明。

第一，从类别看，韩礼德(Halliday 1985/1994：118)将心理过程分为"情感"(Affection)，"感知"(Perception)和"认知"(Cognition)三个次类；周晓康(Zhou 1997：425)分为五个次类，即还将韩礼德说的"行为"(Behavioural)和"言语"(Verbal)包括在内。笔者取韩礼德的分类方式，理由如下：（一）根据韩礼德的阐述，心理过程涉及两个参与者，但如果将周晓康说的"宝宝笑了"这样的行为过程包括在内，就不符合上述标准；（二）直觉上我们很难说"宝宝笑了"或者"孩子们在说话"与这里说的"心理体验"有多少直接关系，虽然两者都可能受心理因素支配。但如果是这样，所有的过程类别就都可能划入心理类，这样就失去了分类的意义。尽管"宝宝笑了"一类的小句可能与心理感受有关，但在社会交往中的确存在主体没有任何高兴的情感，却装笑或傻笑,以维系或增进既有的人际关系。所以,在本书的体系中,笔者坚持韩礼德关于心理过程的基本分类体系。

第二,笔者基本赞同周晓康沿用的方案,即仍分单纯与复合参与者。从"自主性"(Volitionality)看,在典型的单纯感知者心理过程中,事件性过程成分(动词)都是"非自主动词"(马庆株 1988/1995:13—46);从现象看,存在"引动者"(Causer)与"现象"重合的语用方式,如"此事让他很着迷"中的"此事",一方面是引动者,引动"他""着迷";但它又是"他""着迷"之所在,故又为现象。当然,引动者也可能与现象分离,如"这事儿使他想起了自己的过去"中的"这事儿"(引动者)、"他"(感知者)和"自己的过去"(现象)。

第三,心理过程是一个很特殊的及物过程类别。即是说,除了上述情况外,还有以物质和关系过程的隐喻方式出现的心理过程。例如,"这一想法猛烈地撞击着她的心"和"他只好把这种思念深深地埋在心里",前一句表面上看来像物质过程,因为过程成分是"撞击",后一句像处所过程:"他"同于载体,"心里"是处所。这样的小句均可用物质和关系过程的有关模式去分析,但毕竟都是描述主体的心理状态或心理体验的,所以仍应作特殊类别的心理过程看待,或者说是以物质和关系过程的方式识解的心理过程。

第四,心理过程与包孕关系之间有纠葛,如"他很痛心"与"他对这事儿感到很痛心",前一句像包孕关系:"痛心"是描述"他"的;但与后一例比较,我们则很难将该小句排除在情感心理类之外。可见这里存在过渡情况:情感心理过程与包孕关系过程连成一体。但在具体处理上,我们仍然坚持一条规则:有两个参与者的(包括感知者或现象隐没或省略),就作为情感过程看;否则为包孕关系过程。但不能据此忽视甚至否认其间存在的过渡性和连续性。

第五,还有几种情况。(一)感知者或现象,其一隐没;例如,"这事儿很难想明白"和"他感觉到了",前者是感知者隐没,后者是现象隐没。(二)在复合心理过程中,感知者可能与施动者重合,也可能错位。例如,"她有意讨好她父亲"和"她让我想起我的妹妹",前一例是施动者与感知者重合,后一例中两者错位。(三)有环境成分被同时选择为引动者和现象的,如"娅为这个臆念激动不已"中的"这个臆念"既是引动"娅""激动"的起因,也是"激动"的范围(现象)。因此有非典型参与者——"起因环境现象"(Phenomenon of Cause)和典型参与者"非环境现象"之别。(四)还有"载体性感知者",例如"你的话使我感到温暖"中,"我"是感知者,但"温暖"又具有描述"我"的归附属性的特点;但这样的句子主要的还是心理性的,所以这里把"我"看作同时具有载体特征的感知者(对比前一章的"感知者载体")。

图(1)是心理过程的系统模式图。

（1）

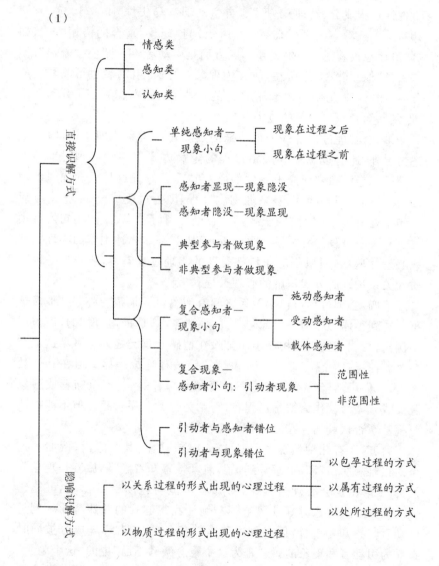

2.1 基本感知者—现象过程

这里主要从单纯感知者—现象的角度,讨论情感、感知和认知三个基本心理过程。我们说"主要",是因为典型的单纯句和典型的复合句之间不是截然分开的。

2.1.1 情感过程

情感过程指那些包含一个存在体对另一个存在体产生的"喜欢""害怕""惶恐""讨厌"等情感。例如(本小节中没有直接标明出处的语料,均出自姜利敏的中篇小说《且乐》),

(2) 娅不仅爱他,更打心眼里尊重他,赞赏他的艺术气魄和敏锐头脑。

这三个小句中的"爱""尊重"和"赞赏"都是同一个存在体"娅"对另外三个存在体"他""他"和"他的艺术气魄和敏锐头脑"发生的情感。因此,三者都是情感类心理过程。"娅"是共同感知者,系单纯类。

该类小句又可根据过程成分本身,分为若干次类,如"喜欢""希望""感激""介意/担忧""赞同/认可"等等。以下是与喜欢有关的实例。

(3) 普通中国老百姓喜欢这些
(4) 我喜欢他偎在我怀中。
(5) 也许你曾爱过谁?
(6) 他很着迷这些
(7) 索恩似乎也迷上了娅
(8) (越是意识到这点)我还越是醉心于他
(9) 而且(我)依然日甚一日地痴情于他
(10) 所有外国人都会因此而垂涎于娅
(11) (索恩)非常热衷中国民乐
(12) 并不是所有的中国女人都稀罕洋鬼子
(13) 有一些住在豪华富丽的五星酒店的异国游子,常常在厚厚的帘幕后面,注视着、品味着、怜悯着又常常是羡慕着你们?
(14) 可是娅无意于他
(15) 他反而可能会轻视甚至厌倦你
(16) 她憎厌那些人烟鼎沸的大排档,痛恨那些放肆吃喝、高声大笑的闲人;却又更加看不得摩肩接踵、娓娓蜜语的一对对恋人。
(17) 但他极其反感一切粗劣的东西
(18) 我用不着他们心疼(郭宝昌:《大宅门》)

喜欢类过程成分又分两类："爱"类和"憎"类。前者是喜欢的肯定极,如(3—13),相关过程成分是:喜欢,爱,着迷,迷上,醉心(于),痴情(于),垂涎(于),热衷(于),稀罕,品味,怜悯,羡慕等;其他相关成分如:喜爱,喜好,爱慕,恋,好(hào),嗜,宠爱等等。"憎"是喜欢的否定极,如余下各例中的是:无意(于),轻视,厌倦,憎厌,痛恨,看不起,反感;其他如:嫌恶,憎恶,痛恶,羞恶,恶,憎,嫌,烦,腻烦,腻味,腻,头痛,作呕,嫌弃,厌弃,恨,怨,怨恨,恼恨,仇恨,仇视,嫉妒等等。

其中不少现象成分之前有引导性介词,如"于";有的虽然没有,但可以加上去,如(11)。后面的成分,"他""他""娅""他"等,均可连同介词不出现。因此,这一类成分具有间接参与者的特征。这样成分就是系统模式中说的"间接参与者现象";它们与相关过程的关系不如"喜欢"等不需要中介成分的过程所带的现象紧密,后一类系直接参与者现象。

下面是感激类实例。(19)中"一辈子"一类的成分系度量性范围。

(19) 为此,我感谢你一辈子。

(20) 他不知该感谢或咒骂造物者的安排(于晴:《为你收藏片片真心》)

(21) 我不但常常感念我的父母……(《冰心文集第三卷》)

(22) 他知道苏小姐的效劳是不好随便领情的(钱钟书:《围城》)

(23) 他还能不对他们感恩戴德吗?(梁晓声:《一个红卫兵的自白》)

(24) 我一家子八口人谢谢七老爷(郭宝昌:《大宅门》)

下面是有关指望/希望类小句的实例。

(25) 娅总是希望自己象个非常现代的女孩

(26) 她实际上是日甚一日地渴望着这个目标。

(27) 此去的地方按月有二十几元工资,我便很向往(阿城:《棋王》)

(28) 小祖宗,我就指望你了!(出处同上)

(29) 他们不指着下棋吃饭。(出处同上)

(30) 大家就纷纷找了各种藉口请假到总场,盼着能见着王一生。(出处同上)

(31) 我期待他们再相遇的时候。

(32) 虽然小林不盼望自己老家来人,却盼望老婆那边来人。(刘震云:《一地鸡毛》)

(33)(你们)以后不要图你们面子好看(出处同上)

例(27)中的现象"二十几元工资",出现在过程成分"向往"之前,甚至在感知者"我"之前。其他希望类过程成分有:巴望,指望,梦想,望,盼,神往,希图,觊觎,贪图,憧憬,渴求,恳求,探求,追逐,谋求等。这一现象与属有关系中"缺"类连在一起(见前一章有关感觉属有者的实例)。

感激类过程成分常见的有:感谢,感念,领情,感恩戴德,谢谢等。例如,

(34) 他知道苏小姐的效劳是不好随便领情的(钱钟书:《围城》)

该句的感知者在句中间的"是"前省略了,当为句首的"他",现象成分是"苏小姐的效劳",基本过程成分是"领情"。

希望/指望类指相关主体的希望的,例如,

(35) 此去的地方按月有二十几元工资,我便很向往(阿城:《棋王》)

其中的现象"二十几元工资",出现在过程成分"向往"之前,甚至在感知者"我"之前。其他希望类过程成分有:希望,渴望,向往,指望,盼(望),期待,巴望,指望,梦想,望,盼,图,神往,希图,觊觎,贪图,憧憬,渴求,恳求,探求,追逐,谋求等。

其他还有"害怕"和"担心"类,如:患,(害)怕,担心等;"满意/自豪"类:(不)满意,自豪,"同情"类:同情,理解;"谅解"类:原谅;"高兴/悲哀/愤怒"类:迁怒(于),高兴;"感触"类:动容,激动;以及"得意/失望"、"灰心/惆怅"、"安心/紧张"等类。

由此可见,(一)感激类和希望类似乎不完全是纯粹的单纯类别,尤其是后者,事实上,希望类与认知类的关系紧密;同时,这些现象有主体的自主因素参与,还有施动特征,因此,这一类可以看作典型单纯类和典型复合类的过渡现象。(二)对于有些情感过程而言,后面无法直接跟现象,仍然以介词为标志,出现在过程成分之前、甚至感知者之前。此时,这些现象成分带有已知信息的性质。例如,

(36) 起先索恩也是很为自己这点儿优越感自豪的

如果"自己这点儿优越感"直接出现在过程成分"自豪"后面,就得用"于"加以引导。但这样的成分无论以哪种方式出现均具有间接参与者的性质(现象)。

下面是其他类型的实例。

(37) 人不患贫,不患难,怕就怕毫无希望

(38) 我是怕你们从中作梗(于晴:《为你收藏片片真心》)

(39) 她……甚至也有点害怕这些情景。

(40) 对可能出现的任何结果她都不曾担心过

(41) 她同情我的处境(巴金:《怀念肖珊》)

(42) 我不能原谅自己

(43) 他迁怒于你

(44) 席间傅氏谈到民十七年涿州入城守城之役,及去年抗日之战,大家均为之动容。(《冰心文集第三卷》)

(45) 娅为这个臆念激动不已

(46) 这再一次使她对弟弟大为惊讶。(同上)

(47) 潜意识中的你对自己目前的境况无疑很不满意。

(48) 起先索恩也是很为自己这点儿优越感自豪的

(49) 保罗显然很高兴别人这么说他们。

这其中有"害怕"和"担心"类,如(37—40);"满意/自豪"类,如(47)和(48);"同情"类,(41);"谅解"类,(42);"高兴/悲哀/愤怒"类,(43)和(46);"感触"类,如(44)和(45)。其他还有"得意/失望","灰心/惆怅","安心/紧张"等等。

可见,对于有些情感过程而言,后面无法直接跟现象,仍然以介词为标志,出现在过程成分之前、甚至感知者之前。此时,这些现象成分带有已知信息的性质。以(48)为例。如果"自己这点儿优越感"直接出现在过程成分"自豪"后面,就得用"于"加以引导。但无论以哪种方式出现,这样的成分均具有我们前面说的间接参与者的性质(现象)。

下面一例的过程成分"看中"是从两个基本过程成分"看"(生理性物质)和"中"(心理情感)演化来的,因此"看中"可以看作一个介于情感和感知之间的过程成分,或者说是基于感知的情感成分。

(50) 他们一起看中了一处较理想的商品房。

还存在现象隐没的情况。例如在下面这个实例中,"懊悔"的范围

(现象)是什么,在这里给隐没了,单凭这一句看不出来,须借助语境。

(51) 然而她并不懊悔。

而对于以下一类实例,它们一方面是心理的,但主要的还是生理的,因而应当归入物质类,或者说介于物质和心理之间:"惊"是心理过程成分,"醒"是生理性的行为,"惊醒"演化成一个词以后,重点落在"醒"上面。

(52) 正在睡觉的香秀被男人低沉地吼声一阵惊醒(郭宝昌:《大宅门》)

总之,(一)情感类单纯感知者过程所关涉的,是对主体的心理体验的描述,如是"爱"还是"恨","喜欢"还是"讨厌","得意"还是"失望",以及"感激","满意","恐惧","在意","同情","同意/赞同","谅解","高兴/悲哀","安心/紧张"等等;(二)现象既可能出现在过程成分之后,也可能出现在这之前,甚至感知者之前;(三)在过程成分之前的现象既可能是间接参与者,但也可能是直接参与者。

2.1.2 感知过程

感知过程主要与人感觉到的心理意识状态有关,因此,其现象就是眼、耳、鼻、舌、身等人体(或动物)器官等所"看见/到"、"听见/到"、"闻到"、"嗅到"、"尝到"、"感觉到"的东西。参照马庆株(1988/1995)的见解,这一类过程成分都是非自主动词,即这里所关涉的过程都是心理状态,不受主体自觉意识控制;而其中的"看"、"听"、"闻"、"嗅"、"尝"和"感觉"等都是自主动词,即主体可以通过意愿是否去实施相关行为。有相关自主动词参与的小句是行为性物质过程,而这一类复合性的非自主动词所关涉的则是心理过程。例如,

(53) 没有几分钟的时间,连云涛梳洗完毕走进客厅,注意到一地的杂乱。(于晴:《为你收藏片片真心》)

最后一个小句的过程成分"注意到"表明相关主体("连云涛")通过视觉输入了有关"客厅"状况的信息:"一地的杂乱"是一种心理反映。但这里涉及到两点:"注意"的过程与结果,故为"感知":由"感"而"知"。又如,

(54) 他特别注意到娅的嘴巴
(55) 明天你就能见到娅啦。

(56) 突然,娅看见了索恩

(57) 熊澧南,印鉴远,你见我兄弟老二吗?(《沈从文散文选·我上许多课仍不放下那一本大书》)

(58) 娅迷迷糊糊地觉察了他的意图

(59) (少安)隐隐地可以嗅到一种泥土和青草芽的新鲜味道。(路遥:《平凡的世界》)

(60) 你嗅见了玫瑰花的香气了没有?(王蒙:《组织部来了个年轻人》)

(61) 你连敲门声都没有听见!(于晴:《为你收藏片片真心》)

(62) 敏儿感到有人用力踩了她一脚。(出处同上)

(63) 她咬住下唇,直到尝到一股血味,她才惊觉自己在不知不觉中已咬破了下唇。(出处同上)

(64) 有一天,我正在山上干活儿,远远望见山下小路上有一个人。(阿城:《棋王》)

常见的典型感知过程成分如:注意到,见到,看见,见,觉察,嗅到,嗅见,听见,感到,尝,觉和望见等;现象分别是"娅的嘴巴","娅","索恩","我兄弟老二","他的意图","……新鲜味道","香气","敲门声","有人踩了她一脚","一股血味","自己在不知不觉中已咬破了下唇"和"一个人"。现象成分既可能是词组,也可能是小句;大多出现在过程成分之后,但也可能出现在之前,如"玫瑰花的香气,你也嗅见了"。这主要是出于信息组织上的考虑。

注意载体出现在过程和现象之后的。例如,

(65) 听见了没有,景琦!(郭宝昌:《大宅门》)

(66) 见过钱吗你!(出处同上)

下面这些实例中的相关小句也应当归入这一类。

(67) 一个护士来打针,才发觉她的心脏已经停止跳动了。(巴金:《怀念肖珊》)

(68) 他随着这声音从路坎上一间玻璃房子旁发见了一株小草。(《沈从文散文·小草与浮萍》)

(69) 我们……在门口遇见了表妹。(出处同上)

(70) 有一次,我见到一个战士(魏巍:《谁是最可爱的人》)

(71) 我听说有这种报纸,但又听说是内部的,看不上。(路遥:《平凡的世界》)

(72) 他半天才留意到润叶已经不梳辫子,变成了剪发头。(出处同上)

(73) 于是,她听到了表扬,这是她进厂十几年来第一次听见表扬。(理由:《中年颂》)

(74) 我却认出来人是王一生——棋呆子。(阿城:《棋王》)

(75) 他在这片湟水滩上的大小村庄里学到了很多东西。(张承志:《北方的河》)

(76) (小林)后来渐渐……学会了说"不,这事我办不了!"(刘震云:《一地鸡毛》)

下面这些成分做基本过程的相关小句也应当归入这一类:发觉,发现,遇见,见到,听说,留意,听到(见),认出等。注意下面的实例。

(77) (小林)后来渐渐……学会了说"不,这事我办不了!"(刘震云:《一地鸡毛》)

其中的"学"既可能是自主性的物质过程成分,也可能是非自主性的感知性动词。比较以下两例。

(78) 女小彭这些天忙着去日坛公园学气功,就把这事给压下了。(出处同上)

(79) 但他学了不很多(王蒙:《组织部来了个年轻人》)

前一例的"学"是行为性的,整个相关小句表征的就是物质过程;后一例中的"学"是感知性的,因为其后有"了"和所"学"之量。当然,并非后面跟上"了"就是感知性的。例如,如果我们说"他都学了快一年了,还没有学会","学"显然就是自主动词,因而相关小句也就是物质过程了。又如,

(80) a. 我小的时候,读到一段波斯的故事,我非常地喜欢它(《冰心文集第六卷》)

b. 他已经朦胧地读到了一首真正的诗篇。(张承志:《北方的河》)

(81) a. (我)只和人家见过几次面(刘震云:《一地鸡毛》)

b. 慧看过那么多娅在她的家庭环境中不可能看到的书。

两个 a 句中,过程成分"读到"和"见过"都是感知性的,而 b 句中的"读到"和"看(到)"则带有一定的过程特征。

还有一个成分"觉得",在不同的语境中可能是感知性的,但也可能作为认知过程看待。

(82) 他觉得他的手很有劲(张承志:《北方的河》)

(83) 这时小林倒觉得老婆上床就入睡是个优点(刘震云:《一地鸡毛》)

前一例是一种直接的感知认识,是生理机能传递给意识的一种感觉;后一例则是认知性的,与"认为"之类的见解性意义相当。这后一例所关涉的现象就是下一小节要讨论的基本议题。

又如,"觉得",在不同的语境中可能是感知性的,但也可能作为认知过程看待。后一种情况拟在下一小节讨论。

也有自主动词用为非自主动词的情形。如在以下一例中,"看"是"看见"的意思。

(84)(我)远远就看你呆头呆脑(阿城:《棋王》)

也有现象隐没的,如下面加下划线的小句,其中隐没了现象成分"这句骂人的话"。

(85) 娅斟酌了一下,又教了他一句:王八蛋!黄瓜蛋!索恩立刻学会了:黄……瓜蛋!黄瓜蛋……

可见,有关过程成分大都是复合性的。以"听到"为例。该成分是由行为性事件"听"和由此产生的认知结果"……到"组成。后者是前者的动作性结果(action result)。前者是自主性的,整个事件则是非自主性的。这在英语中也有分别,而且有时使用的还是不同的词,如 listen (to)和 hear,look (at)和 see。因此,从语法功能的角度说,这种结构当为学界说的"动结式"中的一种(见吕叔湘 1980:17,127;张涤华等 1988:105;另见梁银峰 2006;宋文辉 2007;施春宏 2008 等)。

2.1.3 认知过程

认知过程指那些与明白、理解、看法、记忆、熟悉或习惯、思考等意识活动(或者说是意识状态)有关的小句。例如,以下各例分别代表了上述各次类的具体语用现象。

(86) 娅觉得她完全成了一个被启蒙者。

(87) 我清清楚楚记得男同事一个也不少
(88) 地区管文教的书记我认得(阿城:《棋王》)
(89) 当然他起先并不知道你是位女作家。
(90) 她已经习惯了宋劲飞的存在(于晴:《为你收藏片片真心》)
(91) 所有这些我都反复考虑到了

其中,观点/看法类常见的其他基本过程成分有:认为,看待,小看,重视,看不起,漠视,鄙视,貌视,赞同,同意等。以下语境中的"想象"和"反对"也属于这一类。

下面拟就这其中的每一例提供更多实例,并加以扼要说明。先看观点/看法类。

(92) 呆子认为外省马路棋手高手不多(阿城:《棋王》)
(93) 索恩,你怎么能这么看待娅呢?
(94) 难道中国人就是这样想象他们的客人的吗?
(95) 几代沉下的棋路,不可小看。(阿城:《棋王》)
(96) 省委并没有特别重视有关田福军的这些告状信。(路遥:《平凡的世界》)
(97) 姐姐,我知道你看不起我姐夫!
(98) 因为我单凭直觉就知道,只有在真正的野地里,人可以漠视平凡,发现舞蹈的仙鹤。(《张炜小说选·散文与文论》)
(99) 他们既不鄙视普通人的世俗生活(出处同上)
(100) 我突然觉得很泄气,有些同意他的说法。(阿城:《棋王》)
(101) 我完全赞同。(于晴:《为你收藏片片真心》)
(102) 我一向不反对新女性(出处同上)

这一次类还应该包括"相信/怀疑"等认知心理状态。例如,

(103) 我真不敢相信他会为我吃什么醋。
(104) 此时,娅已深信自己已经无所谓索恩了。
(105) 他也知道,他们是信任他,才又求告到他门上(路遥:《平凡的世界》)
(106) 她坚信他最终一定会响应她爱情的呼唤的(出处同上)

(107) 幸亏人们没有都去信奉"庄子主义"（出处同上）

(108) 就连她都会怀疑他是不是个揽工汉呢！（出处同上）

(109) 当然，我们毫不怀疑整个社会将奋然前行！（出处同上）

(110) 有一点他们深信不疑：那一定是个好地方。（出处同上）

(111) 可我又不信人们说的那些王一生的呆事（阿城：《棋王》）

还有行为动词用作认知动词的。例如，(112)中的"看"实则是"认为"之意。

(112) 我看她恐怕太自信了

其他相关过程成分有：主张，认为，感到，发觉，发现，以为，当，坚持等。根据以上实例，这一个次类其实还可以进一步细分。例如，(92—94)可以分为一组，(95—99)可以分为第二组，(100—102)为第三组，(103—112)为第四组。值得深入研究。

下面是有关记忆/遗忘类的实例。

(113)（他）很小就会背诵上百首唐诗

(114) 可妈的话你得记着（出处同上）

(115) 这以后，大家没事儿，常提起王一生，津津有味儿的回忆王一生光膀子大战脚卵。（出处同上）

(116) 但愿善良的读者还能记住他（路遥：《平凡的世界》）

(117) 多少年来，他一直记得和女儿的那一次对话。（出处同上）

(118) 不用吃了上顿惦记着下顿（阿城：《棋王》）

(119) 我迷象棋，一下棋，就什么都忘了。（出处同上）

(120) 他们似乎忘记了一整夜的唇枪舌战（路遥：《平凡的世界》）

(121) 他忙乱和劳累，常常想不起她，但并不是已将她遗忘。（出处同上）

(122) 我忘了问您老二位了（王蒙：《坚硬的稀粥》）

记忆/遗忘类心理过程的基本过程成分，常见的有：背诵，记（着），记得，回忆，记住，惦记，忘，遗忘，忘记，想不起等。如，

(123) 可妈的话你得记着(阿城:《棋王》)

(124) 不用吃了上顿惦记着下顿(出处同上)

(125) 我迷象棋,一下棋,就什么都忘了。(出处同上)

相关过程成分还应该包括"怀念"等,如:缅怀,追忆,思念,想念,惦念,思量,渴想,念,悼念,追悼等。

下面一个大类是有关"明白"或"了解"的语用现象。例如,

(126) 可他怎么体会不到我心里其实有多么苦啊!

(127) 我还从来没有经验过这样一种发自深心的死去活来的爱呢。

(128) 我突然意识到他的情绪的真正源由了

(129) 他不用多接触便能领悟一个情境、一个女人的心理。

(130) 我也是女人,当然体会得出你这种心情。

(131) 现在娅已经感到了新生活的魅力。

(132) 他从那极富民族特质的音乐中才真正感觉到了中国的精神。

(133) 他通常懂得体贴娅

(134) 哦,我明白你的意思了。

(135) 这些道理其实你比我更明白

(136) 娅对索恩的话大惑不解

(137) 詹妮仿佛早已洞察了索恩的心思

(138) 我算彻底看透你了!

(139) 你不了解索恩。

(140) 你怎么知道是我?(阿城:《棋王》)

(141) 但我大致觉出是关于活着的什么东西。(出处同上)

其中(134)还出现了比较对象"我";还有例子中的过程成分是隐喻性的,如(130),(131),(136)和(137)。又如,

(142) 他能从艺术中窥探到中国的实质性的精神。

(143) 可是现在,他突然清楚地看到了一个尖锐的事实

(144) 但是我看得出他的思想矛盾得很厉害。

明白或了解类认知过程中,常见的基本过程成分有:体会(得到/不到),经验(过),意识(到),领悟(出/到),感到,懂得,明白,洞察,看透,知道等。这一类成分还可能是隐喻性的,如(145);还可能出现比

较对象,如(146)中的"我":

(145) 我算彻底看透你了!
(146) 这些道理其实你比我更明白

这一类还应该包括"疑惑"(不明白)等相关现象。

(147) 大家又奇怪是谁赢了(阿城:《棋王》)
(148) 娅正奇怪他们怎么会知道自己的。
(149) 全家人顿时都停止了干活,瞅着他的脸色,想知道外面的事态究竟怎样了?(路遥:《平凡的世界》)

下面是有关熟识或习惯类的小句。

(150) 哥哥认得他们(《沈从文散文选》)
(151) 自然他们不认识王一生(阿城:《棋王》)
(152) 现在大家只晓得倪云林是元四家里的一个,诗书画绝佳,却不晓得倪云林还会下棋。(出处同上)
(153) 他毕竟已经习惯妻子的这一套把戏
(154) 俊山精通乡俗礼规(路遥:《平凡的世界》)

在熟识或习惯类小句中,常见的基本过程成分有:认识,认得,晓得,习惯,精通等。

注意,在以下例子中,过程成分"熟悉"和"认识"对感知者和现象来说,是相互关系。在这种情况下,我们把介词"对"和"与"引导的成分"我父亲"确认为现象。

(155) 他们……对这地方熟悉得就象自己的身体一样。(出处同上)
(156) 他早年在我们市里,与我父亲认识(阿城:《棋王》)

还有"关心"或"介意"类,基本过程成分如:操心,体谅,在意,顾(及)等。

(157) 婚姻的事我们不操心也不行(路遥:《平凡的世界》)
(158) 后人们完全能体谅来你老人家的心情儿(出处同上)
(159) 其实(你)完全不必在意这种现象(出处同上)
(160) (她)完全不顾任何禁忌或道德束缚(出处同上)

下面是有关想象/预料类的几个实例:

(161) 根据岑对她的印象,岑能<u>想象</u>得出她在那种单位是如何的如鱼得水。

(162) 十多年来,小小一直<u>幻想</u>着毛叔叔到底是怎么样的一个人呢?(于晴:《为你收藏片片真心》)

(163) 我不能不<u>联想到</u>法律、规则等等与个人生活密切相关的种种问题。

(164) 但她无法<u>想象</u>居然能到这样的地步!

(165) 她原来<u>估计</u>二哥会支持她(路遥:《平凡的世界》)

(166) 人们早就<u>预料</u>砖瓦厂会在这小子手里成为一棵摇钱树。(出处同上)

(167) 她原来就<u>猜想</u>少平的日子过得艰难(出处同上)

下面是思考类。

(168) 田福堂听玉亭这么一说,倒开始认真<u>思考</u>这个大胆的设想(出处同上)

(169) 他也<u>琢磨</u>不来这孩子长大以后会成为一个什么样的人。(出处同上)

(170) 润生<u>盘算</u>就在这里吃点东西(出处同上)

(171) 她甚至还这样<u>想</u>过:将来能寻二哥这样一个男人就好了!(出处同上)

还有思考类:思考,琢磨,盘算,想(过),思量,忖量,思忖,思虑,考虑,合计,寻味,揣摩,想,构思,寻思,斟酌,衡量,掂掇,酝酿;猜想,揣测,推断,估计,估摸,料想,预计等等。

下面这样的例子应该作为同类复合过程看,即"认知+情感"(172)和"认知+感知"(173),这是由过程和现象一起确定的。

(172) 我从来没<u>经历</u>过这种情绪震荡。

(173) 而王运丰也<u>感受到</u>一种意识到自己的价值的愉快。(陈祖芬:《祖国高于一切》)

下面是现象隐没的实例:前一例隐没的现象应该是一个对象,后一例隐没的是一个事实。

(174) 其实他是<u>误会</u>了。

(175) 索恩把话筒朝向仍然开着的水笼,娅立刻<u>明白</u>了,咯咯地笑起来。

上面讨论了单纯参与者心理过程,具体涉及情感、感知和认知三个大类以及不同的次类。下面将以此为基础,集中探讨典型的复合参与者心理过程。不过从前面的实例我们已经认识到,单纯参与者和复合参与者之间存在过渡现象,而不是截然分界的。

2.2 复合参与者心理过程

就复合参与者而言,这又分三个大类,一是复合感知者—现象心理过程,二是复合现象—感知者心理过程,三是引动者置身于感知者和现象之外,从而使整个小句带上一定的包孕关系特征。先看前一类。在这里,感知者既可能是施动者,也可能是受动者。例如,

(176) 什么时候,为什么自己忽视了娅,淡漠了娅?
(177) 我都被你吓坏了

就前一例而言,"自己"是"忽视"和"淡漠"的感知者,但同时是施动者,因为它是实施这两种行为的主体,两个"娅"则是"忽视"和"淡漠"的作用对象(受动者)和现象(被感觉的对象)。可见,无论是施动感知者还是受动感知者,相关过程动词都是自主性的,而典型单纯感知者—现象心理过程中,其基本过程成分都是非自主性的。下面这些实例可以进一步说明这一点。

(178) 娅有意讨好父亲
(179) 你别站在这儿恶心我(郭宝昌:《大宅门》)
(180) 但金富和金强几个人还在那里贪心地挖着,气得玉亭又跑下去,吓唬这几个人说(路遥:《平凡的世界》)
(181) 这么说,你还是容忍了他?
(182) 索恩似乎抓住了她的心理变化。
(183) 听说你钻研象棋?(阿城:《棋王》)

前四例是情感性的,但"娅"、"你"、"孙玉亭"和"你"四个参与者都是主动实施"讨好"、"恶心"、"吓唬"和"容忍"四类心理行为的,因此四个参与者都是复合性的:施动感知者。后两例是有关认知心理的:(182)的基本过程成分"抓住"是隐喻性的,仍然属于认知心理过程;(183)"钻研"是主体"你"主动实施的认知思考行为,所以两个感知者也都是施动性质的,为施动感知者。这一语用现象所关涉的主要是情感类和认知类心理过程。

过程成分的施动特征还存在程度上的差异，对比(178—183)与下面这些语用现象。

(184) 可是这几匹牲口却没人关心它们。(张贤亮：《绿化树》)

(185) (你)让人总是无法摸透你的真实心思。

(186) 大家你望望我，我望望你，搞不清是怎么回事儿。(出处同上)

(187) 这里的知青在城里都是平民出身，多是寒苦的，自然更看重王一生。(阿城：《棋王》)

(188) 地区各部门和各机关的干部就开始纷纷猜测谁将是专员的继任者(路遥：《平凡的世界》)

前面对比(178—183)中的"讨好"、"吓唬"、"容忍"、"抓住"、"钻研"和"求"与(184—188)中的"关心"、"摸透"、"搞不清"、"看中"、"猜测"，我们能明显感觉出前一组过程成分的施动性比后一组的强，而(188)中的"猜测"就是单纯感知者—现象过程。如果这一认识基本成立，那么单纯感知者—现象过程和复合感知者—现象过程是连在一起的。这一点我们还将在下面的受动感知者—现象过程中获得更具体的认识。

而像下面这样的句子，实则是两个过程成分在同时起作用："说"和"服"，因此这不仅是复合性的，而且不是绝对单纯小句所能完全囊括得了的。

(189) 但他当时无法说服这家伙。(路遥：《平凡的世界》)

下面是有关受动感知者的实例。

(190) 我准备忍受一切屈辱

(191) 娅已被索恩对保罗的态度激怒了

(192) 他深深地感动了(张承志：《北方的河》)

(193) 别人倒吓了一跳(阿城：《棋王》)

第一例是通过过程"忍受"来表明"我"是受动者的，而"一切屈辱"是现象。第二例中"娅"是"被""激怒"的，所以是受动感知者，而"索恩对保罗的态度"则是现象；但很明显，我们也不能说这个现象就是引动者，只有"态度"的主体"索恩"才是引动者。第三、四两例中显然"他"和"别人"是受动感知者。

再看第二类,即复合现象—感知者过程。在这里,引动者与现象重合。例如,

(194) 没有一首歌曲使我如此感动(张贤亮:《绿化树》)

此例中"我"是受动感知者,"歌曲"是引动者,同时是现象。因此,笔者把这一类现象成分叫做"引动者现象"。如"你想死我了"(你让我很想你)中的"你"就属于这种情况。这一用法很普遍,且看实例(有下划线者为引动者现象)。

(195) 即使梦中,<u>他</u>也那样动人而令我着迷
(196) 有过索恩,从此不再会有<u>任何中国男人</u>让我有兴趣了
(197) <u>这样的交流</u>总是让人愉快。
(198) <u>这些</u>明显令索恩不快。
(199) <u>他的态度</u>令我十分失望
(200) 难道<u>索恩</u>就这么令人讨厌吗?
(201) (<u>我</u>)更不想惹他厌烦
(202) 到底<u>什么人</u>把她迷成这样?
(203) <u>这简直象一条悬在猫头顶上的鱼</u>,令它垂涎而焦灼。
(204) 虽然<u>这</u>令娅失望,却也使她感动。
(205) <u>如何使自己看起来既有魅力又不显得过于人为</u>,可真让娅伤透了脑筋。
(206) <u>这么回答</u>似乎自己心里也舒坦些。
(207) <u>这个大义凛然的发言</u>,怎能不使满座动容(《冰心文集第六卷》)
(208) <u>一绺绺白生生的花发</u>让我爱怜而酸涩

在这些实例中,感知者无疑都是受动者,而相关行为正好是由感知者所感知的现象引发的。其中,(195)中的"他",是"我""着迷"的对象(现象),又是"我着迷"的引动者,所以也是引动者现象。(196)中"我"所"有兴趣"的是"中国男人",但也是后者令"我"陶醉(负值),所以该成分也是引动者现象。余者相类。

不过,上述例句中现象与引动者之间已经开始分化:最后几例中的引动者的现象特征不如开头几例的典型。事实上,这是开始向两者分离的转化。而在下面的实例中,引动者则完全和感知者和现象分离开来。

(209) 这样下去,不仅苦了别人,也苦了你自己!(路遥:《平凡的世界》)

(210) (我)不能再把润生当小孩看待(出处同上)

(211) 这使润叶联想起了她父亲(出处同上)

(212) 可我让他明白了一个真理

(213) 张俊开始被徐文霞的叙述弄得不知所措(陆文夫:《小巷深处》)

这里的第一例是方式环境成分做引动者,其他的都是典型参与者,最后一例是间接参与者。

留心以下语用情况。第一,以别的过程的方式出现的心理过程。如"天热/冷/冻死我了","你气死我了"和"这水烫死我了"等,其中的第一个成分"天"和"这水"是引动者,"我"是受动者;同时"我"感觉到"热/冷/冻"和"烫",所以"我"又是感知者;两种功能相结合,"我"就是受动感知者。问题是,现象何在?看来这应当归属到后面要讨论的、以物质过程的形式出现的心理过程。当然,"你想死我了"中的"你"和"我",仍然分别为引动者现象和受动感知者。

第二,前面已有实例表明感知者或现象可能隐没。又如,

(214) 他的想法是要有一个象娅一模一样的女孩,娅经过仔细思考后同意了。

(215) 如果那老家伙打你的主意,你必须立即让我知道。

就相关小句而言,前一句中的现象"他的想法"在"同意"后隐没了;后一句所隐没的现象是"那老家伙打你的主意"这件事。下面一例是有关感知者隐没的语用现象。

(216) 娅也常常想解开这个谜,但这个谜非但解不开……

后一小句中的施动感知者在这里既可看作是省略,也可看作是隐没。

第三,有感知者与现象重合的现象。例如,

(217) 原来他们早几天已经在一次宴会上认识了。

(218) 很早他们就互相倾慕了。

(219) 他们断断续续地有一些不愉快。

前一例是认知性的,后两例是情感性的。当然,也有不重合但彼

此所指相同：

(220) 至少从目前看来,似乎一个比一个还要不信任对方

如果加以改造,(220)变成"他们彼此不信任",感知者与现象重合在一起。

第四,还有一种很特别的复合感知者—现象过程。例如,

(221) 我越来越生自己的气
(222) 但是娅不大忍心扫别人的兴
(223) 店主陈根本不上他的当
(224) 好几个老外打她主意
(225) 娅的模样、气质、观念都特别容易讨得外国人的欢心

第一句中引动者就是感知者自己"我"。第二例的"娅"为施动者,"别人的兴"显然是一个融感知者和范围的范围性准参与者。第三句中的"店主陈"当为受动感知者,"他"为施动者,但后者也是相关名词词组的一部分。最后两例与前三例有所不同。第四例中"好几个老外"既是引动者也是感知者,但现象"她"具有受动特征,后面有范围出现。最后一例的情形与前一例大致同前：感知者"外国人"是作为名词词组的一部分的形式出现的；所不同的是,前面的"娅的模样、旗帜、观念"是现象,而不像前一例那样是引动者；该例有些获得性属有关系的因素,这从过程成分"讨得"可以看出其前后两个参与者之间的关系。这与我们下面要讨论的问题有关。

这里小结一下。第一,从上面的分析我们看到,单纯感知者—现象与复合参与者心理过程之间并不存在截然的界线,其中好些过程成分既可以当作自主动词看待,也可以作为非自主动词使用。第二,在上面涉及到的这些实例中,有些引动者现象成分在句中同时做环境,引动者和现象三位一体。第三,从我们找到的语料看,这种现象基本上以情感类居多。

2.3　以关系和物质过程的隐喻方式识解的心理过程

在前面的分析中,我们谈到了过程成分本身通过隐喻方式体现心理过程的情形；这里来看另一种隐喻现象,即整个小句以物质或关系过程的方式出现,但实际上符合心理过程的定义：(一)心理性描述,(二)有感知者,(三)有现象。当然,过程隐喻和小句隐喻两者无法截

然分开。这里仅就典型的小句隐喻现象做一说明。

典型的隐喻性心理过程,即将相关心理过程以物质或关系过程的方式加以识解,从而以相应的过程的方式出现。例如,

(226) 那天索恩真是开心极了。
(227) 娅却又渐渐陷入了强烈的疑虑的包裹之中。
(228) 后来,(他)甚至还产生了许多美妙的欲望
(229) 霎时,象一道电光般明晰的直觉击穿了她的魂魄
(230) 事实上她这时也无力再承受什么新的打击了。

先看第一例。一方面,"开心"是用来描述相关主体"索恩"的,但它又是"索恩"的情感状态。因此这是一个同时具有心理过程与包孕关系过程的小句。前面说过,类似现象一律作为包孕关系过程处理,但这毕竟只是一个作识别用的硬方法;事实上,这一类小句同时具备包孕过程和心理过程的特点,尤其是当该句中出现"与我家人共度周末"这样的起因性连带成分时,其心理过程的特点就十分突出。因此,这是一个以包孕关系过程的方式出现的心理过程:它在形式上是包孕关系,但它本质上是心理体验性的。

再看其他几例。描述主体处于某个时间或空间中的状态的小句,当为处所关系(彭宣维 2000),因此(227)应为处所关系,但这里关涉的是主体"娅"的情感状态,所以这一类小句被看作以处所关系的方式出现的心理过程。(228)是以属有关系的方式出现的心理过程。(229)则是以物质过程的方式出现的心理过程,"……直觉"是施动者。(230)也是以物质过程方式出现的心理过程,"她"是受动者,但这里描述的是"她"的心理承受能力。

下面是以包孕关系的方式出现的心理过程。

(231) 那天,岑回家后不知怎地,总有些心神不宁
(232) 一出停机坪,娅的心就狂热地欢呼开来
(233) 我又害怕了
(234) 娅向索恩解释后,索恩反而更不高兴了
(235) 他的心境陡然又变得阴暗起来
(236) 那时的娅怀着的几乎是一种纯功利的愿望。
(237) 那一群群行色匆匆的路人揣着的是怎样的一种意绪

比较以下一例。

(238) 娅现在的心情是十分矛盾的。

该句的侧重点是就整个"心理"状态说的,而不是情感状态;因此,该句主要应当看作包孕关系。

(239) 这一行不对我的心思(张承志:《北方的河》)
(240) 这正合少平的心意。(路遥:《平凡的世界》)

这两句从形式上看很像前一章讨论的包孕关系;但它们说的主要的是心理的。因此,两例都是以关系过程的方式出现的心理过程。

下面是以属有关系的方式出现的心理过程。

(241) 她猛然产生一个强烈到无可自制的愿望
(242) 何况我初来中国后就一直存有这个野心。
(243) 太突然了,我一点没有思想准备
(244) 他……有一种过去年代里长久未曾重温的复杂情感。
(245) 有时候他便有了种疲累的感觉。
(246) 岑越听越觉得娅这事实在太复杂,令她有一种黔驴技穷的感觉。
(247) 它怀有深切而无奈的自卑、自罪感。
(248) 我想他根本还抱着侥幸心
(249) 她……老有一种讨好主子的欲望
(250) 娅很快泄掉了怒气
(251) 他丧失了兴趣

下面是以处所关系的方式出现的心理过程。

(252) 大写的"我"展现在她脑海
(253) 心理上竟有了种不适应似的感觉
(254) 岑的思绪不知怎么仍在娅那儿飘摇
(255) 丈夫没再吭声,心里却莫明其妙地生出种想见见这个娅的愿望。
(256) 不经意中,微微的一缕情愫悄悄飘漾在丈夫的心田。
(257) 一种愉悦的欣快感开始涌遍全身。
(258) 这类念头时不时地会在娅脑海中闪出
(259) 我愿意从此溶化在这种醉人而伤人的情感里。
(260) 至少它会令你不至于过于盲目地沉沦在情网中。

下面是以物质过程的方式出现的心理过程。

(261) 我不想让我的坏心情破坏你的心情
(262) 你的显意识几乎完全被他占据了嘛……
(263) (你)至少也可以转移一下自己的兴奋点
(264) 所以她乘机狠狠晾了索恩一把。
(265) 这个念头却死死地缠住了她的意识
(266) 母亲费了多少多余的心思呵
(267) 每天都品尝着简直是生离死别似的孤独、思恋和翻来复去的焦虑。
(268) 两人短促地调整了一下心态
(269) 这么些天来,也正是这些难以确认的信息在支撑着我,诱导着我。
(270) 一句话又触及自己的痛处
(271) 一种越发强烈起来的对索恩的厌恨唤起了她的自尊。
(272) 心情花儿一样砰然绽放
(273) 大学以后,娅的心态才慢慢恢复正常。

除最后两例外,其余各例中前面的参与者表面上看都是施动者;最后两例中的"心情"和"娅的心态"是中动者。

最后看下面这些小句。

(274) 她准适应那种环境。
(275) 难怪我会做那样的梦。
(276) 娅作过多少稀奇古怪而又美妙无比的白日梦呵!

该小句的主体"她"既可能是心理上,也可能是生理,"适应""那种环境";所以,这应当看作典型的物质过程和典型的心理过程的中间地带。第二例和第三例按理应作心理过程看,因为按照弗洛伊德的见解,"做梦"是一种心理行为,但在语言中,基本过程成分"做"通常是物质性的,因此,这两个小句仍然看作典型的物质过程和典型的心理过程之间的中间现象。

从上面的分析我们看到,即便我们严格坚持以结构作为语义分析的基本对象的标准,我们仍然无法仅就隐喻识解后的语义结构本身做出"自足"性的分析。这清楚地表明,语义结构分析是离不开对语境(事理)的参照的。也就是说,语义并不是自足的(autonomous)。

总之，心理过程同物质过程和关系过程一样，都存在单纯和复合参与者的分别。这里有几种情况，一是同一过程内部的单纯类别之间有连续现象，二是同一过程内部的单纯参与者与复合参与者之间有过渡现象，三是不同过程之间有过渡和连续现象。这最后一种现象还表明，小句在这里通过参与者和过程的功能复合，便初步脱离了纯粹小句的范围，多多少少带有一定的复句特征，只是这样的特征在有的过程类别中不明显，但在另一些类别中十分突出，尤其是当两种过程以一个句子的方式融合在一起的时候。同时，如果参与者跨出词组的范围，整个相关句子就有复句的倾向（如心理过程中的现象由一个句子体现时）。事实上，物质过程和关系过程存在类似特征，甚至更为突出，如包孕关系。小句也只是一个连续体上的典型范畴；而一旦进入复合参与者小句，相关句子就带有复句的特点。由此可见从小句到复句之间的连续性。

附录:主语是人际性的吗?——主语及主语结构的概念形式特征[①]

摘 要:经典系统功能语法将主语看作一个人际性的语法范畴;本文通过识别主语的标准以及相关语言现象对经典主语理论的性质提出质疑。作者认为,主语(以及主语结构)不是人际性的,而是体现小句概念意义"及物性"的语法形式范畴"句法";原语气成分中叫做主语的成分,在这里叫做互动语。定式成分具有双重功能:同时协作体现概念性的时间意义"时间性"和人际性的社交意义"社交性",其自身的语法功能则分别叫做时态操作语和语气操作语。因而,社交性→语气[语气成分(互动语+语气操作语)+剩余部分];在概念相度上则有:概念意义→主语结构。

主题词:主语、概念形式、句法、语气、定式成分、互动语

1. 引言

经典系统功能语言学("经典理论")将主语(Subject)看作小句人际性的语法范畴,即语气成分(Mood Element)中除了定式操作语(Finite Operator)之外的另一个成分;但本文作者发现,无论从定义还是从识别看,经典系统功能语法中的主语理论,都存在问题。笔者此前虽然持同一观点,但没有给予应有的理论阐述,和传统语法的主语范畴几乎没有什么两样(彭宣维 2002:100-110),因此应予检讨。

这里先扼要介绍本文的理论前提及相关对象。根据工作记忆原理,具体语言过程可以归纳为两个基本加工阶段,一是有关语义、语法和语音的经验图式的激活过程,且称为"第一阶段的加工";二是在语用原则和策略的认知调节作用下,从已经激活的相关语义、语法和语音系统中,选择有关成分,从而生成相关结构的过程,称为"第二阶段的加工"。只有第二阶段的加工过程中被选择和识解的语义关系,才是本文说的语义层,而不是此前的阶段,后者帕默尔(Palmer 1964)称

[①] 本附录原分二文、分别发表于下:"试论主语及主语结构的概念形式特征",《中国外语》,2006(1);"主语是人际性的吗?",《外语与外语教学》,2007(3)(与尚惠敏、刘娟、刘芳合作)。

为前语法阶段(见 Halliday 1966/1976：98；对比 Halliday 1973，1978；Langacker 1987，1991；Lakoff 1987；Lakoff & Johnson 1999；Fawcett 2000；Jackendoff 2002)，接近Jackendoff模式中"语义"和"语法"之间的"界面"(Interface)，只有这样的语义观才符合意义源于语用的功能主义精神(Malinowski 1923；Firth 1957，1968；Wittgenstein 1955/1999；Austin 1962；Harris 1998)。因此，经典理论中的"及物性"、"时间性"和"归一度-情态"是体现概念元功能(意义潜势)的语义范畴，它们是"主语结构"识解的结果。此外，本文只涉及陈述句，不涉及疑问句和祈使句：三类基本句子都发挥人际性的言语功能，但陈述句的基本功能同时传递概念意义，而疑问句和祈使句的基本作用只是人际性的。

本文将具体涉及四个方面的议题：(一)韩礼德的语气理论，(二)主语识别中存在的问题，(三)主语的语法形式特征，(四)相关理论阐述。

2. 经典理论的语气理论和主语范畴

这里暂不涉及韩礼德(Halliday)在1970年及以前的观点，只介绍此后比较定型的看法。韩礼德关于主语的基本观点是，主语是语气成分的一个基本构成要素(另一个是定式操作语)，它们和剩余部分(Residue)一起，构成小句的人际语法范畴"语气"(Mood)，相关语域范畴是语式(Tenor)。这一有别于传统语法的处理方案，似乎不仅能满足其模式建构需要，还有充分的理论依据。

首先，语气理论中需要一个功能成分，以便解释它如何维系和推动言语交往。一方面，韩礼德(Halliday 2004：107-108)将有关人际意义"言语功能"，即社交意义，归纳为两种交换关系：一是商品交换(Commodity exchange)，包括物品—服务(goods-&-services)与信息(information)交换；二是角色交换(Role exchange)，包括给予与索取交换(giving and demanding)。两种变量在选择中可以生成四种语义范畴：

  (i)["物品—服务"＋给予]→提供(offer)：would you like this teapot?；

  (ii)["物品—服务"＋索取]→命令(command)：give me that teapot；

  (iii)[信息＋给予]→陈述(statement)：he's giving her the

teapot;

(iv)［信息＋索取］→询问（question）：what is he giving her?

前两种被概括为提议（Proposal），其功能是物品—服务交换，因而有如下体现模式："物品—服务"交换→提议（提供＋命令）；后两种则是命题（Proposition），其功能是信息交换，体现模式为：信息交换→命题（陈述＋询问）。与命题和提议相应的语法范畴就是语气。

另一方面，他将语气的构成具体化，包括"语气成分"和"剩余部分"；而维系和推动言语交往的核心成分，则是其中的语气成分。例如（同上，第 69 页；下划线为笔者所加）：

(1) Speaker：　　　　　　　　Listener (becoming Speaker in his turn)：
Would you like his teapot?　　Yes, I would. No, I wouldn't.
Give me that teapot!　　　　　All right, I will. No, I won't.
He's giving her the teapot.　　Oh, it he? Yes, he is. No, he isn't.
What is he giving her?　　　　A teapot. I don't know; sha'n't tell you.

即是说，正是小句中那些"在一系列修辞性交换中被颠来倒去的"部分，发挥了相关交际功能（第 111 页）。这一点集中体现在主要以类似成分交替出现的言语交往中，如 I would，I wouldn't，I will，I won't，is he，he is，he isn't 等。在韩礼德看来，这个核心成分正是人们普遍接受的"主语"和"定式成分"；说话人使用主语来行使一定职责，使小句作为交际事件而发挥作用。说话人将其交际意图负载于"主语＋定式操作语"这一结构上，"要求听话人予以承应。"（第 117 页）其测试手段是附加疑问句：被复制到附加疑问句中的是主语和定式操作语。至此，一切历史遗留问题似乎就得到了完满解决。

其次，当韩礼德将主语确认为一个人际语法范畴时，其立足点是功能定性和理论传统。一方面，他试图给主语指派一个语义性的功能地位（第 112 页）：

"主语"这一术语与早先的"语法主语"一致；但在这里我们拟从功能的角度给予重新解释。主语不是一个纯粹的形式范畴；像其他语法功能一样，从根源上讲它是语义性的。

他进一步说：主语为一则命题的形成提供某种东西，即相关命题内某种可以被肯定或否定的东西（第 117 页）。于是，将主语看作人际性的语法范畴似乎便有了充分理由（第 110 页）：

当语言被用来交换信息时,小句以命题的形式出现。于是,命题就成了某种可以争论的东西——某种可以肯定或否定的东西,还可以被怀疑、反驳、强调、有保留地接受、限制、调节、悔恨等等。

这一点似乎显得尤为有力,因为有整个西方传统作支柱。而无论是从语言学还是从哲学的角度看,这一传统至少在亚里士多德时期就开始了。例如,亚氏在论述肯定命题和否定命题以及全称命题与非全称命题时,就提到了"断言或否认"所关涉的"可能性、不可能性、偶然性、必然性"(《亚里士多德全集》第一卷第 69 页;简称《全集》)。这似乎就为韩礼德将主语重新解释为一个人际性的语法范畴、对命题实施各种操作的手段,提供了理论来源。

然而,上述观点对我们认识有关语言现象,实际上是误导。笔者的基本问题是:为什么不能将"语气+剩余部分"分析为一个独立于主语结构的范畴、而主语结构另做解释呢?下面首先说明两者分离的事实依据,然后指出经典理论以命题作为出发点存在的问题。

3. 经典模式中主语识别存在的问题分析

韩礼德说小句的语气成分是由主语加定式操作语构成的;但在具体分析中"主语结构"和"语气结构"则被分别处理为两个层次,即(一)主语结构:"主语+定式操作语+述语+补语+状语",(二)语气结构:"语气成分+剩余部分"。本文以为,如果将两者看作一体,会显得很牵强:这显然是两种彼此独立的结构关系。尽管有不少系统功能派学者对"主语+定式操作语"的人际性,从不同角度做过阐述,但何以将两者看作一体而仅仅体现社交功能?此外,巴特等人(Butt *et al* 2000:91)阐述道:"语气和语气成分是给予主语、定式范畴和归一度的称谓"(the name **given** to the Subject and Finite plus the polarity)(黑体为笔者所加;也见 Eggins 1994 第 6 章)。因此我们就有可能在主语结构和语气结构之间划分一条界线,因为"给予"这一行为可能完全是人为的。

从韩礼德的分析看,是"主语+定式操作语"被看作语气范畴的内在构成成分的;但笔者认为这只是巧合:英语中仍然存在主语和语气成分中相关构成范畴分离的现象。而将语气成分中名词组所体现的范畴看作主语,其实是将两种性质不同的范畴混为一谈了。

这里涉及主语的识别问题。一方面,按照传统语法,作主语的名词组与谓语定式动词之间有数的一致关系(如 Biber *et al* 1999:180-192;这个问题很复杂,可另见 Sun 1979)。据此,以下句子中加下划线的成分即为相应各句的主语[①]。

(2) <u>The schedule</u> leaves a wide margin of time for self-study, doesn't it?

(3) There were <u>two caterpillars</u> on the leaf, weren't there?[②]

(4) In the garden are planted <u>three orange trees</u>, aren't there?

但另一方面,"主语在附加疑问句中以代词的形式复现"(Quirk *et al* 1985:725;也见 Lakoff 1987:547)。这样就只有(2)一类的句子才同时符合两条标准;(3)和(4)都有问题:据前一标准,两个名词组为各句的主语;据后一条,there 为(3)的主语,但(4)呢?

为此,一些语言学家提出了补救措施。例如,Jespersen(1949Ⅶ:109)将存在句中的 there 看作准主语(Quasi-)。夸克(同上,第1403-1406页)则叫做语法主语(Grammatical),与名词性实义主语(Notional)相对,如(3)中的 two caterpillars。但仅仅贴上一个标签并没有从理论上解决问题:如果主语存在"语法"和"实义"之别,那么"主语"应该是一个什么样的范畴呢,语义的、语用的、还是语法的?无论哪一种定性说明都成问题;there 与所谓的实义主语之间,缺乏像"先行主语"(Anticipatory)和"后置主语"(Postponed)那样的内在关系,例如,

(5) <u>It</u> was on the news <u>that income tax is to be lowered</u>.

此外,我们找不到别的直接语义关系。所以,笔者很难将(3)中的 there 与 two caterpillars 以及(4)中的 in the garden 与 three orange trees 均看作同一类范畴。

那么,附加疑问句的功能是什么呢?附加疑问句有升、降两种语

[①] 三例均系作者自拟,并分别得到三名被询人(英语为本族语,分别来自英国、加拿大和澳大利亚)认可。此外,他们还一致认为,对于(3)的附加疑问句,除了 aren't there 之外,还可以说 don't we 或 don't they。

[②] 有人向我指出,用存在句的"例外"情况来反驳底气不足,理由是这只是一个孤例。笔者的看法是,这里所举的确只有一例,但存在句广泛存在:(2)所代表的是一大类语言现象,且相当复杂(如 Lakoff 1987 等),在笔者看来,有关问题还远未解决。

调,分别体现两种功能。升调是说话人指望听话人对相关陈述的命题做出真实与否的决断;如果是降调,说话人则希望听话人对相关陈述给予肯定回答,因而具有感慨而不是疑问的功能(Quirk et al 1985:811)。因此,无论是升调还是降调,其基本功能都是人际性的,即促动听话人参与话语交际,做出相关应答。而这正是语气成分所体现的基本人际功能。据此,笔者主张将带有附加疑问句的句子看作两个相对独立的小句:前面的陈述句同时发挥概念和人际功能,而后面的附加疑问句则只有人际意义(对比 Fawcett 1999)。

这样看来,传统语法中由识别主语的两条基本标准所确立的语法范畴,应该是两个不同的概念。换言之,以名词组与相关动词的数的一致关系为标准所确立的范畴,与以附加疑问句作为测试标准所识别的语法范畴,是两个概念而非同一范畴。一方面,韩礼德采用了后一条标准,这样识别出来的范畴就是人际性的,而由此确立的、关于语气的整体框架则合理地解释了有关现象,这是他的重要贡献。但附加疑问句中那个复制成分所回指的,并非总是主语!另一方面,由一致标准确立的是一个什么样的语法范畴呢?这个问题的确存在,因为传统语法指出的这一类现象,经典理论并没有给出合理解释;2004年以前韩礼德对这个十分重要的问题忽略不计。虽然新版《导论》补充指出,相关动词的人称和数的格标记在当代英语中已基本消失(Halliday 2004:119),不足为虑①;但任何一个懂英语的人都知道,有关单数主语的动词后加-s的情况,仍然普遍存在;如果将德语、法语和俄语等其他印欧语考虑在内,无论何种人称都存在类似标记现象。

下面是有关德语、法语和俄语的例子,并配相应的汉语译文;目的是试图表明这些语言中句子主语的性、数、格与谓语动词的形态变化之间存在对应关系。

先看德语。德语中主语与谓语的对应关系非常严格,谓语动词受不同人称(我、你、他/她/它、我们、你们、他们、您/您们)的制约,谓语动词必须随主语变化。例如:

---

① 其实这个问题与经典理论一向主张的"概率"问题有关。这虽然是经典理论的基石之一,但这并不意味着:概率就是一切,韩礼德也从来没有这样说过或暗示过;而据笔者所知,语言学界也没有任何其他人说过"概率"就是确立范畴的首要和唯一条件。其实,历时语言研究中对许多范畴的构拟,从来都不是从概率出发的;相反,研究语言的历时发展进程的语言学家们,通常最担心(也是最小心)的,就是从现当代语言现象的概率出发来考察其历时演化过程。

（6）*Ich* **komme** zu dir.（我到你这儿来）

（7）*Er* **kommt** zu mir.（他到我这儿来）

（8）*Sie* **kommen** zu mir.（他们到我这儿来）

以上三个例句为现在时，谓语动词 kommen（来）随主语的人称变化而变化。又如，

（9）*Du* **kannst** zu mir kommen.（你可以到我这儿来）

（10）*Er* **kann** zu mir kommen.（他可以到我这儿来）

（11）*Sie* **können** zu mir kommen.（他们可以到我这儿来）

这三个例句也为现在时，但带有情态助动词 können（能、能够、可以），它与主要动词的不定式（即：动词原形）一起构成复合谓语。情态助动词须随主语的人称变化而变化，主要动词以不定式的形式位于句末。

（12）*Ich* **bin** in Beijing angekommen.（我到达北京了）

（13）*Er* **ist** in Beijing angekommen.（他到达北京了）

（14）*Sie* **sind** in Beijing angekommen.（他们到达北京了）

以上三个例句为现在完成时，表示在说话之前动作已经完成，但与现在仍有关系。德语的现在完成时由"时间助动词 haben 或 sein（随主语人称而变化）＋主要动词的第二分词"构成，时间助动词的选用须视主要动词而定。例句中的 angekommen 是主要谓语动词 ankommen（到达）的第二分词，要求的时间助动词是 sein。句中的 bin、ist、sind 是时间助动词 sein 与主语"我"、"他"、"他们"的对应变化形式。

再看俄语：

（15）*Мальчик* каждый день **опаздывает** на урок.（男孩每天上课都迟到）

（16）*Мальчик* сегодня **опоздал** на урок.（男孩今天上课迟到了）

（17）*Мальчик и девочка* каждый день **опаздывают** на урок.（男孩和女孩每天上课都迟到）

（18）*Девочка* сегодня **опоздала** на урок.（女孩今天上课迟到了）

（19）*Мальчик и девочка* сегодня **опоздали** на урок.（男孩和

女孩今天上课都迟到了)

在俄语中句子的谓语动词与主语之间存在着严格的对应关系。它不但受到主语的性、数的制约,还取决于主语行为的时间和状态。例句(15)中句子的主语 мальчик(男孩)的行为是经常性的,所以与之相对应的谓语动词以完成体的现在时形式 опаздывает 出现。(16)中"男孩"的行为是已完成的一次性行为,所以使用的是谓语动词完成体的过去时 опоздал。(17)中主语是复数,其行为是经常性的,因此谓语相应的则是未完成体的现在时的复数形式 опаздывают。(18)中主语是阴性,故谓语动词是 опоздала,而不是 опоздал。(19)表示的是两个人已完成的一次性过去行为,所以谓语动词是 опоздать 一词的复数形式的过去时 опоздали。

法语虽然不及德语和俄语的变化丰富,但毕竟这种对应关系很明显。例如,

(20) *Je* **pars** pour l'Amérique avec quelques amis intimes.(我和几个好朋友动身去美洲)

(21) *Nous* **partons** d'un éclat de rire.(我们有时会突然大笑起来)

(22) *Elle* **est partie** à trois heures.(她三点钟走了)

以上三句话的谓语动词存在明显的形态变化,它们分别是 pars, partons, est partie,其实都是从同一个动词 partir("离开"的原形)变化来的,因主语 Je(第一人称单数名词),nous(第一人称复数名词)和 elle(第三人称单数名词)不同。事实上,法语中所有定式动词都要随主语数、性等的变化而变化;第三句是复合过去时,过去分词因主语是阴性而要加 e。

这些现象足以说明,小句中有一个名词词组与相关动词有内在联系;这个名词词组就是主语。按照我们的理解,即便其间没有上述形式标记,这种内在联系也能通过语义关系得到间接说明。因此,相关名词组的功能不能避而不谈;而存在句只不过是把相关功能揭示出来了。

但是,与英语不同,德语、俄语和法语中有关存在句反疑问句,与英语不同,倒是与汉语接近,即前面的相关名词词组没有关系。例如,以下各对实例中的反疑问成分都一样(斜体成分为相应小句的主语):

(23) In Deutschland gibt *es* viele chinesische Studenten,**nicht wahr**?（es 为形式主语，viele chinesische Studenten 为宾语；翻译：在德国有许多中国大学生,是不是?）

(23') Sind *Sie* Stefan Holz,**nicht wahr**?（您是施特芬·霍尔茨先生,是吧?）

(24) У *них* есть много денег,**правда**?（他们有很多钱,是吗/不是吗?）

(24') *Эта девушка* очень красивая,**правда**?（这个女孩很漂亮,是吧?）

(25) Il n'y a plus de *doute* possible,**n'est ce pas**?（不会再有疑问了,对不对/不是吗?）

(25') *Les concierges* ont toujours tenu une grande place dans la vie parisienne dans la littérature,**n'est ce pas**?（守门人在文学作品所描写的巴黎人的生活中总是占有重要位置,对不对/不是吗?）

至于新版《导论》认为的"结构主义传统下的主语是一个纯粹的语法成分,在句法层的操作中没有语义可言"（同上），则是另一回事;本文说的主语是有语义的,即小句的概念意义（彭宣维 2011：290—325）。就是说,与动词有数的一致关系（无论显、隐）的那个名词组就是主语,附加疑问句中以代词身份出现的那个成分不一定同时是主语,而那个代词本身的功能也并非主语。主语结构和语气结构应当分离开来处理;即便多数情况下,复制代词就是前面陈述句中的名词组（主语）,但这只是重叠问题,此时相关名词组具有双重功能:既协作构成语气成分,也做主语。试比较对(2)和(3)两例所做的分析：

(a)

the schedule	leaves a wide margin of time for self-study
主语	谓语
语气成分	剩余成分

(b)

there	were	two caterpillars	on the leaf
谓		主语	语
语气成分		剩余成分	

此外,经典理论从命题的角度寻找理论依据也值得商榷;我们拟

从根源上来梳理这一点。其实命题是一个同时具有概念性和人际性的复合概念；韩礼德所以将主语看作一个人际性语法次范畴，其理论出发点直接与命题和提议有关。而这一点可以追溯到古希腊哲学家那里。例如，亚里士多德在论述命题的基本类别时，涉及到命题的肯定与否定、全称与非全称、简单与复合、矛盾与非矛盾等问题。这些均同时涉及命题的概念意义。以矛盾命题与非矛盾命题为例，亚氏有以下论述（在哲学领域 subject 被译为"主项"；出处同前，第 54 页）：

> 如若两个命题的主项相同，肯定命题的主项是全称的，否定命题的主项不是全称的，那我们就把这两个命题称为相对立的矛盾命题，如"所有的人都是白的"和"并非所有的人都是白的"，以及类似的命题。再如，"有些人是白的"，在我所说的矛盾意义上，就与"没有一个人是白的"相对立。

而矛盾命题所牵涉的则是经验事理，后者与概念意义所体现的经验知识范畴有关，属于语场的范围。这一点在亚氏之后的语言学研究中屡有论及，如 19 世纪法国的魏尔（Weil 1844/1978）在论及表达出发点时就是以命题的概念意义为依据的。

又如，肯定命题与否定命题，在系统功能理论中被概括和阐述为一种语义范畴，即归一度（Polarity）；它同时与经验意义和人际意义有关；而与此相关的全称命题与非全称命题（ALL and NON-ALL Propositions），在当代诸多文献（包括 Halliday 理论）之中被进一步阐述为情态（Polarity），在系统功能语言学的理论阐述中也同时涉及概念意义和人际意义（见 Halliday 2004：126—130；胡壮麟等 2005：124—125）。

此外，命题还与动词的时态有关，而这一点所体现的经验意义十分突出。如亚里士多德所述（《全集·解释篇》第 5 章 52—53 页）：

> 所有命题都含有一个动词或一种动词的时态。甚至'人'的定义，如若不增加'现在是'、'过去是'、'将来是'或某些这一类的词，那么它根本无法形成命题……在各种命题中存在着简单命题，如肯定某事物的某种东西，或否定某事物的某种东西，另一种是复合命题，如由简单命题构成的命题。简单命题是一种有意义的表述，它肯定或否定某一事物在过去、现在或将来的存在。

这里除了命题的时间性外，还涉及到了简单与复合命题。这些阐述显然与小句的概念意义有关(参阅 Halliday 2004 年第 6、7 章有关动词词组和复句的概念意义的论述)。因此,鉴于命题同时涉及概念义和人际义,我们就很难说与命题有关的主语一定就是人际性的了。

这里就相关议题做一小结。第一,在多数情况下,那些作主语的相关名词组,具有双重功能:一是韩礼德确认的人际性语法范畴,另一个则是体现概念意义的语法形式范畴。但这两种功能并非总是重叠在同一成分上的,如(3)和(4)。第二,命题是一个复合概念,至少亚氏笔下的命题如此;而在由此发展而来的系统功能语法中,命题就该同时是概念意义与社交性和情态性的人际意义。经典理论仅仅以命题的一个侧面为依据来确认语气成分的构成要素之一,显然有些经不起推敲。

现在的问题是:我们这里确立的主语究竟是一个什么性质的范畴呢?我们将在下面说明:主语范畴与人际意义的体现毫无关系;主语是一个语法形式范畴,起支配作用的是底层的概念意义。

4. 主语的语法形式特征

这里拟说明,主语是一个语法形式范畴,起支配作用的是底层的概念意义"及物性"。笔者将从两个方面来阐述这一点。第一,经典理论中缺乏这样一个形式范畴;第二,我们拟从语言学史上人们对主语的一些共识的角度,来梳理主语的语法形式特征。先看前一点。

把主语看作概念意义的语法形式范畴有理论上的需要。经典理论在分析词组和复句时均涉及到两个侧面;但在分析小句时只涉及到一个侧面;主语结构正好可以填充这个空挡。

首先,韩礼德(2004 年第 6 章)在分析名词组和动词组时,讨论了它们的经验结构和逻辑关系。以名词组为例,他自拟了一个典型例子,能囊括名词组内的所有基本语义范畴:those two splendid old electric trains with pantographs,其中的语义范畴依次为指别(those),数量(two),主观特征(splendid),客观特征(old),类别(electric),事物(trains)和限定(pantographs),并将由此组合而成的结构,称为经验语义结构:指别+数量+主观特征+客观特征+类别+事物+限定。与上述语义成分相对应的是语法类别:限定词(those),数量词(two),形容词(splendid/old),形容词(electric),名词(trains)以及介词(with)和名词(pantographs),它们构成以 trains 为中心语、其前后成分均为修饰语的逻辑结构:前置修饰语+中心语+后置修饰语(对比 Bloomfield 1933/1955 年第 12 章;也见后文)。

注意,其中的限定范畴与其他语义范畴不同:它不是由一个词、而是由一个介词短语体现的。但介词的基本功能并非经验性的,而是体现经验范畴之间的逻辑语义关系的,认知语言学则看作体现认知空间关系。因此,韩礼德此处说的经验语义结构,正是他在别处(Halliday 1973)说的概念意义,即经验意义与逻辑意义的总称;他叫做逻辑关系的范畴,实际上是一个更为抽象的概念,应属于语法形式的范围,因为这是一个基于经验意义的抽象结构关系。即是说,他对词组的分析实际上已经涉及到笔者说的语义和语法两个层面,即"第二阶段加工"过程中被诠释的语义关系、以及由此进一步抽象产生的语法关系。这种语法关系与传统语法所说的、在所指对象上基本一致,只是彼此的理论框架不同(见后文)。

其次,韩礼德对复句内部两个小句之间的关系也做了类似区分。其一是逻辑语义关系,其二是相互关系(2004 年第 7 章)。笔者认为,前者名符其实;而后者同样是一个更为抽象和更为形式化的范畴,这也是传统语法涉及的基本议题之一,惟理论框架有别。因此笔者建议称之为逻辑语法关系;这也正是笔者理解的语法形式范畴(见后文)。

按照这一思路,介于词组级和复句级之间的小句,其概念意义(及物性、级差性、时间性)为何无类似逻辑关系(见 2004 年第 5 章)?笔者主张,主语结构与概念意义之间应有体现关系,只是主语结构是基于概念意义、但已脱离了具体语义特征的、更为抽象的认知范畴,故称为概念形式,即句法关系,与语言认知诠释过程中出现的概念意义以及诠释前被激活的概念元功能相对:[概念元功能/意义潜势]→[概念意义]→[概念形式:主语结构]。

下面从柏拉图和亚里士多德的有关论述来梳理主流主语观的句法特征。斟酌以下引文(粗体系本文所加)。

(i) 陌生人:一个句子必须而且不能不有一个**主语**。

　　费:是的……

　　陌:我给你说一个句子,由一个**名词**和一个**动词**把一个**事物**和一个**动作**组合在一起。你得告诉我这个句子说的是谁。

　　费:好的,我尽力而为。

　　陌:费亚提特坐着——句子不长。费:不长。

　　陌:这个句子**说的**是谁……你得告诉我这个句子说的**主**

语是谁。

费：是我；我是主语。

(ii) 肯定判断是一个有关**主语**的事实的陈述，这个**主语**要么是一个**名词**，要么是一个无名称者；肯定判断中的**主语**和**谓语**必须各自指向**一个单一的事物**。

主语在这两段话里是多个概念的总称，从当代语言学的角度看至少有三种相关但又不同的内涵：一是外在实体性范畴；二是与主题相近；三是我们现在理解的语法形式特征。

第一种主语观是一个外在实体。根据当时的认知水平，I am the subject 一句中的 I 是指特定情景中的说话人：鉴于 I 和 subject 是识别关系，subject 也是外在的，因为前一引文中由"名词"和"动词"所组合的"事物"和"动作"在柏拉图的认识中肯定不是两个认知范畴。如果这一理解基本合理，那么这一主语观当然就很成问题。从当代认知语言学的角度看，I 则是一个经过认知处理而获得的经验语义范畴，subject 也一样。

第二种主语概念在以后两千多年的历史过程中演化出了一个独立的范畴地位，这就是"主题"（Topic），即相关信息片段中所谈论的那个基本对象。这一概念成型于公元前一世纪狄奥尼修斯（Dionysius）有关词序功能的论述；到十八世纪的法国和德国时已有广泛讨论，如法国的狄德罗（Diderot，1713—1784），孔狄亚（Condillac，1714—1780）以及瑞法洛（Rivarol，1753—1801），德国的博德默尔（Bodmer，1689—1783）和黑德尔（Herder，1744—1803）等（出自 Scaglione，载于 Weil 1844/1978：ix）；在十九世纪中叶以后得到充分发展（Weil 1844/1978；Gabelents，Wegener，Ammann，后三者出自 Sgall et al 1986 和 Hajicova 1994）。美国的结构主义学者霍凯特（Hockett，1958：201）则是明确区分语法主语和语义性主题的第一人。

第三个主语概念是以相关经验范畴为基础的语法形式范畴，这一点明确地贯穿于整个西方语言学史直至当代，如古希腊时代的斯多葛学派（主要体现在"格"理论中）、亚力山大学派（如 Thrax & Dyscolus）、古罗马时代的瓦罗（Varro）和普利西安（Priscian）、13 到 14 世纪的摩的斯泰学派（如 Thomas of Erfurt 关于 Dependency 与 Terminancy 以及 Suppositum/subject 与 Appositum/ predicate 的相互关系)(见 Robins 1997)。20世纪上半叶丹麦学者叶斯帕森(Jespersen)的主语概念本质上也是语法形式的(如1949Ⅲ,尤其是206—208页;另见陈脑冲1993)。布拉格学派区分"句子的实际切分"和"句子的形式切分",后者就是指语法主语和语法谓语(Mathesius 1939;钱军 1998:294—295)。类似主语概念也出现在当代其他学派的有关论述中,只是角度及理论框架彼此相异。而夸克等(Quirk *et al* 1985:717—799)接受这一形式概念的事实,尤能表明经典理论之外其他学派的学者,一般都是把主语作为一个语法形式范畴看待的。

再回过头去看,如果说柏拉图和亚里士多德笔下的主语概念还显得有些驳杂和粗疏的话,那么此后学界确有一些学者明确地阐述过主语是一个基于经验意义的语法形式范畴这一观点。例如,马泰修斯(Mathesius 1975:100—101)指出:

> 英语倾向于选择某种具体的成分作句子主语,尤其是那些指人的词……在当代捷克语和英语中,主语可以实施以下功能:既可能是由述谓结构表达的施动者,也可能是动作的受动者,但其分布在这两种语言中有很大差别……

这里阐述了词序演变和语用目的的关系;但结合其"形式切分观"我们看到,第一,尽管这里强调的是功能词序观,但主语的本质并没有改变,仍然与主题概念相分别;第二,被保留下来的主语概念在于它体现经验性的语义范畴"施动者"和"受动者"。不过,"在英语中,动作者和主语并非总是一致的"(Hill 1958:267;另见 Weil 1844/1978:37)。这在当代一些代表性著述中也有回应;而且与主语对应的还不仅仅是施动者和受动者。例如,一些代表性学者(如 Quirk *et al* 1985:740—747;Biber *et al* 1999:123—124)在总结主语的有关特征时,均认为主语可能对应于多种经验语义角色,诸如"施动者,即一个动作的有意识的发动者"、"一个事件的无生命的外在启动者"、"某一施动者为了实施某种动作所使用的工具或手段",以及"好些非施动性的角色",如"接受性主语,用以指示一个有生命的个体,即一个被动接受者,或者某一动作或状态的经验因素"。总之,主语和谓语来源于我们现今所理解的主题和述题的内涵,但已经与后两者分离开来,发展和进化成为一对独立的语法概念。因此,无论是从系统功能语法理论完善的需要看、还是从语言学史上主流主语观的继承与发展历程看,主语都应当作为一个经验性的语法形式范畴来看待。

而在系统功能学派内部,也已经有将主语结构作为一个语法形式范畴看待的。例如,韩礼德本人早先(Halliday 1970/1976:24)就是将主语结构和人际性的语气结构分离开来处理的:

	// the sun	was shining	on the sea //
概念	受事 Affected	过程 Process	处所 Locative
人际	语气 Modal	命题 Propositional	
语篇	主位 Theme	述位 Rheme	
	新信息 New		
	主语 Subject	述语 Predicator	状语 Adjunct

这里的主语和三类词汇-语法范畴没有任何直接关系;福赛特(Fawcett 2000:72)在引述该图时,于最后一个结构范畴前添上了COMBINED(组合性的)这样一个总括性的称谓,并认为这里的句法分析为整合性分析。其实,我们完全有理由把它理解为一种更为抽象的形式关系,否则它何以游离于三个基本语法范畴之外? 在笔者看来,只有将其理解为一个基于三者但又更为抽象的形式范畴才能给予合理解释。

这一思路启发了福赛特(Fawcett 1999,2000)。其主语概念指从系统网络中选择语义特征(对比 Halliday 2004)到纯粹的语法形式关系的说明过程,由一系列体现运算构成(如第 180 及 281—282 页),从理论上揭示了韩礼德模式中缺乏句法层(Syntax;韩氏甚至反对使用这一术语,如 1994:xiv)的局限。福赛特的具体分析如下(上图出处为 2000:148,下图为 2000:247;上图中的句法范畴缩写符是:S(ubject),O(perator),M(ain verb),C(omplement),A(djunct);为省篇幅,上图恕不提供术语汉译):

						S Y N T A X
S/Ag	O	M	C/Af	A		
we	would	visit	Mrs S	every sunday		
						TEXT
experiential	overt agent	repeated past	social action	overt affected	periodic frequency	S E M A N T I C S
interpersonal	information—giver					
polarity		positive				
validity		unassecced				
thematic	subject theme					
informational					unmarked new	
(no realizations of 'logical relations' or 'affective' meaning)						

因篇幅所限，这里无法对该理论框架及有关术语甚至它的合理性逐一做出说明，但只需对比其中 Syntax（句法）和 Semantics（语义）的相互关系，即可看出主语结构的地位和性质，即一种整合各种意义的、相对独立的结构关系。

总之，这里梳理的主语应当是一个句法概念，一种从底层概念意义基础上抽象而来的、纯粹的结构关系。这种分析性思考不仅可以回应"主语结构缺乏语义关系"的误识，对笔者来说还是十分必要的，因为这样能明确实例性语义和语法层次及其动态特征。

5. 进一步理论阐述

接下来就有三个相关理论问题需要解答：第一，语气成分中原先叫做主语的范畴究竟应该如何称谓？第二，定式操作语这一称谓所体现的语义功能又该如何确定？第三，本文所说的语义和语法范畴，其间究竟是什么关系？

就第一个问题而言，笔者主张将建构语气成分的、原先叫做主语的范畴，称为"互动语"（Interactant），即实施社交互动的基本功能成分；而定式操作语是另一个功能成分；根据韩礼德，两者合称为语气成分，体现话语的社交意义，从而达到物品—服务或信息交换的目的。按汤姆逊（Thompson 1996：45）："只要当前命题处于运作状态"，互动语就是"非协商性的"(同前)。笔者认为,这种非协商性是与定式成分的"有效性"相对而言的。

此外,如果把支撑性 there(存在句)结合起来考虑,将先前叫做主语的那个范畴改称为互动语尤其符合逻辑。即是说,既然先行成分 there 是主语,即所谓的"傀儡主语",或者说"语义上空洞(或无指代)"(Quirk et al 1985:740—47;Biber et al 1999:123—24),那么从逻辑上讲,没有语义内容,又何来形式呢?因为体现程序是"意义→形式"。可见,存在性 there 并非主语,而是一个建构语气成分发挥交际功能的范畴。也就是说,there be 存在句型中只有与定式动词有一致关系的名词组才应该被当作主语;其他句型中作主语的名词组则同时发挥相关人际功能。在后一种情况下,同一个成分同时发挥着两种语法功能:一是体现概念意义中的有关范畴,二是协同体现社交人际意义。据此,存在句 there were two caterpillars on the leaf, weren't there? 中的 there 则是语气成分的构成要素"互动语";而 In the garden are planted three orange trees, aren't there? 附加疑问句中的 there 仍然可以看作是对前面陈述句中处所成分 in the garden 的复制,故 in the garden 为相关语气的互动语。

顺带提一句,此前学界认为存在性 there"不具备地点副词 there 的处所意义"(Quirk et al 1985:1405),所以有处所性/指别性 there 与存在性/呈示性 there 之别(Adamson 1999/2002:606;Lakoff 1987:462—585;Bolinger 1977:90—123)。但从这里的具体情况看,there 并没有完全脱离处所特征,除非这里的 there 不作 there be 句型中的 there 理解。

就第二个问题而言,定式成分也是双功能的,因为它能同时协作体现概念性的时间意义和人际性的社交意义。因此,我们需要区分定式范畴的语义功能,并确立相应的语法功能称谓(另见 Halliday 2004:115—116;Jespersen 1949IV 第 1,3 和 22 章)。一方面,定式操作语具有体现概念意义中时间范畴的作用,即时间性;其语法功能则是协作构成时制范畴,因而定式操作语的这种语法功能可称为时制操作语或时制定式语。于是有以下体现模式:时间性→时制操作语/定式语。另一方面,定式操作语也是人际导向的:它同时发挥另一种功能,即协同体现社交意义,所以也称语气操作语。或如汤姆逊所说:定式成分引导"听话人推导相关命题所主张的有效性","并将这种有效性与此时此地言语事件的现实性、或者说话人的态度联系在一起"

(同前)。因此有以下体现模式:社交性→语气[语气成分→互动语＋语气操作语/定式语)＋剩余部分]。

至此,我们的目的是试图重新确认主语的语法功能性质、以及原先叫做主语的那个范畴的称谓,附带涉及定式成分的语法和语义功能问题。而要使前面的论证过程落到实处,还有一个重大的理论问题需要解答。这就是前面提出的第三个问题:如何从理论上说明语义和语法之间的关系?事实上,这一点已另有讨论(彭宣维 2011)。现将主要观点引述如下。虽然这是基于汉语分析取得的,但结论具有普通语言学意义(对比彭宣维 2002:100—110)。

笔者赞同米勒(Miller 1985)对传统语法的评价:传统语法的主要问题在于将语法和语义混在一起;但对语言的这两个层次是彼此独立生成的(第 193 页)这一观点持保留态度。第一,这两个层次是同时生成的:语法形式是在音系成分序列化和结构化过程中同时生成的;而语义则是这一形式化编码过程中从经验知识范畴中附带出来的语义特征、以及由语义特征在选择过程中序列化和结构化的结果;第二,多种底层语义范畴在体现过程中可能表征为为数较少的数种形式结构;第三,语义和语法之间只有抽象程度的不同,没有明确和硬性分界,或如学界常用的比喻,是一个硬币的两个面。

第一点需要很大的篇幅来阐述,此处引用结论,且仅对后两点做扼要概述。笔者在讨论现代汉语由语法结构确立的语义范畴时,涉及到诸多语法形式范畴,包括"得"字结构(补语),"连"字句,"把"字句,"被"字句,"领主属宾句",兼语句,存在句,"形容词谓语句","名词谓语句"。我们看到,同一种语法结构对应于多种语义结构。如语法形式上的"把"字结构,对应于好几种语义关系,包括物质过程("他把那家伙揍了一顿"),心理过程("张三把这事又想了一遍")。又如"得"字结构,可能有物质过程("张三打得很重"),心理过程("这事儿张三想得太多了"),还有增强复句("张三打得儿子昏了好几次")(另见 Fawcett 1987; Zhou 1997)。这些事实不仅能为本文的基本观点提供支持,也与认知语义学"意义—形式影射关系"或意义—形式"合成关系"的观点基本一致(Goldberg 1995; Talmy 2001:11,25)。

同时,由于语义范畴所包含的语义特征与经验范畴所包含的经验特征从本质上讲是同质的,因此,即便语义范畴是语法编码过程中所产生的附生物,前者在认知空间距离上也更靠近于经验范畴,而其类别相对来说要复杂得多,变化的幅度也要大得多;语法范畴于是可以看作是在语义范畴的基础上的进一步抽象,用认知语言学的话说,是进一步的"勾画"(Profile;Langacker 1990)。因此其结构范畴不仅比语义范畴抽象,而且变化的幅度和范围也要小得多。事实上,这一点对于词组和词亦如此。例如,词的形式构成和词的语法类别(词性)总是有限的,但其语义特征和范畴千差万别;在名词组中,其语法形式结构要么是前置修饰语+中心语(如 those trains),要么还有后置修饰语(those trains with pantographs);但名词组的语义结构范畴,不仅在数量上远远多于前置和后置两个成分,在构成上也复杂得多。

总之,语义范畴是人的认知能力通过音系手段从语境启动的经验知识中提取语义特征、并经过入列条件的选择而生成的;语法范畴则是对选择过程中被识解的语义范畴和经验知识范畴的抽象化和结构化。抽象化就是概括化或象征化的认知过程;对语法层次的深入分析,有赖于语义结构,对语义结构的深入分析,有赖于有关经验事理;而经验事理的隐喻化,就意味着语义表达方式对经验知识或多或少的认知"勾画"和重新处理,从而可能出现与经验事理相悖的语义关系,如 the fifth day saw them at the summit;这也正是 Halliday(1995,1999)把上述过程看作对"经验"范畴的"重新整形"(reshaping)的原因。可见,语义和经验知识之间并非对等,而应当从理论上区分开来。这样做既有认知上的依据,也符合"语义即是语言的使用"这一功能主义原则;而从语义范畴到语法范畴,就意味着抽象程度的加大和范畴数量的减少。据此,"概念意义→主语结构"的体现模式,不仅符合前人有关主语性质的基本认识,尤能清楚地区别于语气成分的构成要素之一。

6. 结语

这里将本文阐述的、有关主语的功能属性总结如下。第一,主语是一个狭义的语法范畴;它只与概念意义有关,是直接体现小句概念意义的形式范畴。第二,主语与语气不发生任何关系,更不存在体现关系,连性质也不相同;同时,主语与主题已经分化。第三,主语是主语结构的基本构成要素之一;另一个是谓语,包括定式动词、述语、补语和状语等次范畴;此外,主语结构还应包括语态和时制等形式范畴。

因此,经典理论意义上的"提议"与主语无关;事实上,祈使句句首被省略的成分,就不宜再叫做主语。

参考文献

Adamson, S. Literary Language. In R. Lass (ed.) *The Cambridge History of the English Language* (III). London: CUP, 1999; Beijing: Peking University Press, 2002: 539—653.

Aristotle原著,秦典华(译),"解释篇",苗力田(主编),《亚里士多德全集》(第一卷),北京:中国人民大学出版社,1997年,第47—80页。

Austin, J. L. *How to Do Things with Words*. Cambridge, Mass.: Harvard University Press, 1962.

Biber, D., S. Johansson, G. Leech, S. Conrad & E. Finegan. *Longman Grammar of Spoken and Written English*. 北京:外语教学与研究出版社,1999年。

Bloomfield, L. *Language*. London: Allen & Unwin, 1933/1955. 北京:外语教学与研究出版社,2002年。

Bolinger, D. *Meaning and Form*. London: Longman, 1977.

Butt, D., R. Fahey, S. Feez, S. Spinks & C. Yallop. *Using Functional Grammar: An Explorer's Guide* (2nd edition). Macquarie University: National Centre for English Teaching and Research, 2000.

Chao, Y. R. (赵元任) *A Grammar of Spoken Chinese*. Berkeley, Los Angeles & London: University of California Press, 1968. 吕叔湘译,《汉语口语语言》,北京:商务印书馆,2001年。

Daneš, F. 1960. Functional sentence perspective and the organization of the text. In F. Daneš (ed.) *Papers on Functional Sentence Perspective*. Academia & The Hague, Prague: Mouton. 1974: 106—128.

Eggins, S. *An Introduction to Systemic Functional Linguistics*. London: Pinter, 1994.

Esser, J. Functions of intonation. In R. Dirven & V. Fried (eds.) *Functionalism in Linguistics*. Amsterdam: Benjamins, 1987: 381—393.

Fawcett, R. *Cognitive Linguistics and Social Interaction*. Herstellung: Groos, 1980.

Fawcett, R. The semantics of clause and verb for relational processes in English. In M. A. K. Halliday & R. Fawcett (eds.) *New Developments in Systemic Linguistics*, vol. 1: *Theory and Description*. London: Pinter, 1987: 130—183.

Fawcett, R. On the subject of the subject in English: two positions on its meaning (and on how to test for it). *Functions of Language*, 1999, 6(2): 247—273.

Fawcett, R. *A Theory of Syntax for Systemic Functional Linguistics*. Amsterdam: Benjamins, 2000.

Firth, J. R. The technique of semantics. F. R. Palmer (ed.) *Papers in Linguistics 1934—1951*. Oxford: OUP, 1957: 7—33.

Firth, J. R. S synopsis of linguistic theory. F. R. Palmer (ed.) *Selected Papers of J. R. Firth 1952—1959*. London: Longman, 1968.

Goldberg, A. E. *Constructions: A Construction Grammar Approach to Argument Structure*. Chicago: University of Chicago Press.

Hajicova, E. Topic/Focus and related research. In P. A. Luelsdorff (ed.) *The Prague School of Structural and Functional Linguistics*. Amsterdam: Benjamins, 1994: 245—275.

Halliday, M. A. K. Deep grammar: system as semantic choice. In G. R. Kress (ed.) *Halliday: System and Function in Language*. Oxford: OUP, 1976 (1966): 88—98.

Halliday, M. A. K. The form of functional grammar. In G. R. Kress (selected and edited) *Halliday: System and Function in Language*. Oxford: OUP, 1976 (1970): 7—25.

Halliday, M. A. K. *Explorations in the Functions of Language*. London: Arnold, 1973.

Halliday, M. A. K. *Language as Social Semiotic: the Social Interpretation of Language and Meaning*. London: Arnold, 1978.

Halliday, M. A. K. *An Introduction to Functional Grammar* (3rd edition). London: Arnold, 2004 (1985/1994).

Halliday, M. A. K. Language and the reshaping of human experience. In B. Dendrinos (ed.) *Proceedings of the Fourth International Symposium on Critical Discourse Analysis*. Athens: University of Athens Press, 1995.

Halliday, M. A. K. The grammatical construction of scientific knowledge. In R. Rossini, G. Sandri & R. Scazzieri (eds.) *Incommensurability and Translation*. Cheltenham: Elgar, 1999.

Harris, R. *Introduction to Integrational Linguistics*. Oxford: Pergamon, 1998.

Hill, A. A. *Introduction to Linguistic Structures*. New York: Harcourt, Brace and Company, 1958.

Hockett, C. F. 1958. *A Course in Modern Linguistics*. New York: Macmillan.

Jackendoff, R. *Foundations of Language*. Oxford: OUP, 2002.

Jespersen, O. *A Modern English Grammar: on Historical Principles* (III, IV, VII). Copenhagen: Einar Munksgaard; London: Allen & Unwin, 1949.

Lakoff, G. *Women, Fire and Dangerous Things*. Chicago: University of Chicago Press, 1987.

Lakoff, G. & M. Johnson. *Philosophy in the Flesh: the Embodied Mind and its Challenge to Western Thought*. New York: Basic Books, 1999.

Lamb, S. *Pathways of the Brain*. Amsterdam: Benjamins, 1999.

Langacker, R. W. *Foundations of Cognitive Grammar* (*vol. I*). Stanford: Stanford University Press, 1987. 北京: 北京大学出版社, 2004 年。

Langacker, R. W. *Concept, Image, and Symbol: The Cognitive Basis of Grammar*. Berlin: Mouton, 1990.

Langacker, R. W. *Foundations of Cognitive Grammar* (*vol. II*). Stanford: Stanford University Press, 1991. 北京: 北京大学出版社, 2004 年。

Long, R. J. (龙日金) *Transitivity in Chinese*. University of Sydney, MA Thesis, 1981.

Malinowski, B. The problem of meaning in primitive languages. Supplement to C. K. Ogden & I. A. Richards. *The Meaning of Meaning* (10th edition). London: Routledge, 1966 (1923): 296—336.

Mathesius, V. On the so-called Actual Division of Sentence. 张惠芹、武爱华、于淑杰译,朱威华校,王福祥、白春仁编,《话语语言学论文集》,北京: 外语教学与研究出版社, 1989 (1939) 年, 第 10—17 页。

Mathesius, V. *A Functional Analysis of Present Day English on A General Linguistic Basis*, ed. by J. Vachek, and tr. by L. Duskova. Hague: Mouton, 1975.

Miller, J. *Semantics and Syntax: Parallels and Connection*. Cambridge: CUP, 1985.

Palmer, F. R.. Sequence and order. In C. I. M. Stuart (ed.) *Report of the 15th Annual Round Table Meeting on Linguistics and Language Studies*. Washington D. C.: Georgetown University Press, 1964: 123—130.

Plato. Sophist. In *The Essential Plato*. B. Jowett (trans.). New York: Quality Paperback Book Club, 1999: 1179—1189.

Quirk, R., S. Greenbaum, J. Leech & J. Svartvik. *A Comprehensive Grammar of the English Language*. London: Longman, 1985.

Robins, R. H. *A Short History of Linguistics* (4th edition). London: Longman, 1997.

Sgall, P., E. Hajicova & J. Panevova. *The Meaning of the Sentence in its Semantic and Pragmatic Aspects*. Boston: Reidel, 1986.

Sperber, D. & D. Wilson. *Relevance: Communication and Cognition*. Oxford: Blackwell, 1995.

Sun, L. (孙骊) English subject-verb concord: an overview. 《外语教学与研究》, 1979 年第 1 期, 第 13—20 页。

Talmy, L. *Toward a Cognitive Semantics* (Vol.1). Cambridge, Mass.: MIT, 2001.
Thompson, G. *Introducing Functional Grammar*. London: Arnold, 1996.
Tsao Feng-fu, *Sentence and Clause Structure in Chinese: A Functional Approach*. 台湾:学生书局,1990年.
Weil, H. *The Order of Words in the Ancient Languages Compared with That of the Modern Languages*, new edition with an introduction by A. Scaglione. Amsterdam: Benjamins, 1844/1978.
Wittgenstein, L. *Philosophical Investigations*, translated into English by G. E. M. Anscombe. In *Philosophy* 17. Beijing: Chinese Social Sciences Press, 1955/1999.
Zhou, X. K. (周晓康) *Material and Relational Transitivity in Mandarin Chinese*. Ph. D. Dissertation. Melbourne: University of Melbourne, 1997.
曹逢甫,"台湾闽南语的 ka⁷ 字句",第一届国际汉语方言语法研讨会宣读论文(2002年12月26—28日,哈尔滨),2002年.
陈脑冲,"论'主语'",《外语教学与研究》,1993(4)年,第1—9页.
戴耀晶,《现代汉语时体系统研究》,杭州:浙江教育出版社,1997年.
郭　锐,《现代汉语词类研究》,北京:商务印书馆,2002年.
胡壮麟,《语篇的衔接与连贯》,上海:上海外语教育出版社,1994年.
胡壮麟、朱永生、张德禄、李战子编著,《系统功能语法概论》,北京:北京大学出版社,2005年.
李临定、范芳莲,"试论表'每'的数量结构对应式",《中国语文》,1960年第11期;收入《李临定自选集》,开封:河南教育出版社,1994年,第1—11页.
李　泉,"'形+动态助词'考察",胡明扬主编《动词问题考察》,北京:北京语言文化大学出版社,1997(a)年,第190—206页.
李　泉,"'形+宾'现象考察",胡明扬主编《动词问题考察》,北京:北京语言文化大学出版社,1997(b)年,第168—189页.
李　泉,《汉语语法考察与分析》,北京:北京语言文化大学出版社,2001年.
梁银峰,《汉语动补结构的产生与演变》,上海:学林出版社,2006年.
刘一之,《北京话中的"着(·zhe)"字新探》,北京:北京大学出版社,2001年.
陆俭明主编,《面临新世纪挑战的现代汉语语法研究·98现代汉语语法学国际学术会议论文集》,济南:山东教育出版社,2000年.
陆俭明、沈阳,《汉语和汉语研究十五讲》,北京:北京大学出版社,2003年.
吕叔湘,"把字句法研究",《金陵、齐鲁、华西大学中国文化汇刊》(第8卷);收入吕叔湘著《汉语语法论文集》(增订本),北京:商务印书馆,1948/1984年,第176—199页.
吕叔湘主编,《现代汉语八百词》,北京:商务印书馆,1980年.
马庆株,"自主动词和非自主动词",《中国语言学报》,1988年,第3期,北京:商务印书馆;收入马庆株著《汉语动词和动词性结构》,北京:北京语言学院出版社,1995年,第13—46页。

彭宣维,《英汉语篇综合对比》,上海:上海外语教育出版社,2000年。

彭宣维,《语言过程与维度》,北京:清华大学出版社,2002年。

彭宣维,"SFG作格分析的地位及其系统配置新探",载张克定等主编第9届中国功能语言学学术研讨会文集《功能·语用·评价》,北京:高等教育出版社,2007(a)年,第51—64页。

彭宣维,"作格关系、语态类别和信息推进",《外语研究》,2007(b)年第3期,第41—48页。

彭宣维,《语言与语言学概论——汉语系统功能语法》,北京:北京大学出版社,2011年。

钱 军,《结构功能主义:布拉格学派》,长春:吉林教育出版社,1998年。

施春宏,《汉语动结式的句法语义研究》,北京:北京语言大学出版社,2008年。

宋文辉,《现代汉语动结式的认知研究》,北京:北京大学出版社,2007年。

宋玉柱,"动态存在句",《语文学习》,1982年,第6期;收入宋玉柱著《语法论稿》,北京:北京语言学院出版社,1995(a)年,第62—67页。

宋玉柱,"可逆句",日本《中国语研究》,1982年第21号;收入宋玉柱著《语法论稿》,北京:北京语言学院出版社,1995(a)年,第200—207页。

宋玉柱,"略谈'假存在句'",《天津师范大学学报》,1988年,第6期;收入宋玉柱著《语法论稿》,北京:北京语言学院出版社,1995(b)年,第95—100页。

王 力,《中国语法理论》(上),上海:商务印书馆,1947年。

《现代汉语词典》(修订本),北京:商务印书馆,1995年。

张涤华、胡裕树、张斌、林祥楣主编,《汉语语法修辞词典》,合肥:安徽教育出版社,1988年。

张国宪,"现代汉语形容词的体及形态化历程",陆俭明主编,2000年,第613—632页。

周晓康,"现代汉语物质过程小句的及物性系统",《当代语言学》,1999年,第3期,第36—50页。

朱德熙,《语法讲义》,北京:商务印书馆,1982年;收入《朱德熙文集》(第1卷),第1—260页,北京:商务印书馆,1999年。